ROUTLEDGE LIBRARY EDITIONS:
WW2

Volume 22

OUT OF STEP

OUT OF STEP

A Study of Young Delinquent Soldiers in
Wartime; Their Offences, Their Background and
Their Treatment Under an Army Experiment

JOSEPH TRENAMAN

Routledge
Taylor & Francis Group

LONDON AND NEW YORK

First published in 1952 by Methuen & Co., Ltd.

This edition first published in 2022
by Routledge
2 Park Square, Milton Park, Abingdon, Oxon OX14 4RN

and by Routledge
605 Third Avenue, New York, NY 10158

Routledge is an imprint of the Taylor & Francis Group, an informa business

© 1952 Methuen & Co., Ltd.

British Library Cataloguing in Publication Data
A catalogue record for this book is available from the British Library

ISBN: 978-1-03-201217-9 (Set)
ISBN: 978-1-00-319367-8 (Set) (ebk)
ISBN: 978-1-03-204396-8 (Volume 22) (hbk)
ISBN: 978-1-03-204402-6 (Volume 22) (pbk)
ISBN: 978-1-00-319302-9 (Volume 22) (ebk)

DOI: 10.4324/9781003193029

Publisher's Note
The publisher has gone to great lengths to ensure the quality of this reprint but points out that some imperfections in the original copies may be apparent.

Disclaimer
The publisher has made every effort to trace copyright holders and would welcome correspondence from those they have been unable to trace.

JOSEPH TRENAMAN

OUT OF STEP

A study of young delinquent soldiers in wartime; their offences, their background and their treatment under an Army experiment

with a Foreword by

GENERAL SIR RONALD ADAM, Bt.,
G.C.B., D.S.O., O.B.E.,

and a Preface by

PROFESSOR SIR CYRIL BURT

METHUEN & CO., LTD. LONDON
36 Essex Street, Strand, W.C.2

First published in 1952

CATALOGUE NO. 3970/U

PRINTED IN GREAT BRITAIN

This book is dedicated,
with infinite gratitude, to
MARGARET,
who has given me so much

BUT MAN IS A NOBLE ANIMAL,
SPLENDID IN ASHES AND POMPOUS IN THE GRAVE,
SOLEMNIZING NATIVITIES AND DEATHS WITH EQUAL LUSTRE,
NOR OMITTING CEREMONIES OF BRAVERY
IN THE INFAMY OF HIS NATURE

(*Sir Thomas Browne*)

FOREWORD

By GENERAL SIR RONALD ADAM, Bt., G.C.B., D.S.O., O.B.E.,
formerly Adjutant-General to H.M. Forces

THE Special Training Units mentioned in this book were an experiment, and a valuable experiment, for they gave a chance to many difficult young men, and this was impossible in an operational unit in war time. The originator of the idea was Geoffrey Gilbey, but much credit was due to Lt.-Gen. Sir Ralph Eastwood, G.O.C., Northern Command, who encouraged and supported the first experiment at what later became No. 1 S.T.U.

It was not surprising that we had difficulties with the Young Soldiers battalions from whom the bulk of the young men came in the first years. These battalions were formed at a time when the Army's resources in officers and N.C.O.s were strained to the utmost by the re-formation of the returned divisions from France and the increased number of infantry battalions formed in the summer of 1940 to resist invasion. The Young Soldiers battalions were the final straw, and it was impossible to provide the numbers or types of officers and N.C.O.s required. At this time personnel selection had not been introduced; and, as a result, many young men were unhappily put into jobs that were too much above their capabilities or below them. That is bound to lead to unhappiness in any organization.

Much of the best work of the S.T.U.s was, however, carried out at a time when the Army was still hard pressed for resources. The writer remarks on the lack of trained psychologists to help. As the Army went overseas, and as the personnel selection work and officer selection work expanded, we had too few psychiatrists and psychologists to do the tasks required.

The three S.T.U.s were given a pretty free hand as to how they tackled the problem. In No. 1 S.T.U. much was done by letters and occasional visits to parents to enlist their help in making their sons into good soldiers, and I was always much struck by the help the parents could give if they were properly approached. This method was also adopted and developed by the other S.T.U.s.

I think we can say that the experiment was a success; and much is due to the officers and N.C.O.s, some with considerable experience in youth work and all enthusiasts, who, under considerable difficulties and misunderstandings, did a remarkable job of work. In particular the Commandants, Majors Gilbey, Hooker and Long, who contributed their own experiences to the experiment, and each in his own way worked out suitable methods of treatment.

I hope that something may be learned from this book to help to solve the problems of peace, which are no less acute than those of war. The industrial revolution has left us a problem that must be solved.

PREFACE

By Professor SIR CYRIL BURT

AMONG the many novel experiments that were initiated, in the very midst of war, by General Sir Ronald Adam, was the formation of Special Training Units to deal with young soldiers who had failed to fit in with the disciplinary requirements of the Army, and were rapidly drifting into delinquency. It was hoped that, with the aid of appropriate training and careful individual treatment, many if not most of them might gradually develop decent habits of conduct, regain the self-respect that they had usually lost, and even take a pride in working efficiently with active units. As will be seen from the following chapters, the venture proved a remarkable success.

In an army, what is necessarily regarded as delinquency includes, not only acts that would constitute criminal offences in the eyes of the civil law, but various misdemeanours, such as deserting, being late or absent without leave—appearing on parade with a broken boot-lace or a rusty bayonet—many of which would scarcely call for official censure in ordinary civilian life. Nevertheless, there appears to be a close association between the two types of offence; and the military problems present many analogies with those that confront the criminologist who seeks to study the causes, the treatment, and the prevention of crime under the normal conditions of peace. Moreover, there are certain advantages in studying cases in the forces. The organization of the Army in wartime enables closer and more continuous observations to be carried out, and various types of treatment to be more systematically tried. As a member of the Advisory Committee of Psychologists, appointed by Sir Ronald Adam in the earlier years of the war, I myself took a personal if somewhat indirect interest in these and similar experiments, and can testify to the useful work then done. It was work which had both an immediate practical value and a theoretical significance of its own.

The guiding idea underlying the formation of such units was based on a principle for which psychologists have long been pleading, namely, that, with rare exceptions, the treatment of incipient delinquency must be thought of not as something that can be disposed of by summary punishment or settled once and for all by a medical diagnosis: it is essentially a psychological problem.

Now, when a man's actions cannot be altered by swift or sudden agencies, such as penalties, rational persuasion, or the influence of a new emotional incentive from outside, like falling in love, there is only one alternative—training. This must consist in systematic training in the widest sense of that word, in a training which will be concerned, not so much with educational or vocational accomplishments, as with the building or re-building of character.

Psychological research has taught us a good deal about the methods of training and the processes of character-formation in the young. Children of school age are readily accessible to the investigator; and, since during the years of growth they are still pliable and plastic with habits barely formed, they are comparatively amenable to educative influences. But very little is known about the development or reconstruction of character in men who have already passed beyond the stage of adolescence. Moreover, what little we have learnt from reformative attempts with older criminals is far from encouraging; and the psychologist's first comment on an experiment of this type is that it should be used, as far as possible, as an opportunity for study and investigation. Hence, the careful observations carried out by Mr. Trenaman among these units will, I am sure, be of interest, not only to those concerned with the more immediate military problem, but to all who are interested in the practical treatment of crime. Indeed, his work forms the first comprehensive study, by case-history methods, of a group of potential or actual delinquents who have already reached full maturity.

Hitherto the few investigations which have been undertaken with adults of this type have been of necessity conducted, so to speak, from a distance. Broad statistical reviews have been attempted of the abstract nature of the problem as a whole. And a few individual studies have been made by magistrates, by psychiatrists, and by social reformers; but for part-time investigators like these, the persons observed have nearly always been no more than passing acquaintances. To examine a man once or twice in your consulting-room, if you are a psychiatrist, to have one or two talks with selected convicts, if you are a prison visitor, will not enable

you to reach the heart of each man's problem. Mr. Trenaman has
spent many months in the closest personal contact with each of
his cases. He has shared their day-to-day life, and approached
them as a fellow-soldier and a friend. And in this way he has been
able to compile a first-hand series of observations, collected according to a pre-arranged plan.

Those of us who have been directly engaged in the study of
delinquent boys and girls know all too well how inadequate are the
data obtained when such youngsters are referred merely for brief
examinations, or called up for special investigations in the artificial
surroundings of the laboratory, the child guidance clinic, or the
school. Even to work with them at a residential institution, like
the old-fashioned reformatory or the Borstal school, seldom yields
a genuine insight into their real character. To understand such
children intimately, it is essential to know them in ordinary life—
to stay with them in their homes, to join in their spontaneous games,
to share for a while their everyday transactions under free and
natural conditions. With boys and girls it is not difficult to find
suitable occasions: with adults it is, in ordinary circumstances, all
but impossible. But the Special Training Unit presents a unique
opportunity; and Mr. Trenaman is to be congratulated for having
been one of the first to see and seize it.

Readers who have not the privilege of knowing Mr. Trenaman
personally will, as they turn over his pages, quickly discover that
he possesses just those rare gifts which make a man a good observer
of his fellow-creatures—gifts which cannot be imparted by academic
courses on psychology and which an academic course may even
spoil. He seems to have by nature that tolerance of outlook, that
sympathetic and imaginative insight, which the born psychologist
alone enjoys. He is at once objective and alert. He is prejudiced
by no preconceived theories about mental mechanisms or hypo-
thetical motives. He describes the facts as he observes them. His
interest lies, not in proving some pet conclusion of his own or of his
favourite psychological school, but in the human beings themselves.

As a result, his book is a mine of reliable observations and data.
They are stated plainly and without unnecessary technicality.
Where percentages and numerical tables are helpful, figures are
appended. But the real value of his work lies, not so much in the
statistics, as in the numerous case-histories that he has reported
and discussed in full and vivid detail.

It will be impossible to treat delinquency scientifically until we have arrived at scientific understanding of the causes that produce it. And one of the most valuable parts of Mr. Trenaman's investigation consists in his detailed analysis of causal factors. Here the special conditions under which he has worked have again been of great assistance since, in the case of many of the characteristics which he wished to examine, it was possible to obtain comparable figures from control groups.

The employment of a parallel group of non-delinquent individuals has formed a distinctive feature of British investigations; and its value in deciding which particular conditions are to be regarded as genuinely causal is still not fully appreciated. When, for example, Healy records that among 823 recidivist cases (chiefly youths aged 11 to 19) 33 per cent were found to suffer from abnormal physical conditions and 4·6 per cent from parental neglect, it is difficult to tell what significance is really to be attached to the figures, because for all we know, similar percentages might be found among law-abiding youths of the same social class. It is therefore urgently to be hoped that, if any further researches are planned along these lines in the near future, arrangements will be made for gathering similar information from a non-delinquent control-group, comparable in all relevant respects, except delinquency, with the group of delinquents.

Mr. Trenaman's inferences are doubly valuable, because for so many of the conditions he has studied a comparison of this sort can be made. To the psychologist it is encouraging to find that, to a large extent, his principal conclusions are in keeping with those reached by earlier investigators in very different fields. Much the same set of causal factors has been noted in studying delinquent youngsters while still at school. In the past the writer on criminology has too often been tempted to carry over his findings into other fields, as though they had a kind of universal validity. But in psychology such extensions are highly precarious. They must be verified afresh for each new class or age-group. And then, in the rather rare instances in which the new results agree with the old, we may safely infer that we are at last reaching basic principles.

The first point on which Mr. Trenaman is able to confirm earlier conclusions is one of the most important: there is no such thing as an innate or inherent criminal disposition. It follows that, in spite of many pessimistic statements to the contrary, no delinquent, however hardened, is irrevocably beyond all hope of reform. No doubt, as many of the cases show, there are certain peculiarities of temperament and mental constitution which make it easier for one person to succumb to temptation than another. But, when we are dealing with young adults of nearly twenty-one, these innate qualities have been largely overlaid by the effects of personal experience. Hence in the present inquiry we are confronted, not so much with the difficulties due directly to inborn disposition, but with the habits and ways of thought superimposed on what is innate by the incidents and accidents of childhood and of early adolescence. Accordingly, at this stage of life, by far the most important of the factors that we must examine and deal with are the conditions prevailing in the social environment in which this or that individual was living until his entrance into the Army.

The next step to determine is which of these various environmental conditions is commonest and most influential. And, before answering this further question, there is one helpful feature in Mr. Trenaman's procedure that deserves special commendation, namely, his division of causes into major and minor factors. Too often in the past those who have studied such influences have been inclined to infer that, when a particular condition is found more frequently among delinquents than among non-delinquents, it therefore plays a crucial part; the factor may be merely contributory, and the relation quite indirect.

And here perhaps it may be useful, at the very outset, to attempt a broad classification of the twenty-six factors that Mr. Trenaman finds to be 'strongly associated with delinquency'. There seem to be five main groups—physical, intellectual, emotional, economic, and what we may call domestic.

(i) Physically, the men in the delinquent groups are, on the average, weaker, feebler, and more ill-nourished. They have suffered more frequently from early ill-health, and have more often been the victim of minor accidents. But, in the main, physical weakness would appear to form only a supplementary cause. Except in a few rare cases it does not seem to have been directly responsible for delinquent behaviour. Indirectly, however, by causing repeated absence from school, over-indulgence at home, and inefficiency at work, it would appear in at least a small proportion of the cases to have played an essential part. The practical corollary, both for prevention and treatment, is obvious.

(ii) Intellectually, we are told, though a little below the average level in innate intelligence, the delinquents were not markedly subnormal. Thus the familiar notion that habitual delinquency is

commonly an outcome of congenital dullness or borderline deficiency is not borne out by his findings.   However, in educational
attainments, the majority proved to be decidedly backward; and
many were semi-illiterate.   The striking inequality between potential
capacity on the one hand and actual attainments on the other
appears with many individuals to have directly produced a cumulative series of untoward events—truancy during childhood, incom-
petence at work later on, constant changing of jobs, and a growing
sense of frustrated ability and aspiration, all tending to issue in a
succession of criminal outbreaks.

(iii) Emotionally, the men in the delinquent groups were far
more immature, restless, and adventurous than those in the control
groups.   They were highly unstable themselves, and they came as
a rule from highly unstable families.   One might perhaps imagine
that, among those who had lived in homes where conditions were so
insecure and uncertain, a strong and powerful yearning might arise
to seek conditions of greater security.   On the contrary, the large
majority seem to prefer a life of hazard to a life of safety, and hanker
after situations which may afford some measure of excitement and
some outlet for a spirit of adventure.   Many, as they grew up, had
wished to go to sea; most of them had volunteered for the Army;
nearly all had found it difficult to settle down in any safe and permanent job.   As compared with the control group, their leisure
activities showed a far greater tendency to seek emotional excitement in its simplest and most accessible form, particularly at the
cinema.   On the other hand, few had developed any quiet or progressive hobbies, such as are comparatively common among youths
of a more stable character.   No doubt, the gambler's attitude
towards life, which is typical of such persons, is itself largely an
effect of home conditions where the future was unpredictable.   Yet,
after working through the family histories of many such cases, it is
difficult to resist the inference that the instability is often a hereditary trait, and that the unstable conditions of life at home are the
effect rather than the cause of a characteristic which distinguishes
just the case in front of us.

(iv) Economically the majority had come from poor and overcrowded homes.   They were members of large families, and of
households living near the borderline of downright poverty.   Mr.
Trenaman has shown how multifarious may be the consequences,
both direct and indirect, of these more material limitations.

(v) Nevertheless, when all is said, it is the psychological

conditions of early life rather than its economic conditions that are ultimately decisive. By far the commonest and most conspicuous feature, distinguishing these groups from the rest, is to be found in the social and emotional atmosphere of their parents' homes. Parental neglect was noted in nearly half the cases, and was by far the most frequent of all the major factors. Ten per cent were homeless. Friction, quarrelling, and irregular relations between the parents is noted as a contributory cause in about two-fifths. But in almost every instance the relation between the son and his parents had been abnormal. In some cases one or both parents were invalids; in others, punishment had been excessively severe; in far more the home discipline had been irretrievably weak; and in quite a number there was a definite record of over-indulgence. Excessive affection on the part of mother or father was observed as well as lack of affection; and it is curious to find that an exceptional attachment to the home was much commoner than a history of rebellion against the parents or of running away in childhood. Broken homes were reported in about one-quarter of the cases; but in general this appears to have acted as a minor rather than a major factor. Mr. Trenaman's observations suggest that it is perhaps unwise to regard such circumstances as forming a direct or powerful factor (as so many recent writers have done) without inquiring more precisely how they have actually affected the child. Some of the men seem to have been greatly disturbed by the loss of a mother in early childhood, and by the intrusion of a step-mother who at times lived up to a step-mother's reputation. But, as many social workers will testify, in those large and erratic households, where instability is accepted as a permanent feature of family life, such changes do not always produce the reactions which statistical investigators, who have themselves been brought up in relatively secure and stable middle-class families, are so often tempted to imagine. Often, indeed, they are shrugged aside with the same lighthearted humour as life's other little calamities. 'My first mother was quite nice,' writes one, adding, 'Father has been married three times, a proper Henry VIII, as you might say.'

   This brief summary furnishes a fairly clear and detailed picture of what might almost be called the delinquent type—the kind of person to be met with in the following pages. However, if we are to speak of a 'type', we must beware of assuming that all who constitute this 'type' stand out as different from their fellows or as closely similar to each other. Glancing more closely at the numerous illustrative case-histories, we cannot help being impressed by the point that Mr. Trenaman's descriptions bring out so clearly: each man in the Special Training Unit formed a unique and individual personality, with his own particular outlook and his own peculiar problems. Only when we approach him as an individual, not as one indistinguishable member in a vast homogeneous army, is there any chance of arousing his better motives and bringing him back to decent behaviour.

In my list of causes I have not made a separate group for pathological conditions, although we are told that as many as 19 per cent of the men in the Special Training Unit (including a large proportion of the total failures) were eventually discharged as 'psychopathic' personalities. My reason is that, in common with many other investigators, I find it difficult to discover what precisely the term 'psychopathic' means. Different psychiatrists interpret the term in very different ways. With some, indeed, the mere persistence of an apparently incurable delinquency is accepted as a sufficient indication of a psychopathic disposition; but that is merely to give an unfamiliar name to a very familiar condition. Moreover, in view of the absence of any definite or agreed set of symptoms, many psychiatrists are now disinclined to use the word; and Dr. William Moodie, the former Director of the Child Guidance Council, has recently stated that 'the term "psychopathic personality", like the diagnosis of moral defect, is now gradually being given up'.[1] Perhaps its frequent appearance in the descriptions of the men here studied means that the group as a whole contained a large proportion of persons who were by innate constitution emotionally unstable. Mr. Trenaman's contribution to this issue is itself instructive. Having compared the characteristics reported for the psychopathic cases with those reported for the remainder, he finds that the similarity between the non-psychopathic and the psychopathic is so close that, in his view, 'so far as environmental and other factors are concerned, the psychopaths do not represent a different population'.

A knowledge of the commoner causes is of great help to the practical investigator in dealing with this or that individual; and, when in such a case he has at last succeeded in unravelling the chief factors at work, the appropriate treatment often becomes obvious

---

[1] *Modern Trends in Psychological Medicine* (1948, p. 191). He adds: 'it is useful as a lay description which scientifically means little or nothing.'

as a matter of common sense. In the vast majority of instances, as Mr. Trenaman's records show, there is no need (as so many have contended) for prolonged psychoanalytic treatment or for special psychotherapeutic measures in the technical sense. General methods of training, supplemented by an appropriate individual approach where the problem presents special difficulties, will, in at least 75 per cent of the cases, achieve a striking measure of success. To discover in what precisely such measures should consist, the reader must turn to Mr. Trenaman's own chapters.

The social importance of his work is demonstrated in a most illuminating way. In one of the supplementary studies which he has appended to the main body of his work he seeks to estimate the likelihood that any given person will succumb to delinquency in each successive year of life. His method resembles that of an actuary compiling a life-table to show the probability that a man will succumb to a fatal illness before such-and-such an age. By this device he and Mr. Emmett have computed that, out of 100 male persons born on any particular date, as many as eleven will, under present conditions, succumb to delinquency at some stage of their lives—a surprisingly large proportion, over one in ten. Any well-attested suggestion for reducing these alarming figures deserves our most earnest attention. And, as Mr. Trenaman's final chapter shows, there is an encouraging side to the picture. He tells us—and he is able to cite many first-hand observations in support of his contention—that even the worst offenders possess redeeming features in their character. With suitable and intensive training, and with the co-operation of the various social agencies available to help them, there is every reason to believe that a very large proportion of these potential criminals can eventually be reclaimed.

B

ACKNOWLEDGEMENTS

THE years of observation and analysis that went to the making of this study would have been fruitless but for the generous help of friends who lightened the burden of the donkey work, of several officers at War Office who believed in the undertaking and went out of their way to help it forward, and of some distinguished psychologists and sociologists whose criticisms and encouragement and practical help are here acknowledged.

From the first I had the advice and gentle wisdom of my old colleague at the Special Training Unit, George Jamieson; he has contributed two chapters, XIII and XX, on the scholastic work of the Unit. I must thank Miss Alma Spoor for her kind assistance, and Dr. J. C. Penton, Principal Scientific Officer, Army Operational Research Group, for every sort of help most generously given; Brigadier D. H. Cole, formerly Deputy Director of Army Education and Brigadier W. G. Pidsley, Director of Army Education; Major W. S. Hooker, Mr. L. Atkinson and Mr. W. S. Theaker, without whom nothing could have been achieved; Mr. Theaker has befriended and kept in touch over some years with a great number of young soldiers from the Special Training Unit, and I am indebted to him for much valuable evidence. I should also like to thank Dr. G. M. Morant, of the Institute of Aviation Medicine; Miss Jean Rowntree, Mr. Seebohm Rowntree, Mr. Eric Cleaver and his friends and Comdr. Russell Lavers, for encouragement in more ways than I can mention; Mr. P. J. Rees of Swansea Technical Institute (Day-Release); Professor Sir Cyril Burt and Professor Philip Vernon, most generous of counsellors. Finally, I remember with gratitude the men who form the subjects of this study and who worked with me to bring it about, especially D.N., killed in action at Salerno.

J. T.

CONTENTS

Part One—Special Training

Part Two—The Offender

Part Three—The Offender in Conflict with the Army

Part Four—The Offender's Background

Part Five—Conclusions

ILLUSTRATIONS

Maps of Home Towns

Part One: SPECIAL TRAINING

CHAPTER I

AN ARMY EXPERIMENT

IN the early years of the War the Army was burdened with a
great number of young soldiers who would not take to discipline
and were running away from their units or making continual nuisances of themselves in other ways. Nearly every unit had problem
cases who were unable, literally or metaphorically, to keep in step,
and in the young soldier (70th) battalions there were large concentrations. They were not only useless as fighting men, but they
were likely to have a bad influence on others. They were putting
the Army to considerable expense in looking after them when they
were punished, or bringing them back to their units when they ran
away. For instance, it cost on average about seven pounds to
retrieve a single absentee.

Normal methods of punishment were tried repeatedly—confinement to barracks or imprisonment in detention cells, but without
reforming the prisoners, who went on with their offences as soon
as they were free, accumulating sometimes as many as thirty or
forty separate convictions. The Army was therefore faced with the
alternative of either continuing to try to fit them into its ranks or
discharging them. As civilians they might have proved an even
worse nuisance, with wider opportunities for misconduct, especially
in the event of invasion.

It was therefore decided to keep them in the Army and to see
whether some of them could be salvaged for useful work. By 1941
the Army was running short of manpower and this factor may have
influenced the Army Council's decision to try new methods of
dealing with the delinquents. It was felt by the Adjutant-General,
Sir Ronald Adam, that the time was ripe for an experiment in penal
reform which had for long been in his mind.

The first step was an instruction signed by Major-General
Douglas Hogg to all units in Northern Command worded as
follows: 'As an experimental measure beginning on Wednesday
17 Sept 41 all soldiers under 21 years of age who are brought before

you and to whom you would give either detention or a long period
of confinement to barracks may at your discretion be sent instead
to the Northern Command Young Soldiers' Training Camp, The
Racecourse, Pontefract, Yorkshire. . . . The training at this camp
will be specially framed with a view to reclaiming young soldiers
from a career of crime and converting them into good soldiers'.

So on September 17th, 1941, the first experimental corrective
unit was started under the command of Major Geoffrey Gilbey,
M.C. Within a few months the experiment was seen to be doing
well: the persistent absentees were not going absent and the assortment of grumblers, malingerers and rebels was participating in the
training. It was, of course, much too soon to know what permanent effect the training would have on the men, but the War
Office were sufficiently impressed to grant the unit a permanent
establishment and to set up two similar units, one in Eastern and
one in Southern Command. The observations and deductions
made in this work are for the most part the outcome of experiences
gained by the writer in one of the S.T.U.s (Special Training
Units) where he was in charge of Education. All three units were
at first identical in purpose and were governed by the same instructions concerning staff, intake and methods of training.

The Army Council Instruction authorizing the units defined their
purpose as follows:

'There are a number of young soldiers under the age of 21 years
who find difficulty in adjusting themselves to the conditions of Army
life. Through thoughtlessness and lack of a sense of discipline they
commit offences which cause them to become a nuisance to their
units. Normal punishments given by commanding officers and
field general courts-martial appear to do them little good and sometimes make them into worse soldiers.

'Special training units have been established to deal with such
men. By careful individual treatment, these units endeavour to
restore to each man his self-respect and to create in him a pride in
his work. After a course of varying length it is hoped by such
methods to return the man to an active unit, ready and anxious to
make a fresh start.

'These units are in no way punishment camps. While under-
going a course full privileges are allowed when off duty and leave
is granted in the usual manner.'

That reference to 'careful individual treatment' was the only
direction ever given as to methods of treatment. There were,

therefore, the widest opportunities for experiment. Naturally, the methods adopted were largely determined by the ideas of the commanding officer and of the staff whom he selected.

The unit establishment was for 60 staff and 240 trainees, a high ratio of one to four. The staff were carefully chosen; some volunteered to come because they were interested; one or two had experience of probation or Borstal work in civilian life.

Stated briefly, the broad assumption behind the method of training was that the offender could gradually be led into sociable ways, first, by getting to know the personal problem inside the man, secondly by relaxing the pressure of normal discipline and substituting a gentler routine, thirdly by appealing to a man's better nature and avoiding punishments as long as possible, fourthly by developing his education and physique, and fifthly by scrupulous attention to important details of hygiene and social habit. A similar assumption has been described by Mr. L. C. Atkinson of one of the units, as follows:

'What is meant by individual attention?

'Initial welcome of him. Earliest possible talks with him by C.O. and other officers, by the Educational and P.T. staff men and by the Welfare men; quiet, encouraging, eliciting talks aimed at (a) gaining knowledge of his background; (b) acquiring an idea of his outlook, his values, the character-defections to be coped with, his particular educational and physical needs. That information should be carefully recorded and unfailingly perused when he is being dealt with in any particular circumstances.

'Helping him to realize that self-discipline of him is our real aim, not merely the requiring of him to conform to the outward show of military discipline, important though that is.

'Making him feel, when he lapses, that he has earned the award and that it is not imposed to satisfy the indignation or offended sense of any one person; that in the main he has offended against himself.

'By teaching him that it matters not so much what happens to him at any time, as how he reacts; that award or disappointment, withstood by steady conduct, subsequently strengthens him in character.

'By not losing faith in his potentiality for doing well and—what is equally important—allowing him to be aware of that faith. At the same time, by precept and example, setting him standards of conduct.

'By improving his literacy and developing his sense of citizenship and need for soldiering—by repeated educational talks and lectures from outside, carefully chosen.'

The method might perhaps be likened to the Japanese game of Judo in which an opponent's lunges are not resisted but invited, so that he throws himself by his own strength—except that the S.T.U. method was to teach him not to fall.

Thus, if a man appeared to be in danger of running away he was frequently given leave and trusted to come back. If he disliked military training he was taken off it and tried at something quite different, like gardening. If he was all the while hankering after a life at sea he was sent out on a minesweeper for a few days (an experience that sometimes had a sobering effect). If he had trouble at home he was sent on leave and given an opportunity of putting things right, and was helped in every way possible. If he was illiterate or backward and wanted to learn he was taught what he most wanted to know. If he defaulted he was given another chance, and then more chances. It was thought that once a man had decided to accept any of these forms of help he had, in a sense, surrendered his hostile position and the process of re-education had begun.

CHAPTER II

METHODS OF TREATMENT

ON arrival at the Unit many of the trainees had only a vague idea of the sort of place they were coming to. The few who arrived handcuffed naturally assumed that they were being conducted to a place of confinement. Most, even those who had been told something of the nature of the unit, were suspicious of what they would find.[1] A questionnaire on the subject of their attitude to the S.T.U. was put to a sample of the intake early in 1944. This formed part of a whole scheme of inquiry which will be outlined in Chapter VI. As many as 40 per cent admitted that they intended to go absent on arrival at the unit. When asked whether 'most men intended going absent' on arrival, 69 per cent answered 'yes'. The fact that only 4 per cent of the new arrivals did in fact run away or overstay leave (mostly the latter, and the percentage amongst new arrivals would be even smaller), shows that for the big majority the first impressions of the S.T.U. must have been favourable.

The intention was that the newcomer should find friendliness and efficiency. The friendliness could only spring from a sincere interest in the purpose of the unit on the part of all members of the staff. The efficiency, most noticeable in matters like pay, allowances for dependants, leave and Army employment, was insisted on by the Commanding Officer.

After a man had been at the unit a little while he formed a pretty clear idea of its purpose. Asked why they had been sent to the S.T.U., all but 15 per cent of the sample gave a reasonable answer. The most common was 'because I had been a nuisance': then, in order of frequency, 'to make me a better soldier', or 'because of my absence', or 'because I couldn't settle down to Army life', 'because I was not up to the standard of the Battalion' and—less than half the truth—'because I was too young'.

[1] One of the two Welfare Sergeants, who met most new arrivals at the station, tells of one man, 'who came off the train with a bulky object concealed under his blouse, which proved to be a large mirror he had unscrewed from the railway compartment'.

Another question was 'Why do you think the Army has set up Special Training Units?' Three-quarters gave reasonably correct answers which show, perhaps as clearly as anything, the impression that the unit had already made on the men. The one most frequently quoted was 'to help young soldiers become good soldiers', and next 'to give us another chance', but one or two individual quotations will illustrate the reaction better: 'To help men who get discouraged and lose confidence and feel they are being unfairly dealt with', wrote one. 'To train nuisance men into fighting men', and 'to make round holes for round pegs'. There was, of course, a core of objectors (numbering about 6 per cent) who declared that the unit was 'no good', 'a waste of time', or, in self-justification, 'because it is N.C.O.s that usually make men go absent so the Army picks certain ones (i.e. soldiers, not N.C.O.s) and send them here'. A revealing statement from an aggressive youngster who was obsessed with the idea that he was being victimized, was 'my reason for being sent to this Camp where I am victimized every day is because I tried to soldier'. One man completed a questionnaire shortly after arrival in which he said 'I have no idea why I was sent here. It was a dirty trick'. He described the staff as 'terrible' and said he would 'shoot them all'. A few weeks later he answered the same questions again. This time he wrote, 'The S.T.U. is to teach boys to soldier and it's a good idea as it has reformed me and hundreds of others.' Besides these two groups, there were about 18 per cent who said that they 'didn't know' why such units were set up.

Two further soundings were taken to measure the depth of understanding of the purpose of the unit. One question was 'Do you think the staff is trying to be fair to you?', to which 93 per cent answered 'yes'. The other was 'Is the unit better or worse than you expected it to be?' The answer of 81 per cent was 'better' but 16 per cent said it was 'worse'. The latter included some of the most difficult cases, many of whom could still see no good in any Army undertaking. One of these, writing on 25th April 1944, found the unit 'worse' than he had expected: he did not know why it was set up and thought the staff were not trying to be fair. Twelve days later, on 7th May, he answered the same question again (having been transferred meanwhile to another platoon). This time the answer to the first question was 'better': the staff, he said, were fair, and he suggested that the unit was set up 'to teach men to keep out of trouble'. He added that 'This is the longest I have been in the Army without a charge'. He had passed his worst moment and was for the time being on the up-grade.

The training programme of the S.T.U. appeared to differ little from that of the normal army unit. There were full periods of P.T. and education every week-day, and regular instruction in drill, the use of weapons and other military activities. A newcomer would be attached to a platoon of forty or fifty men and the morning after his arrival he would parade with them for his day's duties. Thus the programme was sufficiently like normal military training for the young soldier to feel a continuity in his life—he was neither being locked up nor treated as a patient—and, if he were interested, he could feel that he was not wasting his time as a soldier. The 'special' nature of the training was to be found in the attitude of the staff to trainees, in the various outside and after-duty activities, in the wide choice of employment and the carefully adjusted tempo of the work. The training could be said to touch the man at three levels—the moral, the mental and the physical.

On the moral plane the points of contact were the two sergeant specialists concerned with welfare. They were L. C. Atkinson, of the Borstal Association, and W. S. Theaker, a lawyer with wide experience of social work; their experience and understanding of young offenders were of immense value to every side of the Unit's work. To the young offender, not the least point in their favour was that they had friends in many cities who could help distressed relations; since they were counsellors to the Commanding Officer they could influence leave, Army jobs and even pay! This power to recommend a change of job was most valuable, for many a new-comer to the Unit would be willing to conform for a few months in order to obtain a desired posting. A conformity based on expediency was, in itself, unlikely to effect a permanent change of behaviour, but it tended to form a habit and provided an oppor-tunity for the new training to make an impression. The unit was a junction from which men could branch off into almost any job or regiment. It could even post men into the much-coveted Mer-cantile Artillery, or Water Transport regiments. So the prospect of a change of arm or unit was a powerful factor in holding many of these men, and (as will be shown in Chapter XIV) most of them were anxious to make a change of some sort.

A resident psychologist could have contributed much. One would still have needed to refer defective cases to a psychiatrist who could help to sort out the men with profound psychopathic personalities, the borderline mental defectives and the schizo-phrenics upon whom one often wasted time and trouble. But a resident psychologist with established powers would have helped members of the staff to understand the complex personality pro-blems that were so common. But there was only a visiting psychia-trist to whom difficult cases were referred for an interview of half an hour or so. At the end of the interview, and in the light of the man's record and his intelligence and attainment test results, the psychiatrist made a recommendation—sometimes discharge from the Army, sometimes transfer to the Pioneer Corps where the soldier would be more likely to find employment within his competence, or, more often, more training or more discipline. But, as some Army psychiatrists would readily acknowledge, it was not possible to gain a man's full confidence in one interview. Seldom was any practical suggestion offered for treating or training a man who was to stay at the special training unit. And, as happened more than once, a remark like 'discipline firmly applied', appended to the record of a man upon whom the Army's strictest discipline had utterly failed, contributed little.

The two Welfare sergeants were accessible to the men at all times of the day and night, but they were overwhelmed by the work. There was generally a queue of a dozen men or more outside their rooms, lounging on the back stairs, waiting to get in to see them. The job threw out roots. For they kept in touch by correspondence with the men who had been posted away, so that their postbag, after some months, was enormous. And it is still going on.

The second level of training was educational, and a later chapter is devoted to explaining what was attempted in this work. The young soldier had an hour's educational instruction every working day. There was basic instruction in the three R's and a good deal of general knowledge work which seemed to help those who were capable of social adaptation to understand the demands of society and the simple elements of their own nature. Daytime instruction was naturally linked with spare-time activities. It will be seen (in Chapter XIX) that most of the men were at a loss to entertain them-selves. In the pursuit of a hobby they needed continual encourage-ment and supervision. The Education Centre, offering the facilities and the supervisors, soon became a centre of some useful, though some useless, activities during evenings and week-ends.

The necessity for discipline in educational training was apt to present difficulties too. For example, the trainees' entry into class was disconcerting if sometimes amusing. They would tumble in, knocking over desks and chairs and often upsetting any models or displays that were arranged. One man might throw another's cap to the far side of the room. Some model tanks were displayed on a side table and these would occasionally be picked up and used for a mock battle, with simulated machine-gun rattlings from the audience. There would then be a chanting and pounding of boots on the floor. No attempt was made to silence them by shouting or threatening. Threats were useless unless one intended to carry them into effect. To put one of these men on a charge—that is to bring him before the commanding officer for a military offence—would have been an admission of failure to cope with the situation. A joke or two was more effective in getting their tempers right. It was then best to start talking, preferably interrogatively, about some simple matter that was likely to interest them. Sometimes, and more especially with the platoons which had been in the unit some months, they would take the situation in hand themselves, and loud cries of 'quiet', 'shut up', 'pack it up there', would over-ride the pandemonium. These initial outbursts of rowdiness were probably useful as a 'safety valve'. It would have been quite easy to silence them with an angry word but the practice, in the educational centre at any rate, was to permit indiscipline for a few minutes, but only as a contrasting preliminary, for during instruction periods complete silence and attention was the rule and on no occasion were the men allowed to get out of hand.

The question 'Do you think you learn anything worth while in Military Education?' produced some interesting answers. Some 86 per cent answered affirmatively, adding remarks like 'because it showed me where I made my mistakes', or 'it eases your mind', or 'it teaches you to give your opinion and see other men's point of view', or magnificently 'I want to learn as much about the world and things on it while I can'. Not all, of course, were so earnest and the man who wrote that he liked the education classes because 'you have a sit-down' may have been speaking for many.

The third level of training was the physical. The old-fashioned idea of physical training is that it should be a form of vigorous exercise intended to develop muscles, the more tiring the better. Army P.T. was based on almost the opposite assumption. Its purpose was varied according to the condition of the man and the job he was being trained to do. Sometimes it was designed to loosen and relax, sometimes to strengthen and invigorate the whole body. It was a general experience that after a session of P.T. one felt fresher than when one started. At the S.T.U., under first-class instruction, physical training was adapted to the men's condition. It was not hard, yet it was never slow. It was full of fun but no liberties were taken. If any man broke the rules he was tanned on the behind with his own slipper by one of the others, after the group had decided the number of slaps he deserved; and he generally got it hard.

The whole physical programme—exercises, games, running and obstacle course work—was carefully graded from an easy beginning, keeping well within the men's physical powers and confidence. At first some of them felt it was too easy after the tough going at infantry training centres, and at times they even complained of boredom. But the improvements shown in weight, fitness and stamina convinced the staff that they were right to go slow. The men got more individual attention than the Army could spare them in their primary training and field units. The diffident or frightened youngsters were coaxed and encouraged until they could perform feats that surprised even themselves. One young man, when first confronted by the obstacle course, could not attempt it and was excused from most of the jumps and climbs. But he gathered courage until eventually he was jumping ditches, crawling through underground tunnels, climbing over an enormous scaffolding, crossing water on a rope bridge with exploding charges on either side, and dashing through obstacles with the best of them.

The men responded well to this physical programme. Asked, in a questionnaire, how they 'got on with P.T.', a majority of 78 per cent found it to their liking. 'It makes me feel wide awake', said several; 'I don't like it but it does me good' was another typical remark.

The staff were also constantly watching over the men's personal cleanliness, sending them for baths, getting them to wash and change their socks regularly, even cutting their toenails. They were taught to keep their huts clean, and even to polish their badges. So gradually, by gently graded physical exercise, by continual attention and a good deal of 'jollying', they were nursed into health and tidy ways. The secret, if one can call it that, was fellow-feeling and a high staffing ratio.

The whole training programme appears to have been well balanced, for all sides of it appealed to fairly equal proportions of

A P.T. class in the Special Training Unit grounds

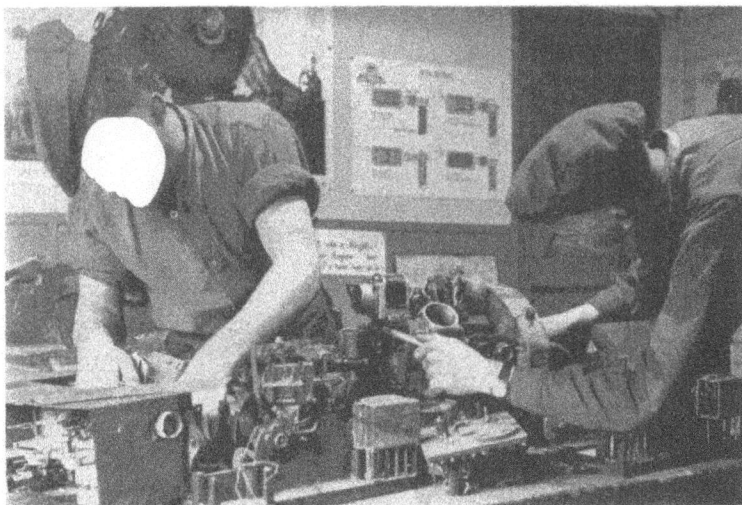

Trainees in the workshop

The old motor boat engine and derelict radio equipment shown above were stripped down to the last bolt, and never reassembled.

the men. A question 'What part of the training here do you like best?' showed roughly similar numbers voting for Education (35 per cent) and P.T. (35 per cent) and the rest (30 per cent) mentioning some form of military instruction, mostly drill or assault course work.

The place of discipline was suggested by the contrast between 'on parade' and 'off parade' manners. On parade, and all daytime duties were parades, strict military discipline was required though it was sometimes conspicuously lacking. After duty there was a friendly mixing between the staff and trainees.

The disciplinary side of the training was perhaps the most difficult to maintain at a proper balance between strictness and laxity. The instructors were dealing with men who had proved themselves hostile to discipline. Yet they had to maintain order, to enforce the basic regulations and they naturally wanted to show some results in military training. At the same time they had to exercise the utmost restraint and consideration for the men who were continually defying them. That was asking a lot of non-commissioned officers who had been brought up in the methods of the regular Army. The results achieved owed much to the splendid work of what Major Hooker often described as his 'backbone', the Sergeants' Mess.

One of the questions put to the sample of trainees was 'What do you think of the discipline here?' It was not well worded for it could and did so easily give rise to ambiguities in the answers. About 20 per cent did not like the discipline and nearly as many described it as too strict, including the anti-social minority for whom 'all discipline in the Army is wrong', to quote one. Nevertheless, the fact that 62 per cent found it satisfactory suggests that it was a fairly light burden. Another question, 'Is it easier to keep out of trouble here than elsewhere?' showed the same distribution in the answers: 63 per cent answering 'yes' and 37 per cent 'no'. Much the same reaction was recorded to a question about the unit's regimental police: 60 per cent were on good terms with them, 13 per cent said they had nothing to do with them, and 27 per cent—much the same group as the objectors to discipline—did not get on well with them. It was evidently no coincidence that many of the men who found the unit so unsatisfactory were also those whose personalities appeared to be most unstable (two-thirds of them are classified as aggressive, immature, introspective or wandering types in Chapter X).

One test of a man's integration into the Army is his willingness to accept promotion. As an inducement to co-operation, the Unit frequently organized cadre courses for the training of potential non-commissioned officers. A dozen or more men would be selected and put through a fortnight's training course, at the end of which the four or five best would be made unpaid lance-corporals and given minor responsibilities. The demotions were numerous and it was not unusual to find a man going up, down, up and then down again. But the general results were good and several men continued to advance to senior ranks. To test the men's attitude a question was put: 'Would you take promotion?'—44 per cent answered that they would. Some of the rest qualified their answers by saying 'not at this unit', feeling that it would be difficult to maintain authority over soldiers who knew their past and would be likely to take advantage of their feelings of inadequacy. Others were constitutionally unsuited and were only giving the sensible answer in saying 'no'. But this question again revealed the minority who were hostile to authority through such answers as 'I'm not the fellow to stand around and tell other people what to do'.

It was not easy to discover what kind of training a man would most readily accept, so he was usually tried out at various occupations until he found something he liked. Besides the basic training programme there were a number of special duties that normally occupied from a third to half of all the trainees. There was work in the large gardens, in the pioneer squads maintaining the camp building, in building squads erecting huts, in cookhouse, sanitary and cleaning squads, and on near-by farms. In this way the man was helped to find a job he was suited for, and the routine and sense of purpose that came from the work itself played some part in his re-education.[1]

The effective group to which the trainee was most firmly attached was the platoon. The four platoons, which bore the names of Auchinleck, Wavell, Smuts and Churchill, were planned as independent communities. They trained separately and their huts were grouped in separate parts of the grounds. There is no doubt that the young offender will more readily attach himself to a small group

---

[1] Rodger, Alec, *A Borstal Experiment in Vocational Guidance* (H.M.S.O., 1937) showed that 69·5 per cent of a group of Borstal trainees for whom work had been found on lines recommended by the author after testing and interviews, proved to be 'satisfactory' whereas only 45·6 per cent of a control group, not so guided, turned out equally 'satisfactory'.

than to a large community. A dozen to twenty is probably the optimum size, though platoons were usually much bigger. In this group the man could grow roots, learn to give and take and begin to assess himself at the value the others placed upon him. On balance, it would probably have been better for a man to remain with the same group during most of his stay at the unit or until he was clearly capable of returning to normal Army life. 'On balance', because there was also a need for graded training through which the offender would pass and this need could most easily be met by grading the platoons and moving a man through them at his own speed of development as was done at the S.T.U. Perhaps the two principles are not entirely exclusive, for it should be possible to select platoons from men of similar type so that the backward would not lag far behind the leaders, and to keep this unit intact while moving it through graded stages in the training. At the S.T.U. the platoons were large and their group life was probably rather weak in consequence.

One of the doubts that haunted the staff was whether the mixing of types in a unit like the S.T.U. would not result in a levelling down towards the standards of the worst. The doubt became a challenge when some desperate character went absent after committing a serious offence, taking with him three or four others whose records were clean by comparison. Yet the unit could obviously only succeed if it managed to weld this diverse human material into an organic whole. They had to learn to work together and to live together amicably. By understanding each other's troubles, and by helping each other they would help themselves. The written work and the group discussions that provided the material for this present inquiry were an important part of that process (see p. 33). An *esprit de corps* did evolve but it was not easy going; it called for a daily, hourly struggle against ignorance, outbursts of temper and defaulting. There were continual petty thefts that inevitably made the men suspicious of each other. Yet there were times, like the occasions of a ceremonial parade in the local town or the response to an appeal to save damaged crops, when they rose to considerable heights. Their attitude to each other was revealed by a question 'What do you think, in confidence, of the other men here?' Some 27 per cent thought they were bad. 'They're the biggest rogues—they would steal off the blind' wrote one virtuous old rogue whose conduct sheet recorded many misdeeds. 'Some are crafty, some shy and some are scroungers', was another description. On the other

c

hand, 73 per cent had a fairly favourable opinion of their fellows, including 42 per cent who thought they were good. 'They are all good but they have had no chance', was one opinion. 'Some have lots of confidence and some none', 'they don't like having to do anything, like me', and 'the bad are the best and vice versa' were other views, more revealing of the writers than of the other men.

The one trait that was common to nearly all of these men was a sense of inferiority. They felt, deep within themselves, not only that they were failures but that they were unable to cope with life; therefore they were acutely sensitive to criticism and were all the time tempted to escape into a world of make-believe. If a civilian stared at them in the main street they felt they were being marked down as 'one of the Borstal boys'. 'Do you think local civilians are prejudiced against you because you come from the S.T.U.?' was perhaps too leading a question, but 76 per cent answered 'yes'. This prejudice they attributed to various causes: some blamed their predecessors who had boasted of their crimes, some remarked naïvely 'they know what we're here for', or 'they have seen our men shouting rude remarks at women'. Their acute suspicion was shown in the suggestion that the words 'special training' in the unit's name were to blame, or that the wearing of a belt when walking out marked them down. 'They call us thieves and hooligans', said some, and 'it shows their low mentality'. Some prejudice on the part of some civilians there may have been but it was far outweighed by the goodwill shown to the camp especially by those in the immediate neighbourhood who helped with dances, canteens and concerts.

This same sense of inferiority prompted some of the men to conceal from their parents the fact that they were at a corrective unit. They were asked 'Do you tell the people at home that you are at the S.T.U.?'; 18 per cent said they did not. Some of those who did were careful not to reveal the special nature of the training, hence the curious addresses that turned up on men's letters— 'Special Commando Training Unit', and 'Staff Training Unit'! Some of the reasons given for not telling their people at home were: 'I am too ashamed, certainly not', or 'they think I'm on a course', or best of all: 'they don't think I'm in the Army because I always wear civvies all the while I'm on leave!'

The men's reaction to the training as a whole was variable and inconsistent. Some would improve and co-operate wonderfully and then suddenly regress. Some would remain apparently un-

affected by the unit and leave, as they came, hostile to all in authority. Some would show an astonishing improvement at first only
to revert slowly to their bad old habits. One of the problems was to
decide whether to let every man stay as long as possible or whether
to post him away while he was on the crest of a wave, if there was
one. The average length of stay at a special training unit was at
first about six months, but in 1944 the period was restricted to four
months except for cases which might be referred to a psychiatrist,
who could recommend that they should stay on up to six months.
It was felt by the staff that most of the trainees did not stay long
enough for the new way to take firm hold. Probably some period
near the Borstal average of twenty months would have been
desirable but one could not expect the Army in wartime to wait so
long for results. Sometimes a man would go away rebellious to
the last, perhaps to serve a long spell of detention before moving
on to his new unit. One felt at the time that such a case was
hopeless or that the wrong methods had been employed. Yet
many a man in that position surprised one by turning out well in
the end. There is always a certain lag in time between the action
of a new environment and an individual's reaction to it. The
relative tranquillity of life at the S.T.U. came to the stormy lives of
some men as an interlude, throwing into relief the harsh reality
that followed. Some of them said in letters, 'We realized what you
had tried to do for us after we left.' One such man was encountered by chance in London in 1947. He had come to the S.T.U.
with fifteen offences on his conduct sheet. He remained defiant
throughout his stay and was finally sentenced by court-martial to
six months' imprisonment. He said that afterwards he regretted
that he had not made better use of his time at the S.T.U. and he
made up his mind to try and co-operate with his new unit. He
managed to keep out of further trouble, served overseas with his
regiment, was promoted to the rank of sergeant, and on his return
to England signed up for regular service. He was engaged to a
pleasant-looking girl who was with him at the time, and he appeared
a very smart and contented young man.

Thus, the response that many of these men appeared to make
to all that was done for them was ingratitude and a succession of
rebellious acts. Yet it was essential that when a man was behaving
badly the staff should remain consistently sympathetic. At such
times he was obviously divided against himself. His old habits
and his instinctive feelings were pulling him down, making him

irritable, urging him to rebel or run away. His new attachments to the unit and to some of the staff were counselling moderation and co-operation. A harsh word or punishment from those he had begun to respect would only rebuff the better side and reinforce the worse. In fact, if there is any law in the treatment of delinquents, it is that sympathy and patience are needed in inverse ratio to the apparent deserts of the man.

Such topsy-turvy principles put a severe strain on the staff. Obviously, men with special qualities were needed for the work. Something more than a sense of vocation was called for, and those who were most anxious to help were not necessarily the most suitable.

Perhaps because many of these young men were physically inferior, it would not have been difficult for a staff of older and generally bigger men to establish a physical ascendancy over them. The young offender's first reaction to camp or prison staff is often much nearer the physical than the mental, especially in the case of those who have been associated with gangs of lads where the leader is usually the physically superior. The problem is to transfer physical fear to moral respect,[1] for unless such a transference is made the official will have to domineer, to fall back on the authority of his rank, and, in the last resort, on the threat of his own force or somebody else's to maintain discipline.

The attitude of the S.T.U. trainees to the more successful members of the staff was almost that of son to father. That may explain why any attempt to promote young soldiers to be N.C.O.s often met with quite strong opposition from the others—because they felt it was wrong to be under the control of someone their own age, just as a boy resents a brother usurping the place of the father.

There were times when a little show of indignation was not a bad thing. It was quite a different matter from losing one's temper. If, even under the sharpest provocation, any member of the staff

[1] An illustration of this problem in an exceptional form is quoted in *Road to Life* by Anton Makarenko (Stanley Nott, 1936). Makarenko was the director of a penal colony in Russia. He was a small, mild man but was once provoked beyond endurance by a rebellious gang of delinquents. In a stormy scene he went up to the ringleader—a truculent fellow much bigger than himself—and struck him on the cheek, knocking him down. The blow obviously shocked the gang as much as it surprised Makarenko himself, for thereafter the whole atmosphere changed for the better. It was not the blow itself, nor any suggestion of terrorism that worked the change; rather the contrary, for it was a token of the utmost indignation from one who was profoundly opposed to any form of violence and whom, secretly, the boys must have respected.

lost his temper he had almost certainly lost the man's respect for ever. Yet it was not uncommon for a man who had defied months of detention, including restricted prison diet and solitary confinement, to be reduced to tears by a single sharp word from the right person. In many respects the offender is like a child; however tough and insensitive he may appear, he is very susceptible to the slightest correction from those he has come to respect.

It is sometimes suggested that close confinement at night and harsh penalties are needed to protect the staff of penal institutions. Yet at the S.T.U., where there was no confinement and the minimum of punishment, no violence was ever shown to a member of the staff, nor were there many thefts from staff rooms. There were one or two raids on the quartermaster's stores and on the officers' quarters, mostly by men intending to escape who were seeking civilian clothes or some means of raising money. The educational staff had a stream of men visiting their rooms but very seldom was anything taken. There was one notable exception. One day the author's bicycle disappeared. When the loss became known several men approached him and said that the culprits were newcomers who did not yet know the ways of the camp. They promised to find out where the bicycle had been taken, and recover it. Days passed and any hope of seeing the bicycle again faded. Then an eager youngster burst into the room with the news that the machine was on its way back. The culprits had been traced and 'dealt with'— no details of the treatment were asked or given—and the bicycle itself appeared in an extraordinary condition. It had obviously been dismantled and put together again because movable parts were in different positions, but the astonishing thing was that in the process of recovery it had acquired a pump and several small fittings that were not there before.

It seems appropriate to conclude this chapter with a quotation from a statement by L. C. Atkinson in which he tried to sum up the unique features of 'special training'. He writes: 'He had gradually to absorb the lesson that it mattered not so much what happened to him from day to day, as how he controlled his reaction; that disappointment or penalty, withstood by steady behaviour, strengthened him.

'Expectation of transfer in due course to the job in the Service to which he felt more drawn or equal, was perhaps the basic hold on him by the Unit, initially. Subsequently, that became of almost secondary importance, when complete rapport with him had been achieved and his self-centred desires modified. But careful placement of him always within his limitations, was obviously wise.

'Incarceration is ugly in sound and meaning. To the growing young man it can be stunting, sometimes beyond repair. "Walls do not a prison make . . ."—only perhaps to the older person of some philosophy. The S.T.U. has been to the detention barracks as the open Borstal to the closed one. Its experience may become regarded as having been progressive in effect. The future treatment of the younger persistent offender, either in Civil or Service life, may well be bound up in establishments that provide working hours full and yielding; that offer full freedom and trust. But the corollary will be ample staff, vocationally gifted men and women of deep-rooted belief in human possibilities—able quickly to win, hold and develop whatever is best in each young person, until social readjustment ensues.'

CHAPTER III

THE RESULTS ACHIEVED BY 'SPECIAL' TRAINING

THE eventual posting away was a matter for the most careful consideration. The man's aptitudes and his own wishes had to be taken into account, though the many requests for a driving job or for service with the merchant navy could obviously not always be met. If a man had found a job that suited him, every effort was made to keep him in it. If his mental powers or his attainments pointed to any particular job—for example, Pioneer Corps work for the dull or a specialist corps for the very intelligent man with mechanical or special abilities—then a request for posting was sent to the appropriate regiment. The finding of a job within, but neither beneath nor above, his competence was known to go a long way towards making a contented soldier. Many men were posted to units where they had friends or to their own county regiments. They were not posted back to their old units, unless the man himself particularly requested it and it was known that his former Commanding Officer wanted to have him back. The following table shows the disposals of 696 men who had been posted away from the Special Training Unit up to the time when the present inquiry was made:

	TABLE 1		%
Posted to Field Force Units		521	76
Transferred to Pioneer Corps		26	4
Discharged from the Army		17	2·4
To Hospital		27	4
To Detention (over 28 days) or suspended sentences put into execution		51	7·3
Deserters		22	3
Convicted by Civil Court (prison or Borstal)		23	3
Miscellaneous disposals		9	0·3
		696	100

Of the large numbers posted to Field Force units, 10 per cent went to a unit of their old regiment, but to a different battalion from the one which sent them to the S.T.U. The remaining 90 per cent changed their regiments.

Was the training successful?

The Adjutant-General allowed a generous margin for failures in saying that even if the units only turned out five per cent of successes' they would have justified their existence. But after the first six months it was with the deepest doubts that some of the staff accompanied these young men to the railway station, assuring them, with simulated conviction, that all would be well. Some showed no noticeable sign of improvement and it seemed such a little time since even the most improved had been indifferent or hostile.

The Commanding Officers of the units to which these men were posted were required by War Office to complete a questionnaire showing how the newcomer had progressed in the first three months since leaving the Special Training Unit. Assessments were required of the man's disciplinary record, his conduct in the unit, his willingness to do an uncongenial job, his efficiency as a soldier at drill, at weapon training and the handling of weapons. These assessments were made on a five-point scale of 'very good', 'above average', 'average', 'below average' and 'very bad'. A mark of 'average' would thus be taken to mean that the newcomer was no worse, if no better, than the usual run of men in the unit, and was therefore an acceptable soldier.

The first few reports returned showed that many of the men posted away were turning out well in their new units, and later counts confirmed this very favourable result. By early 1944, when reports on 356 men from the S.T.U. had been returned, as many as 80 per cent were said to be average or above in their conduct and attitude, as the following table shows:

TABLE 2

Reports on the conduct of 356 young soldiers, made three months after posting from the Special Training Unit—(percentages):

	(a) Very good	(b) Above average	(a) + (b)	Average	Below average	Very bad
	%	%	%	%	%	%
Disciplinary record	18·0	18·8	(36·8)	44·9	11·8	6·5
Conduct in unit	15·0	18·1	(33·1)	48·8	14·1	4·0
Willingness to do uncongenial job	13·4	24·5	(37·9)	43·2	16·0	2·9

A later reckoning, taken shortly before the Special Training Units were disbanded (in August 1945) was based on the reports of just over a thousand men from the three units, as follows:

TABLE 3

Reports on the conduct and military records of 1039 young soldiers, made three months after their posting from the three Special Training Units, expressed as percentages:

	Very good and Above average	Average	Below average, and Very bad
	%	%	%
Disciplinary record	28	48	24
Conduct in unit	25	53	22
Willingness to do un-congenial job	29	50	21
Efficiency as a soldier in:			
(1) drill	21	62	17
(2) weapon training	15	66	19
(3) tactical handling of weapons[1]	13	64	23

Although men were not normally sent back to the units which had posted them to the Special Training Unit, there were exceptions numbering 98 altogether. Follow-up reports on these showed that 64 per cent were said to have improved as a result of S.T.U. training, 35 per cent were the same, and only one was worse. Some men were marked average or above in one or two respects but below average in others. If one counts as 'successful' only those men who were marked at least average in *all three* of the conduct factors listed, then the proportion of 'successes' among the 356 postings was 73 per cent. If, further, some account is taken of the men who were not posted to new units but were discharged or deserted or were sent to prison by a civil court, then the proportion of 'successes' stands at 66·8 per cent.

The way the ratings are distributed in the two tables above—skewed towards the 'above average' level—calls for comment; it would appear from the evidence that the ex-S.T.U. man made a better soldier than the non-offender. That is too much to believe and one must suppose that commanding officers were inclined to be lenient to the 'prodigal son'.

As a measure of the success of the training these figures are, of course, only the first tentative evidence. The Army's standards were necessarily minimal—conformity to the rules, and efficiency as a soldier—and it is highly probable that many men from special

[1] Only 888 cases; some men were posted to units where this subject was not included in the training.

training units learned to accept these standards and yet remained potential delinquents. It is equally probable, as the record in the men's Army documents shows, that some did not become reconciled to the Army for a considerable time after leaving the S.T.U. The evidence from correspondence which various members of the staff kept up with old boys, throws a little more light on the way they turned out, though it is much less complete than the evidence in the discharge reports. The type of man who corresponded after posting with a member of the S.T.U. staff was perhaps finding it harder to integrate himself into the Army or civilian society than the man who was able to stand on his own feet. On the other hand, the obtuse or psychopathic type would probably not write at all. There are records of a regular interchange of letters with 66 men from the Special Training Unit. Of these, 17 (or about 26 per cent) turned out unsatisfactory, 40 could be termed satisfactory and 9 very good. As will be shown in the following paragraphs, this evidence presents rather too bright a picture.

The documents of a sample of 200 men posted from the Special Training Unit enable one to trace their after-histories up to the time of their release from the Army.

Looking first at the records of conduct one notices that there are only 12 per cent with no offences at all recorded against them after leaving the S.T.U. The numbers of crimes entered upon the sheets range from one or two odd lapses to a maximum of sixteen convictions (which included 14 of absence without leave and one of desertion). In the first table below the numbers of those committing various types of offences are shown as percentages of the whole group. The second table records the average number of offences among those men convicted of such offences (not the whole sample). In the first column, under 'Civil and equivalent Army convictions', are listed all those offences like housebreaking for which a soldier must be brought before a civilian court, as well as offences like improper possession (theft) and striking (violence against the person of another soldier) which are normally tried in Army courts but would be breaches of civilian law if committed against civilians. In the column headed 'Personal neglect' are gathered all those minor offences like appearing on parade with long hair, or broken boot-laces, or without a field-dressing, or with a spot of rust on a bayonet scabbard. Under 'Late' are listed offences like overstaying leave by a few hours or missing a parade.

TABLE 4

Percentages of 200 trainees convicted of various types of offence
before and after special training

Period	Civil and equivalent Army convictions	Deser-tion	Absence without leave	Late	Other disciplinary	Personal neglect
	%	%	%	%	%	%
Pre-S.T.U. (1 year)	11	2	74	54	77	51
Post-S.T.U. (Annual average, 3 years)	5·3	2·3	19·3	4·7	14·3	3·7

TABLE 5

Average numbers of various types of offence among those men
committing such offences before and after special training.

Period	Civil and equiva-lent	Deser-tion	Absence	Late	Discip-linary	Personal neglect
Pre-S.T.U. (1 year)	1·3	1·0	3·4	2·5	2·7	2·4
Post S.T.U. (Annual average over 3 years)	0·4	0·4	1·2	0·6	0·7	0·5

Bearing in mind the difference in length of the two periods, there appears to have been a fall in the rate of offences among the men convicted of civilian or corresponding Army offences. Comparisons are difficult because most of the men went abroad where the chances of committing or being apprehended for such offences were fewer, though one or two offences against enemy civilians are included.

The desertion rate fell from an average of once per deserter per year to once every two years. More men deserted in the three post-S.T.U. years but the rate per year was much less. One man cleared off in the Ardennes and another in the Middle East, the former being apprehended and later discharged as a psychopathic personality; the latter was not discovered. Fewer men went absent without leave (and the rate per person affected was much lower) but it should be remembered that in overseas theatres of war running away from one's unit was a hazardous undertaking. The decline in the numbers of latecomers may be accounted for by the fact that privilege leave was rare in overseas service.

The difference in the proportions invoking punishments for disciplinary offences represents a real fall in the crime rate, and this trend is even more marked in the proportions convicted of offences of personal neglect. It does seem that in overseas service many of these men were more willing to conform than they had been at home. The knowledge that they were cut off from escape to their own homes may have strengthened their ties to their Army groups, and the proximity of action and 'real soldiering' may have prompted them to co-operate.

Three men broke down completely in action. One man's company commander reported: 'at the Rhine crossing he was too jittery to fire anything but random shots.' He became a danger to his comrades and was soon discharged for hysteria (sensory). Others did particularly well in times of danger and several were commended in their release testimonials for their bravery. One man's document read: 'He saw considerable active service in Burma and did outstandingly well, receiving a Mention in Despatches. Unfortunately he gets into a good deal of trouble when in a peace station. If kept busy he is capable of behaving well and is a good worker, smart and well turned out.' Or again:

'A volunteer commando and qualified parachutist, he has a high standard in behaviour, loyal and can be confidently recommended.'

In general, these men served well when they were called upon to enter operational zones. As many as 80 per cent went overseas, mostly to Burma, Malaya, Italy and North-West Europe and serious defections were rare. Twelve men (6 per cent) were wounded in action, five of whom died as a result of their wounds. One man was shot by a German child of seven.

The subsequent histories of 196 out of 203 men, whose cases form the basis of the present study, have been traced through to the time of their Army discharge. One man became a sergeant and went through to his release with a clean record and then signed up for a regular engagement. As a regular soldier he had to begin again as a private and within a year had incurred six punishments for disciplinary offences. So, even amongst those who seem most reformed and most stable there may be relapses.

The normal mode of release for a soldier who was serving for the duration of the wartime emergency was 'Class A' or 'transfer to the W.T. reserve'. An alternative was 'Class B' under which tradesmen who were needed for urgent civilian employment could be released before the date indicated by their age-and-service group. If one excludes from the S.T.U. sample the 15 men who may be counted as casualties, three-quarters of all who remain were released in the normal way under 'Classes A or B'. They had at least fulfilled a certain minimum requirement by serving their time and remaining at their posts. The other quarter had either deserted or, in most cases, were discharged. The 196 men whose complete documents were available were disposed in the following ways:

TABLE 6

Manner of disposal	Numbers	Totals	%
(1) *Normal releases*			
'Class A'	116		
'Class B'	13		
Regular Army engagement	8	137	70
(2) *Casualties*			
Killed in action	5		
Died (in hospital)	1		
Discharged, under age	1		
Discharged for physical disabilities	8	15	8
(3) *Unsatisfactory disposals*			
Discharged (para. 390, section XVI, King's Regulations) as psychopathic personalities (with emotional abnormality, hysteria, schizophrenia, psychosis, anxiety state, mental deficiency or homo-sexuality) or psychopathic delinquent	38[1]		
Discharged, for misconduct	1		
Discharged, on civil convictions	3		
Deserted	2	44	22
		196	100

The main purpose of examining these documents was to discover how many of the S.T.U. men had become 'normal' or acceptable citizens at the end of their war service, and neither their conduct records nor their manner of release are alone sufficient to tell one that. There was also the evidence of the military conduct mark which is awarded to every soldier on release and the written testimonial which accompanies it. The range of military conduct marks is from 'exemplary' to 'very bad', but the terms are somewhat misleading by themselves since an award of 'very good' requires only one year's service and not more than 28 days in detention or field punishment; and with not more than 18 months' imprisonment

[1] Eleanor and Sheldon Glueck in an Introduction to *Rebel Without a Cause*, by R. M. Lindner (London, Research Books, Ltd., 1945) say: 'Studies in various prisons, reformatories and jails usually disclose that this class ("psychopathic personalities" or "constitutional psychopathic inferiors") comprises some 15 to 20 per cent of the inmate population.' The thirty-eight listed in the table above represent 19 per cent.

one may merit the mark of 'fair'. The system of awards was wisely codified by Army Council instruction so that the standards were the same throughout the Army, and while they do not limit a commanding officer's discretion in assessing a soldier's conduct lower than the mark prescribed they do prevent him from assessing it higher. One criticism of this system is that a man's bad past may be carried with him right through his Army career; yet there is a limited opportunity for redemption, for two years' service without any entry in the regimental conduct sheet will annul 56 days' detention.

Of the military conduct marks awarded to these men, 20 per cent were 'exemplary', 21 per cent 'very good', 28 per cent 'good', 24 per cent 'fair', 4 per cent 'indifferent', and 3 per cent 'bad'. But this distribution tells us little by itself, for we do not know the normal proportions for non-delinquents.

The release testimonials are not much more useful, and they should be read for what they leave out rather than what they state. Sobriety, efficiency and willingness are attributed to nearly every soldier leaving the service, so that one of the S.T.U. men of whom it was written 'appears to be a sober man' should, by inference of the omissions, have been an inefficient and unwilling soldier. Here and there, however, an independent judgment is revealed in a remark like—'Trustworthy and reliable. He has been responsible for the safe-carrying of secret packages', or 'tidy in appearance, punctual, trustworthy, a keen chap'.

Although no single document was sufficient as an index of general behaviour, it was possible, in the majority of cases, by considering the whole of the evidence, to classify a man with a fair degree of confidence as very good, satisfactory, or unsatisfactory. If a man had no serious offences recorded against him for at least the last two years of his service and had a good testimonial, he was generally put down under this classification as 'very good'. Any non-commissioned officers who continued to hold their rank until release, were also included as 'very good'. All who were discharged as psychopathic personalities were graded as 'unsatisfactory' as were those who continued to commit numerous offences or were released with an unfavourable testimonial. Those, not included in the other two groups, whose releases were normal, whose tesimonials were not unsatisfactory, whose offences were not too many and who did their soldiering reasonably satisfactorily wherever they were sent were classed as 'satisfactory'. There remained about

one-seventh of the sample whose position was obscured by inadequate documentation or conflicting evidence; these are classed as
'doubtful' and are ranked between the 'satisfactory' and the 'unsatisfactory' group.

The result of this classification was:

TABLE 7

Behaviour of a sample of 196 men after posting from the S.T.U.
up to the time of release or discharge from the Army

Assessment	Number	%
Very Good	45	23·0
Satisfactory	60	30·6
Doubtful	25	12·7
Unsatisfactory	63	32·2
Discharged or died on posting	3	1·5
	196	100·0

Thus, at least just over half (53·6 per cent) proved to be satisfactory soldiers. The proportion of successes is smaller (53·6 per
cent cf. 66·8 per cent) than was suggested by the follow-up reports
three months after posting but it is far in excess of what some of
the more experienced members of the staff dared to hope. A further
limitation of the three-monthly follow-up is shown by the fact that
out of every ten men listed after three months as below-average four
were rated as very good or satisfactory in the final assessment.
Not all of the credit for these successes can be claimed by the S.T.U.s
but the differences between the pre-S.T.U. and the post-S.T.U. crime
rates (see Table 4) strongly suggest that for many men 'special'
training was a turning point.[1]

[1] On hearing of these results a lady who has devoted much of her life to
penal reform remarked: 'You seem to get 50 to 60 per cent successes with
prisoners whatever you do—whether you treat them harshly, lock them up or
treat them kindly.' Some ground for such a contention may seem to be
offered by civilian criminal statistics where success is measured by the number
of times a man reappears before the courts. In the Army, where he is under
constant surveillance, where daily discipline may act as a continual irritant
to an unruly youth, and where every transgression is recorded in his documents, the test is different.
    But the Gluecks (S. and E. T. Glueck *After-conduct of Discharged Offen-
ders*) challenge official prison statistics. They write: 'While it had frequently
been claimed that 80% or 90% of the "graduates" of juvenile courts and
young men's reformatories "succeed", that is never commit crimes again,
our investigations proved that practically the reverse is true. . . . Of these
905, some 88% continued to be delinquent during a 5 year span following
action by the Boston Juvenile Court. . . . And during a 5 year span following
completion of the sentence to the Massachusetts Reformatory (similar to
Borstal) some 80% of 422 young-adult offenders continued to commit crimes.'

PART Two: THE OFFENDER

CHAPTER IV

A DELINQUENT POPULATION?

BEFORE going on to look more closely at a sample of these Army offenders, which is the purpose of this second part of the book, one needs to know a little more about the sort of men that were sent to Special Training Units, to see whether they are typical of the general run of delinquents.

At the time the sample was taken (January to June 1944) a large part of the British Army was stationed at home in preparation for the Normandy invasion. The large numbers of troops at that time stationed in the part of England from which the S.T.U. drew its intake were a normal mixture of infantry regiments and specialist arms, including battalions from county units as widely separated as the Seaforth Highlanders, the Duke of Cornwall's Light Infantry, the South Wales Borderers, the Durham Light Infantry, and the Royal Norfolk Regiment. The S.T.U. intake came from more than sixty different regiments and, as will be shown in Chapter XVII, their homes were scattered over various parts of the country in a fairly normal way. Thus, although there were important differences, as will be shown later, between these S.T.U. men and a normal Army sample in respect of physique, skill, attainments and arm of service (they were mostly infantrymen), such differences must be associated with the type of man who became an offender rather than the type of unit from which he was taken.

Although the method of selection should have resulted in a representative sample of Army offenders being sent to the Special Training Unit, a study of the intake during the three years of its existence (1942–45) suggests three distinct phases, each with a different type of soldier. At the time when the Unit was started, the Army was disbanding its Young Soldier (70th) battalions, which consisted of young men of 17 and 18, too young to engage in active service or to go overseas. They were volunteers, many having come into the Army expecting excitement and adventure only to find themselves segregated and under the control of rather elderly N.C.O.s. They were frequently given the job of guarding aerodromes, necessarily situated in flat, exposed positions. They were isolated, static, bored, and not always on the best of terms with the R.A.F. who seemed to be having a more exciting time. Little wonder some of them grew dissatisfied with the Army and became general nuisances. The early S.T.U. intake included many young soldiers of this sort, and they reacted well. But by the middle of 1943 this class had been worked out and larger numbers of Army call-up were finding their way into the Unit. For the next twelve months a varied assortment of 'nuisances' arrived, from physically immature youths to aggressive psychopaths. This was the second phase. In the middle of 1944 a change in the method of selection for Special Training Units was introduced: all candidates were sent to selection centres where they were graded according to whether their chances of redemption were good, doubtful or poor, and allotted to one of the three units which were orientated so that No. 1 took the poor cases, No. 2 the doubtful and No. 3 the good. Of the three periods the first and third were obviously highly selective. In the middle phase there was no selection other than age limit and the natural process by which each unit within the Command turned out its persistent offenders. This probably produced a fairly representative group of young delinquents, and it is from this middle period that the sample for the present inquiry was taken.

It may be asked whether this was not merely a transient problem group, a product of the attempt to convert a civilian male population into an Army in a comparatively short time. That question can only be answered fully by the investigation that follows. Meanwhile one can briefly describe these offenders as they revealed themselves to the staff of the Special Training Unit. One in every three disclosed that they had been brought before the courts for an indictable offence before joining the Army. Incidentally, the civilian delinquents among the S.T.U. intake proved to be no more troublesome to the Army than those who had escaped the notice of the law, for their conduct sheets showed about the same proportions of entries for Army crimes. About one in every five were physically or mentally immature youths who had been unable to keep up with the pace and demands of primary training. But other abnormalities were noticed in nearly all of these immature men; further study revealed that they were not merely young in age or development— there were emotional obstacles to growth. There were one or two men whose home situations were desperate and who had not been shown the understanding and help that was expected of Army officers.

D

Such men needed only time and a little welfare. Their own powers of recovery were sufficient to effect a cure.

But the great majority of the S.T.U. population were found to have deep-seated problems which seemed likely to bring them into conflict with any authority, service or civilian. They were restless, miserable, without confidence in themselves, subject to sudden changes of mood, aggressive or timid or absent-minded. No doubt the sudden immersion into Army life had further unsettled them. The restriction of their freedom, the difficulties of making new friends, the continual criticism of their untidy, irresponsible ways, the separation from a home that, in recollection, seemed far more desirable than ever in fact it was, all this became too much for many of them. In such cases the desire to escape, to stay away from the unit, to desert or to work their discharge from the Army became overwhelming. But it was clearly not solely the change of environment that was responsible for their waywardness. Had it been so, the return to civilian life should have restored them to an original state of normality by putting the process into reverse. But, as the later chapters of this present work show, there was seldom an 'original state of normality' and the return to civilian life often made matters worse. For the Army had much to offer to men whose lives had been dull or lonely, especially the homeless. The emotional life of the group in a service unit is strong—what the soldier sometimes refers to as a 'good mob'. His individual responsibilities are reduced to a minimum: his pay, food, clothing, accommodation, and even his recreation are provided for him. But as a civilian he must pay his way, balance his budget, seek out his own friends and find his own amusements. Thus, by a strange paradox, it often happened that the man who was all the time trying to run away from the Army was in a better position, and sometimes even less discontented, than he had been before he joined up, though he himself would not believe it. He was often growing roots perhaps stronger than any he had put out before, and it was not until he was torn out of that environment that he became aware of his loss.

It is therefore believed that Special Training Units were dealing with normal delinquent types. One-third of them were already manifestly delinquent, and the other two-thirds must have come from that vast fringe of potential delinquents (possibly two or three times as numerous as those convicted, as Sir W. Clarke Hall has suggested) who might well have been brought before the courts had the arm of the law been longer or more active.

CHAPTER V

THE METHOD OF INQUIRY

MOST recent studies of delinquency have proceeded by either psychological or statistical methods. The psychological investigation usually consists of a small number of case studies by a psychologist or psychiatrist working in his clinic at close range, probing the delinquent's mind and dissecting his motives. The sample, however, has often been too small and too unrepresentative to bear generalizations concerning delinquents as a whole. Several statistical inquiries have been undertaken from police court data, measuring the delinquent and his environment and counting his crimes. These have been based on either public officers' records or replies to questionnaires submitted to prisoners. Here the limitation has been the investigator's remoteness from the offender, making it difficult for him to perceive the offender's personality, his motives for misbehaving, and indeed his whole attitude to life. The delinquent himself is seldom heard. Of course he is the subject of the inquiries, but only as the patient in the consulting-room, the prisoner in the dock, or the youngster whose mother answers the door to the probation officer. To understand the delinquent one needs to live with him, to know him as a companion, even as a friend, and to let him, in the course of time and in his own broken way, tell his own story.[1] It was partly to allow these Army offenders an opportunity of unburdening their problems that the present inquiry was initiated.

[1] An observation on this chapter by Sir Cyril Burt may be quoted here: 'When I started my work for the L.C.C. I found it essential to go and live in slum homes as a guest of my delinquents or their families. I invited some of them one at a time to stay with me in my own home in the country. At the Melton Mowbray Colony where everything was free and easy, we lived with them as members of a queer and slightly quarrelsome family. But I think I learnt most of all from haunting low quarters off the Tottenham Court Road, until I became taken for a member of the criminal band that foregathered there. My secretary (a woman) did the same, though, of course, we were never known to be associated outside. Both of us found ourselves in amusing and embarrassing situations when we got let into secrets that I suppose we ought to have divulged to the police.' *The Young Delinquent* and to some extent D. H. Stott's recent *Delinquency and Human Nature* combine the advantages of the statistical and the psychological studies.

The Special Training Unit presented an unusual opportunity for a study of delinquency. Here was a group of offenders in close proximity to the investigator, on terms of friendly equality. The relationship was not one of official to offender, or of prison officer to prisoner, or doctor to patient, but the normal Army relationship of instructor to trainee and, in many cases, that of fellow-soldier. They were within the confines of a camp yet without any feeling of unnatural confinement (as they might have had in a prison or Borstal institution) for their movements were no more restricted than in any other Army camp.

So it was decided at the end of 1943 to begin recording some of the important facts about them. At first only the outlines of the men's histories were recorded, together with any revealing details that had come out in the course of conversation or in writing. The final shape of the inquiry grew out of the educational activities at the Unit.

For one hour every week during the periods of educational instruction the men could indulge in free expression of their ideas. They were encouraged to write, draw, read or compose a letter. They wrote of topical events, of their own early happy or unhappy memories, their holidays, and home towns, or drew maps of familiar places or sketched a scene. At that time the Education Bill was being widely discussed and it was put to the men that they might like to express their views on the matter. It was suggested that a questionnaire would ensure that everybody covered the same ground. The idea was eagerly taken up and it was even proposed by some of the men that an abstract of the findings should be sent to the Minister of Education for his guidance!

They went to it with a will. One little fellow, who was seldom co-operative, would not stop writing until he was forcibly parted from his paper at the end of the session. For several evenings the more expansive writers came back to the class-rooms to finish their contributions. When all the papers were completed the answers and recommendations were summarized. The following week the findings were displayed on a blackboard and several quotations from representative papers were read over to them. Some of the points were debated and refuted or confirmed, and a final draft was then prepared. This document was dispatched, through intermediate authorities, to War Office. There were not a few expressions of pride and approval when a reply was received from Whitehall informing the Unit that the statement had been read with close interest and passed on to the educational authorities.

This method of pooling experiences and debating the findings was adopted as a regular feature in the educational programme, and it was seen that much of the material produced by it would prove valuable in any investigation of the men's background. One day a taciturn and rather aggressive young Scotsman, who was a great favourite with the men, stood up at the beginning of one of these educational periods and said: 'What's the use of writing about schools and holidays? Why not try to find out what got us into trouble and write that up. It might be useful to other chaps.' There were nods of approval from the others. No time was lost in putting this suggestion into effect. It was, on the whole, much better to carry out an inquiry with the conscious approval and co-operation of the subjects than to play the eavesdropper. An outline of the inquiry was put before the men and questionnaires were drafted and duplicated.

So began the process of writing and recording that went on for over six months. After a questionnaire had been completed the principal findings would be displayed on a wall or blackboard. Some of the more interesting papers would be read out in class, without mentioning the writer's name, for it was always understood as a condition of the inquiry that the strictest confidence would be preserved. Experiences would then be compared and the findings debated. It is doubtful whether they would have co-operated in answering such questions, many of a private nature and occasionally of poignant significance, had they come without appreciated antecedents and without the offer of interesting consequences. The questionnaires had to be simply worded (many of the questions and answers are shown in Appendix B) because so many of the men were backward in reading and writing. The illiterates dictated replies which were written down by the instructors. It may be surprising to the reader that so much information was obtained in written form from men who normally found it difficult even to write a letter. It seemed that, having found an outlet for expression, the force of their feelings often impelled them to attempt descriptions for which their vocabularies were barely adequate. Sometimes a man would write half a page and scarcely a word of it decipherable at a first glance.

By this conscious effort the men appeared to uncover memories and experiences that had long been hidden. They gained a certain amount of comfort from telling their stories, and it probably helped them to discover that they were not alone in troubles which they had always imagined were peculiar to themselves. The daytime work spilled over into the evenings, and many of the men visited the writers' rooms after duty to unburden themselves. In fact, some came too often and were given a 'ration' of half an hour a night.

There were only two objectors. One was a small Glasgow youth, mentally very dull, who wrote, to begin with, 'none of your bissniss'; later he changed his attitude and quite forgot his earlier objections. The other was a most unhappy fellow. He sat amongst the others in class, idling with his papers, with an expression of utter hopelessness. During the evening he called to see the writer and said that he could not bring himself to record anything of his life at home. He had quarrelled violently with his parents. During his last privilege leave they had turned him out of the house and said they would not have him in the home again. His father was a drunkard and often attacked his mother, though they both sided against him. He had seen so much violence and experienced so much unhappiness that he could not bear to be reminded of it. He was emotionally unstable and the least one could do was to respect his wishes in this matter.

CHAPTER VI

THE SCOPE OF THE INQUIRY

IN order that common influences might be traced, specific attri-
butes, some two hundred in all, were entered on index cards.
There was a separate card for each of a dozen different aspects of
a man's history, family background, schooling, etc. Each card
was ruled into twenty spaces and each space referred to some particular fact. For instance, on every man's 'family' card the top
left-hand space showed the number of persons in the family; the
next space across, his order of birth; the next, his favourite brother
or sister, and so on, like this:

Specimen 'family' card

SMITH 8	ABC 3	YB	SINGLE OS	+
6 7	+	S	M	
−	+/+	F		
+/+	FD +			

Over 34,000 data were thus recorded. Each man's answers to the
questionnaires and all his written papers, with any notes that may
have been recorded concerning his history, were filed in separate
folders. From this material an assessment was made of his defections and of the probable causes of his delinquency. The various
etiological factors were laid out in tabular form with symbols (cross
or circle) to represent probability or possibility, and colours (red,
blue and black) to represent degrees of influence.

A matter of importance was the size and representativeness of the
sample of offenders to whom the questionnaires were put. Delinquency is so complex a problem, its ramifications are so extensive
and so frequently hidden, that any study of its nature or causes

should, if it is to claim wider application, employ a sample large enough to bear analysis without having its findings blurred by wide margins of error, yet small enough to permit individual study of the cases. Something has already been said (in Chapter IV) of the representativeness of the group which forms the subject of this inquiry. The group numbered 203 and, if it were really representative, conclusions based on a group of that size would accurately reflect the conditions of the population of which it is a sample to within two or three per cent. A margin of error four or five times greater has, however, been allowed in interpreting the present evidence because although these men appeared to be true delinquent types they were by no means randomly selected.

The sample of 200 has been supported by a larger sample of which, to some extent, it forms a part. This larger sample consisted of the 700 men who had passed through the Special Training Unit at the time the present inquiry was concluded. They include 147 names from the 203 of the smaller sample, thus excluding 56. A few selected data were recorded about the two samples in order to lend statistical support to the smaller group. Thus, the medical categories, religious denominations and intelligence test results taken from the Army record sheets are shown for the two groups. For the larger group, particulars of home conditions, civilian delinquencies, etc., were taken from the confidential reports of the two Welfare sergeants. The two sets of statistics are given in Appendix C.

In general the data for the group of 700 are closely similar to those for the group of 203. Such differences as arise concern the background information. To some extent they confirm the suggestion already made that the earlier intake (included in the sample of 700) were more normal than those of the Unit's middle period from which the sample of 203 was taken. It may also be that with the smaller sample the author had more opportunities of obtaining fuller information by following up the evidence of the Welfare staff.

The arrangement of the two samples may be shown diagrammatically, as in the diagram on the next page.

For the statistical part of this inquiry to have much meaning, corresponding figures for the non-delinquent part of the population or for the entire population are needed. If a group of the same age-range and as nearly as possible the same social background is chosen it may be assumed that any significant differences that arise are not the products of age or social environment. But a limitation of a

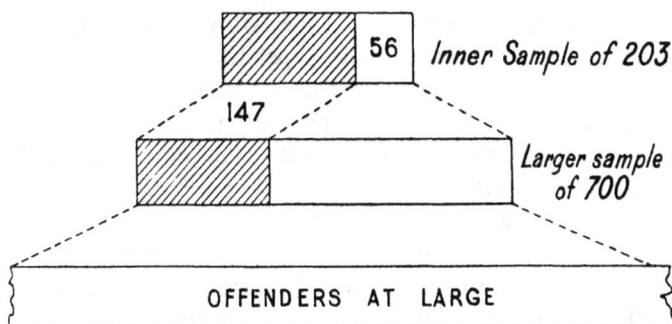

control group of this sort is that it must minimize or obscure those factors in the causation of delinquency which spring from the physical environment common to both, and if, as is suggested in Appendix A, delinquency is very widely distributed, in an active or passive state, amongst a certain section of the community, then it would seem desirable that a control group should be chosen which does not spring from the same background as the delinquents. Perhaps the ideal method would be to employ two control groups, one chosen from non-offenders in the delinquents' own social environment and one from another environment.

For the present inquiry a number of norms for a coeval Army population at approximately the same period have been provided by War Office. These include intelligence and education test results, ratings of combatant temperament, distributions of average heights and weights, average medical categories, and the incidence of illiteracy and semi-illiteracy. In addition, a number of the questionnaires used in the Special Training Unit group were put to controls numbering 200. The controls were composed of three separate elements. The first consisted of 53 young soldiers in two groups. There was one group of men recovering from operations or wounds at an Army convalescent depot. The other was a group of some twenty Service men, mostly in the Army and all under 21, from a London social club. The second element consisted of men from Youth Clubs in Lowestoft, Welwyn Garden City, Kingston, Romford, Dagenham and Plaistow. The ages were 16 to 18, though about a third consisted of Service men on leave. The third element was made up of young men attending part-time day-release centres in Swansea and London as a condition of employment. The average age was a little below that of the offenders. About four-fifths were working-class and the rest lower middle-class youths.

The questions that were put to the Army offenders and to the control groups are reprinted in Appendix B with the answers obtained. With the offenders much more time was available in which to complete their questionnaires, and, in fact, much more time was needed because of their backwardness. The offenders developed many of their answers by written essays or in subsequent interviews, and the process of writing and discussion went on for several months. The control groups answered the questionnaires at single sessions after the investigator had briefly explained the purpose of the inquiry. The questions themselves were then put orally so that the correct emphasis could be placed upon certain operative words, but were answered in writing. They were couched in simple, often colloquial language in order to ensure that even the dullest offender understood what he was being asked. The difficulty was that in making one's meaning clear to the reader the question often lost something in precision. One or two were so blurred by ambiguities that the answers had to be discarded.

CHAPTER VII

PHYSIQUE AND HEALTH

IT is commonly supposed that the young offender is tough; in
fact he is frequently described as a 'young tough'. Yet the
general experience of the Special Training Unit was that the trainees
were noticeably below standard in any physical activity, whether it
was a game of football, cross-country running or route marching.
One man was heard to boast that during his primary training he had
marched thirty miles in a day. Yet on a day excursion to a spot
not eight miles distant from the camp he fell out before he had
marched half-way. His case was exceptional but the performances
of many fell short of their claims. Some did not even pretend to
be strong, and the tendency then was to exaggerate in the other
direction, like the young Irishman who wrote:

> I worry about my helth very much. When I go on P.T. runs my
> hart begins to beet 400 seconds to a minit and it dont agree with me.
> My feet when I do the back and front, my feet go into kramps and I
> no I am not strong enuff, that my helth is going down a awffily much,
> and I dont think I am fit enuff for the Army. The P.T. is killin me and
> I am not agreein with it aniway.

With such conflicting claims a glance at their physical measurements shows the true state of affairs. The tables in Appendix C
show the stature and weights of the S.T.U. sample. When one
looks for comparative background material one realizes how
neglected is the anthropometrical field. The last large-scale
measurements of the stature and weights of the civilian population
were carried out by Sir Francis Galton with a Committee of the
British Association in 1883, when 8585 persons were examined in
one survey alone. Since then improvements in school feeding and
public health have enormously affected the physique of school
children who (according to the Report of the School Medical
Officer of the London County Council, 1951) are today $3\frac{1}{2}$ inches
taller and one stone heavier at the age of 15 than their coevals of
1905-12. Despite this phenomenal increase in size of school
children, the adult male population does not appear to have changed

appreciably in height since 1883 (though the average woman is probably taller by 1½ inches). The average height of men in 1883 was just over 5 ft. 7 ins., as it is in the latest wartime Army figures. So it appears that children are reaching their maximum heights at earlier ages. There is, however, a real difference in weight over the past 70 years, the average person of Galton's day being 20 lbs. heavier than his modern grandson—in fact he was almost the proverbial John Bull. These changes have some relevance to our delinquents who, though generally undersized, sometimes continued to increase in height during their stay at the S.T.U., a fact which tends to confirm the suggestion implied in the figures just quoted, that the effects of undernourishment in the young are to arrest as well as to stunt growth.

The heights in inches of the S.T.U. sample, in the first part of Appendix C, are compared with the proportions obtained by Dr. Charles Goring from his measurements of 1,000 English criminals (published in *The English Convict*, H.M.S.O., 1913), and with those for normal Army intake (all ages) December, 1942. In the second part of the same table the parallel figures include a distribution for 18-year-olds taken from two sample analyses of Army intakes, for various age groups, one in October 1942 and the other in February 1944. These control figures are largely comparable because the age on enlistment of the big majority of the S.T.U. men was 18 years, but some enlisted at 17 and even 16, adjusting their dates of birth to conform to the regulations. Later measurements for several men showed that they had grown sometimes by as much as 1½ inches in two or three years. Dr. Goring's sample of 1,000 prisoners covered a wide age-range and included a large proportion of fully-grown men. Furthermore, the Army norms cover recruits from all classes of the community whereas the S.T.U. men came, in the main, from a lower working-class element, and average stature varies quite considerably according to social group. The 1883 inquiry of the British Association showed differences of two inches between the means for factory operatives (65·92 ins.) and commercial classes (67·95 ins.).

Only the Army intake figures are shown for comparison in the table of weights because the average weights of the population have decreased markedly over the past seventy years. The 1883 mean weights ranged (according to social class) from 142·5 lbs. to 162·1 lbs., whereas the Army intake figures were from 129·4 lbs. for 18 years to 137·3 lbs. for older men (32 and over).

The tables show clearly the physical inferiority of the S.T.U. population compared with the normal soldier. The differences are so apparent that mathematical verification is hardly necessary, but the chi-square test amply confirms them. The significant thing about these figures is not that offenders are short men, for many of them are in fact quite tall, but, as the normal distribution of the figures implies, that they are drawn from a *generally inferior population*. Whether this inferiority is peculiar to delinquents as opposed to non-delinquent members of the same community or whether it is characteristic of the entire social group or groups from which offenders are drawn, is a matter for further inquiry.

One may well ask whether it is possible to recognize the offender by his physical appearance. Imagine yourself standing before a parade of some hundreds of these men at the S.T.U., watching them form up in their platoons, ranged in size from the tallest on the flanks to the shortest in the centre. No one could mistake them for professional soldiers. They slouch, they move rather indolently, they shuffle their feet, one or two may even have their hands in their pockets—a punishable offence on a parade ground.

On parade the normal trained soldier plants his feet firmly down, quickly adjusts his position, snaps his left foot out to the 'at-ease' position, and then stands quite still. These men, one would notice, are fidgeting, turning round to argue with somebody behind, quarrelling about positions or pushing each other, though sometimes in fun. Finally, the sergeant-major reduces them all to silence and calls them to attention. They stand, unnaturally stiff and rigid, some lop-sided, some with shoulders raised, some with heads too far forward or too far back, waiting for the inspection.

As your eye notices face after face you might wonder whether it would register any composite picture of a criminal type.[1] One sees mischievous faces, anxious faces, pasty faces and sullen looks but no common cast of features that one could describe as criminal.

[1] Some years ago C. Lombroso put forward the theory, which was quite widely accepted, that the criminal was a distinct type, a genus of sub-human, a throw-back, having specific skull measurements and facial characteristics—'the characteristics of primitive man reproduced in our times'. (Cesare Lombroso, speech at 6th Congress of Criminal Anthropology, Turin, 1906.) In his later works Lombroso considerably modified his theory of the criminal type. His arguments are summarized in the English version of *Crime, its Causes and Remedies*, Heinemann, 1911. He claims that only 40 per cent of criminals conform to the criminal type and says 'one should receive the *type* with the same reserve that one uses in estimating the value of *averages* in statistics. When one says that the average life is 32 years . . . no one understands by that that everybody must die at 32 years'.

(*Continued overleaf*)

Once or twice one might notice a rather villainous-looking individual and wonder which came first, the bad behaviour or the face. One man with such a countenance proved to be quite a gentle fellow. He said that his looks had often got him into trouble and one was much inclined to believe him. He was like a dog with a fierce face which is always being suspected of a bad temper, driven off or chained up until it actually develops a bad temper. By the opposite process, a pretty child is sometimes petted and spoiled until it becomes vain and self-centred. Another man who had had an orphanage upbringing told how the pretty children got more petting, especially the fair ones, and any child with a mop of curls and big blue eyes was especially lucky. The more intelligent children, too, with brighter ways and quicker responses, were more likely to be given whatever modicum of affection and attention was going, than the dull child.

One is so often inclined to believe that the features reveal the nature of a person; thus one refers to a 'generous mouth', 'eyes wide apart for honesty', 'a high forehead for intelligence', 'a large generous nose', and so on. There may be some truth in these generalizations, but experimental studies have shown that the con-verses—that all honest men must have their eyes wide apart, all intelligent men high foreheads, and so on, are certainly not true.

Sir Francis Galton (*Inquiries into Human Faculty*, Dent, Everyman) believed 'it is unhappily a fact that fairly distinct types of criminals breeding true to their kind have become established, and are one of the saddest dis-figurements of modern civilization', yet he had to admit, after superimposing hundreds of photographs of criminals to produce a composite picture, that 'the individual faces are villainous enough, but they are villainous in different ways, and when they are combined the individual peculiarities disappear, and the common humanity of a low type is all that is left'.

The original theory of a criminal type was based upon skull measure-ments and has long since been utterly refuted by statistical evidence. Dr. Charles Goring (*The English Convict*, H.M.S.O., 1913) carried out a very thorough study of three thousand convicts and concluded that there was no such thing as a physical criminal class. He did, however, find general differ-ences of stature and weight.

CHAPTER VIII

DISEASES AND DISORDERS

ON admission to the Army a man is examined by a medical board of three or more doctors who assess and grade his physical condition. The table below sets out the medical categories in which the larger sample of 700 men from the Special Training Unit were placed, compared with those for a normal sample of Army recruits, taken in 1944 (16 Nov. and including 88 per cent of 18–19-year-old conscripts).

TABLE 8

General Medical Category	Particular Grade	S.T.U. sample %	Normal (18 yrs.) %
A—Men with only minor remedial disabilities, who can undergo severe strain	A1—Minimum fitness	86·8	89·0
	A2—Slight defects of locomotion (feet)	3·6	2·1
	A3—Visual disability (standard 4)	2·4	2·9
	A4—Further defects of vision		(+A5, 0·1)
B—Men with moderate degree of disability who can undergo considerable exertion not involving severe strain.	B1—Second grade constitution	3·3	5·0
	B2—Slight defects of locomotion	1·9	0·6
	B6—Hearing disability (standard 3)	0·4	0·1
	B7—Marked defect of locomotion	0·7	0·2
C—Marked physical disabilities or evidence of past disease.		0·9	—
		100·0	100·0

(The British Army system of classification was based on three broad constitutional levels, A, B, and C, and on standards of keenness of vision, of hearing and of ability to march, denoted by the index numbers 1 to 7.)

It should not be concluded from the fact that 87 per cent of the offenders were classified as A1 that so many were in a state of physical health. The medical category A1 indicates the absence of any disability likely to impair efficiency in battle. For practical purposes the Army's definition is that any man who can march twenty-five miles a day may be classified as A1. A good deal of misunderstanding has arisen over the use of the term A1, which, in its idiomatic sense, is taken to mean 'perfectly fit and well', 'in the pink'. But that was not the Army's definition and if it had been very few men would have gone into battle. There were also the exceptional cases of men who had not reported their diseases when being medically examined, perhaps because they did not want to make too much of their ailments, or because they felt that it was up to the doctors to discover their disabilities.

Physical fitness, in the sense of complete absence of any disease or disorder is apparently rare even in males. According to the findings of the Peckham Health Centre,[1] where 3911 persons of varied social groups were medically examined, only about 14 per cent were found to be in a state of health, about 30 per cent were diseased, and the remaining 66 per cent had some recognizable disorder that needed attention. Judged by such standards the majority of these offenders would have been found far from healthy. With so wide a disparity of standards and without any special medical examination, it is difficult to say how near they were to a state of positive health. One can only speak relatively, and judging by their medical categories and the large numbers who reported having diseases in early life, it would appear that they were less healthy than the general run of young soldiers.[2]

No medical check of any sort was attempted with the non-delinquent control groups, because only a very thorough examination would have provided information really comparable with the Army records and it was not practicable for this to be done. The evidence obtained from questionnaires, however, shows three significant differences between the offenders and the others. One is the larger amount of early ill-health (sufficient to cause them to

---

[1] Innes Pearse and Lucy Crocker, *The Peckham Experiment* (Allen & Unwin, 1943).

[2] Cyril Burt (in the work cited) observed that in his own series of cases nearly 70 per cent were suffering from defects of bodily weakness and ill-health; and nearly 50 per cent were in urgent need of medical treatment. On the other hand, Healy and Bronner (*New Light on Delinquency and its Treatment*, Yale University Press, 1936), working in the U.S.A., found that 50 per cent of their cases had 'good physical condition, with absence of anything except very slight pathological conditions', compared with 65 per cent in a parallel group of normal young persons.

miss at least six months' schooling if they were of school age at
the time) recorded among the offenders. The second is the prevalence of defects of hearing, sight and speech amongst offenders
compared with the controls. The third is the extent to which the
offenders revealed anxieties about their health.

Sickness in Childhood

One offender in every four (25 per cent) reported some serious
ill-health early in life, quite apart from those who had been in
hospital with accidents, ruptures, or common infectious diseases like
measles and scarlet fever (the corresponding proportion in the control
groups was 18 per cent), 64 per cent of the offenders (cf. 59 per cent
among the controls) said they had been in hospital for some reason,
and 46 per cent (13 per cent of the controls) had 'missed more than
six months' continuous schooling because of sickness'. The difference between the last two figures is rather large and it is possible
that some of the offenders were attributing to sickness what should
have been ascribed to truancy. The same question was, however,
put in another questionnaire (on schooling) alongside one about
truancy and almost identical replies were obtained.

The two groups were also asked if they had been 'troubled much
with' disorders of various parts of the body, with the following
results:

TABLE 9

Proportions of S.T.U. sample and control groups reporting
'much trouble with'

	Offenders %	Non-offenders %
Stomach	18	4
Teeth	32	8
Ears	19	4
Glands	20	5
Fits	15	1
Heart	6	8
Feet	10[1]	3
Skin	2	5
None of the above	30	55

With any group of delinquents one looks for sequelae of ence-
phalitis lethargica (sleepy sickness), because it sometimes leaves
serious after-effects including defective mental powers and an

[1] Altogether 6·2 per cent of the full S.T.U. sample of 700 were graded A2.
B2, or B7 for disabilities including defective feet, whereas the proportion in a
corresponding Army intake was 2·9 per cent. Army life was, of course,
likely to bring out any weakness of the feet.

E

impaired moral sense. Burt (op. cit.) records the disease in 4 per cent of his cases (amounting to a major factor in their delinquencies with 2·4 per cent) compared with only half of one per cent in the non-delinquent population. No greater number (3 per cent in a sample of similar size) was found at the Special Training Unit, and only two men showed symptoms that were recognizable by a medical officer as sequalae of the disease. One such case was subject to fits and spells of insomnia and he used to drop off to sleep during the daytime (he explained his behaviour by saying that he was 'touched upstairs').

Much the most common disease in the early lives of these men was pneumonia. Some 12 per cent reported having had acute bronchitis, pneumonia or tuberculosis. Burt found these defects in only 4 per cent of his cases (3·5 per cent among the non-delinquents) and he assesses the condition as never more than a minor disposing factor in their delinquencies. The difference between the two figures is remarkable but it is possible that Burt has counted only the very severe cases or those who still suffered from pulmonary weakness.

Diphtheria was reported in 3 per cent of the S.T.U. cases. Ear, nose and throat operations (necessitating hospital treatment) including mastoid, cover 6 per cent. The prevalence of adenoidal conditions amongst offenders has been noted by Burt. Many such cases at the S.T.U. came to the notice of the Medical Officer and several were sent away for operations.

Abnormal behaviour has sometimes been attributed to the effects of a severe head injury. The two groups, offenders and non-offenders, were asked 'Have you ever had any serious accidents like broken bones or injury to the head?' Among the S.T.U. group 42 per cent answered that they had, and 27 per cent of the controls. The two sets of replies are significantly different and reflect a general difference in behaviour and background between the two groups. But they do not show how far a delinquent career could be precipitated by head injuries. In one or two of the S.T.U. cases the mother, or occasionally the man himself (perhaps echoing the mother), suggested that his troubles could be traced to a bad blow on the head ; as one mother put it in a letter—'when he was at work a door and a coal-bag fell on his head, since when he has been unnaturally quiet'. Yet, in nearly all such cases, the men's own testimonies showed earlier histories of truancy and bad behaviour; mother love being stronger than mother logic, it seems that they were, perhaps unconsciously, trying to find excuses for a situation that would otherwise reflect upon their sons or themselves. Altogether, only 2·4 per cent of the S.T.U. men reported serious injuries to the head.[1] One man had been hit on the head with a brick when he was five, but he also suffered from meningitis at an early age; after leaving the S.T.U., however, he became a very satisfactory soldier (though he had nineteen crimes on his conduct sheet in the year before his S.T.U. training). Another man who had suffered a severe head injury with concussion as a child, necessitating thirty-two stitches, appeared *a priori* to date his misdeeds back to that accident. Yet, after leaving the S.T.U. his conduct improved so remarkably that his final showing was assessed (in the classification in Chapter III) as 'very good'. If the head injuries had indeed affected the brain so that these men had been incapable of normal behaviour it seems unlikely that they could have adapted themselves so successfully to Army life. In all such cases one must turn to medical evidence; otherwise, one might deduce from the case of an S.T.U. offender, who had been a civilian delinquent before joining the Army and who received a severe head injury from a carrier tank but subsequently turned out as a very satisfactory soldier, that it was the head injury that put him right! An amusing sidelight on these early injuries and operations was the tendency of the men to measure the severity of their cases by the number of stitches used to sew up the cuts. The lowest number which was thought worth while recording was five, and the top score thirty-two!

Sight, Hearing and Speech

Defects under this heading were recorded in as many as 33 per cent of the S.T.U. men (against 15 per cent of the control groups), although in many cases—especially with hearing and speech—the trouble had cleared up during childhood. Some 19 per cent reported considerable trouble at some time with their ears, either discharging ears, perforated ear drum, or deafness. Included in these were 6·5 per cent (of the whole group) who still retained some disability, though only three men (in the sample of 200; the proportion in the larger sample was 0·4 per cent) were incapacitated so far as to be medically graded (B6) on that account.[2]

[1] Healy and Bronner (op. cit.): 'A reliable account of severe head injury was obtained in 9 instances (out of 153 = 6 per cent) clearly a much greater proportion than for the general population.' So few cases from a smallish sample hardly justify any conclusions unless norms are known.

[2] Burt (op. cit.) found only 4·9 per cent (including 1·6 per cent with 'marked defect') with defective hearing, compared with only 2·0 per cent

(*Continued overleaf*)

Defective vision was recorded among only 2·4 per cent of the young soldiers, and the same proportion were medically graded because of it. These were cases of partial' blindness or relatively serious disability, and the figures do not include a number of men who were sufficiently affected to have to wear glasses permanently, yet were graded A1.[1]

Defects of speech were noticeably present. As many as 15 per cent reported having had speech troubles at some time (cf. 10 per cent among the controls), and in 12 per cent they were still evident. One or two claimed that the disability followed sleepy sickness, and one, pneumonia. Less than half of this 12 per cent were pronounced stutterers. The rest were slight or occasional stutterers, or lispers, one or two 'only with women', or when excited. Compared with these large proportions, Burt and Healy and Bronner show much smaller percentages.[2] All three samples of offenders show at least that speech defects are much more common among delinquents than among the general population. A defect of speech, whatever the cause, becomes a physical habit, and tends to persist long after the cause has been removed.

It has been assumed by some investigators that the stutterers, the spectacled and the deaf would be persecuted and plagued by their schoolmates, until they were made to feel inferior and inadequate, and that this would affect their subsequent behaviour. The S.T.U. men were asked to report any persecution they may have suffered at school, and about one in five said they were 'picked on'. But the incidence of such 'persecution' was no greater amongst the 33 per cent with marked disabilities of sight, hearing and speech than among the others. Certainly persecution by the other boys at school was more common among the group of delinquents than among the non-delinquents (21 per cent cf. 11 per cent).

In height, weight and general physical condition, this 'per-

---

among his non-delinquent group. Healy and Bronner (op. cit., page 74) found even fewer—only 1 per cent with 'moderately defective hearing', compared with 3 per cent among the controls, and another 1 per cent with otitis media compared with 5 per cent among the controls. It would be a mistake to attach much significance, if any, to the differences between such small sub-divisions of samples of no more than two hundred cases.

[1] Burt's figures were 4·9 per cent for marked defect of vision (compared with 8·5 per cent among non-delinquents) and 8·1 per cent for slight defect (10·5 per cent among non-delinquents). Healy and Bronner speak of 19 per cent with squint or defective vision, 'more than slight', and 7 per cent among non-delinquents.

[2] Burt: 1·6 per cent (0·5 per cent non-delinquents) with defective speech, and Healy and Bronner record 7 per cent. (cf. 1 per cent. among non-delinquents.

secuted' group were not significantly inferior to the rest of the sample. A graph of their stature shows a little bunching around 5 ft. 3 ins. and 5 ft. 4 ins., and it is possible that these shorter men (numbering about a quarter of the 'persecuted' group) suffered at school because they were relatively smaller than their playmates, but with the majority the causes do not appear to have been physical.

It is also claimed by some investigators into the causes of delinquency that these special defects make for increased educational backwardness. Yet the results of Army educational tests did not show any significant difference between those delinquent soldiers who were physically handicapped and those who were not, though it must be admitted that the test ratings were coarsely divided into only six groups, and most of the men were so backward educationally anyway that large proportions (66 per cent in Arithmetic, and 52 per cent in Verbal tests) come into the two bottom groups (normally comprising 35 and 32 per cent respectively), thus effectively reducing the scale of measurement; had one compared the individual scores in a much larger sample, slight differences might have come to light, but they could not have been very marked.

These results are contrary to expectations and one can only explain them by assuming that the delinquent is, in general, so handicapped physically and emotionally that the special defects of the sense organs make little difference to his total discomfort. It is true to say that the Army delinquent was educationally much more backward than the general run of men of his age and social class (see Chapter IX); it is also true that he was more frequently persecuted at school than other men; he also suffered more often from defects of the sense organs; but no marked causal connexions appear between these three characteristics.

Anxieties over Health

Over a third (39 per cent) of the offenders said that they worried about their health (compared with 25 per cent amongst the control groups). Enough has already been said of the offenders' health to suggest that some of this anxiety was justified, and was perhaps only to be expected in those cases where a man who was conscious of some after-effect of a serious illness found himself graded A1 on admission into the Army. One offender claimed that his 'left leg was not working properly' as a result of infantile paralysis, and he did display a limp. Another had had seven operations on his stomach and leg as a child, still had a slight limp, and complained of 'queer pains in the body'. There was also tuberculosis in his family and he felt that he ought to get milk to drink. He too was graded A1. Yet, as mentioned earlier, the medical category A1 was often quite erroneously taken to imply a state of perfect health instead of a minimum standard of physical efficiency.

Not all of the men's anxieties about their health were well founded. 'I had pneumonia when I was two, and I think I've got over it now', wrote one fellow. 'I worry for I had a disease (infantile paralysis) and it can come back, and I still think I have got T.B.' wrote another. Where a particular anxiety was voiced in this way, it was arranged for the man to have a private talk with the medical officer. About one in every seven felt that he had inherited some sickness or defect (15 per cent, cf. 9 per cent in the control groups), and here again their worries indicated only a limited knowledge of the functioning of their bodies. 'I've got a burst ear-drum, and it was passed on from my mother', said one man. Another complained of varicose veins in his upper leg, inherited from his mother. Another wrote, with understandable concern, 'My father died when he was 52 with asthma. My married sister was taken with asthma. She has recently had a baby girl. Will it be affected?' And another: 'Can asthma be catching for my dad has it and my sister?'

Another question: 'Do you think early ill-health has left any harmful effects?' drew the answer 'yes' from 25 per cent of the S.T.U. men compared with 14 per cent of the controls. The fact that so many of the offenders were educationally backward and, as will be shown in a later chapter, in a state of emotional disturbance, may have induced them to believe that they were the victims of early ill-health when they were not. The evidence of their general physical inferiority, however, is strong enough to suggest that there was good reason for a number of them to be apprehensive.

To add to their difficulties some men were fearful of medical treatment. They would report sick and submit themselves to examination, yet were sceptical of any prolonged surgical treatment. So they would often buy patent medicines and treat themselves, sometimes with harmful effects. The most flagrant case was that of a young soldier who developed a poisoned finger. Twice the medical officer made arrangements for him to attend the local hospital to have the septic finger lanced and on each occasion he turned up only to refuse treatment. He was later lectured by several members of the staff at the S.T.U. about the dangers confronting him, and was taxed with being a coward.

'I can stand any pain', he said, 'but I won't have an anaesthetic.'
'Well, then, have it done without an anaesthetic', suggested the
M.O. He finally agreed to this and a further appointment was made
at the hospital. He went into the operating theatre with three
nurses, the doctor and a Welfare sergeant from the S.T.U. He was
quite cheerful at first and said he didn't mind how much it hurt.
He was again offered a local anaesthetic but still refused. So, with
the sergeant at his back, and the nurses holding his arms and wrist,
he boldly faced the surgeon. At the first incision he threw the
nurses aside and jumped around the room, screaming that he
couldn't stand it. The sergeant tried to approach him, but he
retreated behind the operating table. As one of the nurses approached, he seized the table and threatened to tip it over them with
all the surgical instruments, if they did not let him alone. Finally,
the doctor warned him that this refusal of treatment would probably
mean the loss of his hand, if not of his arm. He said that he didn't
care about that but he wasn't having any more. He then signed a
statement certifying that he had refused treatment and was driven
back to camp. He was excused duties and wandered round the
camp with his arm in a sling. Days passed, but fortunately, to
the surprise of most and not least of the man himself, his hand
gradually recovered. He himself always attributed it to faith, but
the top joint of the finger is still useless. The same man was later
discharged from the Army as a psychopathic personality with anti-
social trends. He has since reared a family and works as a long-
distance lorry driver.

Early Undernourishment

It needed no special inquiry to discover that many of these young
soldiers were brought up in very poor homes. They sometimes
spoke of how hard it had been for their parents to make 'ends meet',
or of going without food when they were young, or of never having a
holiday away from home. Yet they were careful to avoid any
reflection on their parents, and it was often not until one knew them
very well that they spoke of distress at home. Altogether, gross
poverty was traced in the early lives of some 15 per cent of the cases,
and the true figure may well have been a good deal higher. Among
the offenders 14 per cent (10 per cent in the control groups) said on
a questionnaire that they went 'short of food through (their) mother
finding it difficult to make both ends meet'. One man spoke of
never having had much to eat except bread and sausage. Another,

a young fellow of charming disposition, and quiet manner (whose
case is more fully described on p. 81) said that he was 'half-starved
for years' because his father was bedridden with sleepy sickness and
his mother only received thirty-six shillings a week. A glimpse of
similar conditions may be obtained through the words of a Scots boy:
    'Our family was a helthy family. My mother had babies and
she was months in bed. The only colds we had were because first
we had no fires in a winter's day, so we got chills in the stumach
and sore heads. We used to pull our teeth out with thred and we
never got a doctor, and I once had perfor(ated) ere.'
    Most of them came from working-class families of which a large
proportion were in the lower income groups. The large size of the
families, too, was a factor here. Yet not all the cases of undernourishment came from homes where the family income was very
small. Working-class families have a habit of pooling their resources, and several instances were noted where the father was in
regular work and one or two of the older children, perhaps step-
children, were bringing in earnings, yet through mismanagement or
neglect the growing child was not properly nourished. In one
family both mother and father were 'out at the boozer' as the boy
put it, 'most of the time', and in another both parents betted heavily.
One man was perhaps echoing more than he knew when he wrote:
    'Well, I think all illnesses what a child has is due to its mother
not taking great care of it when they are first born because at times
she does not feel like looking after them.'

Bed-wetting

Bed-wetting is commonly associated with young offenders. There
were a number of occasional bed-wetters at the S.T.U., but the complaint only came to light in the more acute cases. Soldiers sleep in
blankets, without sheets, and though these have to be shaken and
folded every day, inspections would not normally discover wetting.
On fine days the blankets would be spread out on the grass to air,
but even then wetting would not always show on the heavy, dark-
coloured wool. The more serious cases came to one's notice
because the blankets would become unusable, or kit inspection
would reveal sodden underclothing, or, occasionally, it would
become common talk amongst the men. These excessive bed-wetters
did not number more than a dozen or so in 700 men (perhaps 2 or
3 per cent). But the effects were sometimes lamentable and, in at
least one case, tragic (as the man's later history has shown), though
the enuresis was probably a symptom, not a cause.

One was a fine-looking Irishman, of good figure, open pleasant face and forceful personality. He was outstanding among the men and was soon given promotion. He had had previous promotions, a sergeant once, but had been compelled to relinquish his rank because of his persistent bed-wetting. His weakness had, in time, come to the notice of his mess-mates and he felt so guilty about it that he had decided to revert to the ranks. On one occasion he had been punished for wetting his palliasse. A similar situation eventually arose at the S.T.U. when a mounting sense of guilt drove him to excesses and he lost his stripe. It was indeed a sad business to hear this man talking about a disability that he felt pressed on him like a doom. He was given medical treatment without success. His delinquencies, it seemed, coincided with the fits of desperation that were prompted by the shame of the bed-wetting.

Another man for whom medical treatment proved unavailing, has since been released from the Army and has had a succession of jobs. Again, the continual bed-wetting drove him to desperation and when he felt the situation was intolerable he would move on to another job (he was in domestic employment) and try to start afresh. Unfortunately his mind was eventually affected by the anxiety (or by some deeper disturbance that was also causing the enuresis) and he was finally admitted to a mental hospital.

A third man happened to be reported for having taken some books from the Education Centre. At that time the library had been losing rather more books than was considered reasonable, so a kit search was ordered. The man was fetched and his belongings were turned out in front of him. The books came to light and so did a revolting assortment of saturated clothing. His blankets, too, were sodden, and, confronted by this evidence, he broke into a fit of crying and said that nobody would have anything to do with him and that everybody was against him. One could hardly imagine a more miserable-looking man or one in a more wretched situation. There had been previous suspicions of theft and these were confirmed by the finding of several of the missing articles among his belongings. Later, in the course of a private talk, it came out that his bed-wetting went back as far as he could remember. His home had been very unhappy, his mother left the family when he was very young, and a step-mother took her place. He had made no friends because of his complaint—'I've no mates,' he said; 'they can't stand the smell.' Feeling that the whole world was unsympathetic, he had shown little compunction in helping himself to any things that took his fancy. He was later discharged from the Army for this same complaint.

This weakness of bed-wetting, like leprosy, has a powerful effect on the sufferer's mind. It was certainly closely connected with their delinquencies in the serious cases that came to light at the S.T.U. Yet those who have studied the etiology of the disorder trace it to a reaction in the very young child against feelings of deprivation, of being unwanted or neglected. And such emotional disturbances, as will be shown in later chapters, are among the primary causes of many delinquencies. Bed-wetting is therefore probably only one expression of an emotional frustration, of which truancy, wandering, excessive job-changing, and delinquencies are the more usual outlets; it can and does lead to delinquencies if it has not been accompanied by them all through.

Physical Deficiency as a cause of Delinquency

It has been seen that Army offenders were generally smaller, lighter, and inferior in medical grade than their normal comrades of the same age; they had suffered more early ill-health, and were especially prone to troubles of the chest, and of ears, eyes, nose and throat; they included more stutterers and generally exhibited more anxieties about their health. In all these considerations we have been looking at the group as a whole. As a group the offenders were inferior in almost every physical respect.

One might go on to claim that any soldier who was not, and could not be, physically fit was at a disadvantage because he might well feel that his chances of survival were lessened; he might dread the dangers of service in operational zones and be tempted to cut himself adrift from his unit, especially if he was less integrated into the group than his fellows. In fact, one might ask whether physical inferiority were not a general cause of Army delinquency.[1] Two objections spring to mind. One is that there were a great number of weaklings in the Army whose conduct was exemplary. The other is that many of these delinquents, on being posted away, proved to be very satisfactory soldiers despite their physical weaknesses.

Another matter for consideration is that the group included a

[1] See Rev. William D. Morrison, *Juvenile Offenders* (London, 1896)— 'The results of personal experience among large numbers of juvenile offenders, as well as the evidence just furnished by statistical investigations, have for many years confirmed me in the opinion that among the many causes which produce a criminal life the physical inferiority of the offender is one of the most important.' W. D. Morrison was an experienced criminologist and his conclusions were not lightly propounded.

number of individuals who were physically immature and whose troubles arose from finding themselves unable to keep up with the strenuous infantry training of 1943. Yet here again, immaturity is not a characteristic peculiar to offenders. And in the vast majority of such cases many other factors conducive to delinquency were observed.

In considering to what extent physical handicaps may be held primarily responsible for the waywardness of young soldiers, each case in the sample has been examined in detail with this possibility in mind. The list was reduced to thirty-four men whose state of health was such that they might possibly be included in this category. Yet their records, their own statements about their health and their earlier lives, the opinions of their previous commanding officers and the views of the S.T.U. staff show so many other abnormalities —especially broken homes and early poverty—that one would hesitate to say that ill-health was the prime cause or even a major cause of any of their delinquencies. Of course, early illnesses may have been the cause of subsequent waywardness, even after all effects of the illness had passed away, but such matters cannot be investigated when the subjects have grown up, and we are here concerned only with those offenders whose state of health was still unsatisfactory or who obviously bore the after-effects of earlier disorders. Fifteen men had evidently been severely handicapped by inherited weaknesses or bad health, and a few details of their cases are listed below:

No. 1. Sequelae sleepy sickness. Spoke of 'always being neglected' as a child. Parents 'thought I was in their way'. Medical category A1. Deserted in Ardennes; discharged as psychopathic personality.
No. 2. Infantile paralysis—crippled as a child, producing feelings of acute inferiority. Suffered from occasional brainstorms in the Army. Several sibs and parent tubercular. Both parents invalid. Seventeen children of whom five had died. Medical category A1. Post-S.T.U. service history excellent.
No. 3. Deafness in right ear. Said he had been accused of malingering and that his first offence—of failure to comply with an order—was attributable to his deafness. Five Army offences of absence without leave, and two minor disciplinary. Weight 9 stone 9 lbs. Height 5 ft. 6 ins. Special sick report established deafness while at S.T.U. Medical category A1. Posted to overseas service, and completed Army service satisfactorily.
No. 4. Meningitis, in infancy. Father a permanent invalid. Stated that parents wanted a girl when he was born, having two sons

already. Severe blow on head as a child. Weight 9 st.
11 lbs. Height 5 ft. 6 ins. Medical category A1. Nineteen
offences pre-S.T.U. Satisfactory service after posting until
release.

No. 5. Generally weak condition; fainted on attending hospital.
Brought up in orphanage. Two offences of personal
neglect and three disciplinary, pre-S.T.U. Medical category
A1. Weight 9 st. 4 lbs. Height 5 ft. 7 ins. Physical condition much improved at S.T.U. Excellent service history
after posting—promoted Corporal.

No. 6. Adenoidal; a miserable physical specimen. Strong feelings
of inadequacy. He wrote of his Army troubles—'Well, I
tried my best but I always had something wrong with me.
So I think if I had tried a little harder I would have been
alright. So I could not say I was unlucky.' Three offences
of absence without leave, three disciplinary and one personal
neglect, pre-S.T.U. Much improved by S.T.U. training and
upgraded medically to B1. Weight 7 st. 9 lbs. Height
5 ft. 3ins. Satisfactory service history after posting.

No. 7. Weakly; eight of the fifteen children in the family had died.
Very anxious about health. Underwent operation on leg
while at S.T.U. Three offences of absence, one disciplinary
and one personal neglect, pre-S.T.U. Medical category A1.
Weight 6 st. 3 lbs. Height 5 ft. 0 ins. Four absences after
posting—service history doubtful.

No. 8. Immature physically and mentally. Mother died when he
was young; father died later. Contracted malaria during
Army service. Eight offences of absence, pre-S.T.U. Medical category A1. Weight 9 st. 4 lbs. Height 5 ft. 5 ins.
Post-S.T.U. six absences and generally unsatisfactory service.

No. 9. Sequelae sleepy sickness and meningitis. Very strict upbringing; caned most mealtimes. Unable to explain absences
which were compulsive. Pre-S.T.U. offences, five of absence,
two late for parades, and one personal neglect. Medical
category A1. Weight 8 st. 4 lbs. Height 5 ft. 8 ins. Discharged as post-encephalitic.

No. 10. General physical and mental deficiency. Father invalid after
1914–18 War, since died. Much early bronchitis. Illiterate
and very backward in every respect. Offences pre-S.T.U.,
three absences, two disciplinary. Medical category A2.
Weight 9 st. 5 lbs. Height 5 ft. 9 ins. Discharged as mentally deficient.

No. 11. Chronic pharyngitis. Previously six months in sanatorium
for chest complaint and in three Army hospitals for blood
spitting. Father dead, mother suffering from phlebitis and
in difficult straits. Semi-illiterate. Mother died in workhouse during stay at Unit. Medical category A1. Weight
8 st. 13 lbs. Height 5 ft. 3 ins. Discharged as physically
unfit following wound on active service. (See p. 127).

No. 12. Father and grandfather delinquent. Case quoted on page

173. Medical category A1. Weight 8 st. 4 lbs. Height 5 ft. 6 ins. Pre-S.T.U. four absences including one desertion. Discharged after posting as psychopathic personality.

No. 13. Sent to hospital for adenoid operation. Psychotic heredity. See fuller description of case on page 78. Medical category A1. Discharged as psychopathic personality.

No. 14. Discharging left ear. General physical condition poor. T.B. father; parents separated; reared by elder sister. Most unsatisfactory home background. Medical category A1. Height 5 ft. 8 ins. Post-S.T.U. discharged as physically unfit.

No. 15. Physically small—Weight 8 st. 0 lbs. Height 5 ft. 1 in. Chronic naso-pharyngial infection, also chronic suppurative otitis media (bilateral). Neglectful home, poverty, invalid parents. Six of the fourteen children in family had died. An illiterate. Downgraded, post-S.T.U. from medical category of A1 to B1. Service history after posting excellent despite physical disability.

It was not possible to determine with any accuracy what part physical deficiency had played in the delinquencies of these fifteen men. The psychological condition of No. 13 and the mental dullness of No. 10 were probably more potent factors than their physical defects. It was probable that the physical condition of Numbers 6, 7, 9, 11, 14 and 15 was a major factor in their delinquencies. But in every case there were a number of other contingent factors which also have a bearing on delinquency, and it becomes an impossible task to disentangle any single thread from the whole network of causes. Whether the physical condition has all along been the precipitating factor, whether the physical condition has been aggravated by early neglect which also produced the tendency to delinquency, or whether the emotional frustrations, which are present in nearly every case, operate independently of the physical condition and are primary in determining delinquency, are questions that the present inquiry cannot answer.

The original list of fifteen names was compiled before the post-S.T.U. military histories were known. Six of the fifteen proved themselves satisfactory soldiers (Nos. 2, 3, 4, 5, 6 and 15), but when they left the S.T.U. only three of them looked as though they had any reasonable chance of success. The success of No. 15 in adapting himself to Army life despite serious physical disadvantages indicates the presence of latent reserves of power within the individual which are exceedingly difficult to determine.

The following table sets out a few background particulars of these fifteen men and indicates by a symbol the presence of factors other than physical deficiency that have been observed in each case.

TABLE 10

Number of case	No. 15	No. 14	No. 13	No. 12	No. 11	No. 10	No. 9	No. 8	No. 7	No. 6	No. 5	No. 4	No. 3	No. 2	No. 1
(1) Size of family (incl. parents)	16	8	12	15	5	6	8	8	17	11	6	5	7	20	7
Position in family	11	5	8	10	3	4	3	6	4	8	3	3	2	12	5
(2) Constitution of home	FD	S	S	S	FD	FD	.	O	.	.	O	.	.	.	O
Parents' attitude to child defective (D)	D	D	D	D	.	.	D	D	D	D	.	D	.	D	D
Relation between parents—undue friction (F)	.	F	F	F	.	F	.	F	F	F	.	.	.	F	F
Invalid parent(s)	.	+	.	+	+	+	.	.	+	.	.	+	.	+	.
Gross poverty at home	+	+	+	.	.	.	.	+	+	.	.	.	.	+	+
Excessive punishment by parents	+	+	+	+	.	.	.	.	+	+	+	+	.	.	+
Excessive attachment to home	+	+	.	.	+	+	+	.	.	+	+	.	.	.	.
(3) Emotional type	I	I	A	Int.	.	I	.	I	.	I	.	I	.	A	.
(4) Intelligence test group	3	4	4	4	3	5	4	7	8	4	1	2	3	3	2
(5) Educational tests group	5	5	4	5	5	5	3	7	4	4	3	3	3	5	5
(6) Prolonged absence from school	.	+	.	+	+	+	+	.	.	.	.	.	.	+	+
Truancy	+	+	+	+	.	.	.	.	+	.	.	+	.	.	+
Persecution at school	.	.	.	.	.	.	.	.	.	.	+	.	.	.	.
Anxiety over health	+	.	.	+	.	+	+	.	+	+	+	.	+	+	+
(7) Excessive cinema attendance	.	.	.	+	.	.	.	.	+	.	.	.	.	.	.
Gang associations	+	+	.	+	.	.	.	.	.	.	+	.	.	.	+
Excessive job-changing	.	.	+	+	.	.	.	+	+	.	.	+	.	+	+
Civilian delinquencies	+	+	+	+	.	.	.	.	.	.	.	+	.	.	+
No. of Army crimes, pre-S.T.U. (1 year)	4	4	5	4	9	5	8	8	5	7	5	19	7	4	4
No. of Army crimes, post-S.T.U. (3 years)	0	6	0	3	4	0	0	8	4	1	4	2	2	1	5
(8) Mode of release	A	D(Ph)	D(Psy)	D(Ph)	D(Ph)	D(Psy)	A	A	A	A	A	A	A	A	D(Psy)
Overseas service	+	+	.	.	+	.	.	+	+	+	+	+	+	+	+
(9) Final assessment as serving soldier	VG	U	U	U	D	U	?	U	D	S	VG	S	S	VG	U

(1) Including two parents.
(2) O, orphanage or institution upbringing; FD, father dead; S, parents separated.
(3) A, aggressive; I, immature; Int., introspective; (see p. 75).
(4) and (5) Five selection groups, from 1, high, to 5, low (see pp. 59–67).
(6) More than six months at a stretch.
(7) Four or more visits every week.
(8) A, Class A release (normal); D(Ph), discharged physically unfit; D(Psy), discharged as psychopathic personality.
(9) Assessment made after examination of soldiers' documents (see p. 26); VG, very good; S, satisfactory; D, doubtful; U, unsatisfactory.

CHAPTER IX

INTELLIGENCE AND ATTAINMENT

THE results of Army group tests tell something of the men's mental equipment, of their native intelligence. It is now widely held that there is a general factor of intelligence, an innate, cognitive ability that operates to a considerable extent through practical as well as mental activities.[1] A special test, Raven's Progressive Matrix Test, was designed to measure this quality. It was non-verbal, being composed of progressively more complicated pattern problems, so that the person with a limited vocabulary or even the illiterate should be at no disadvantage.[2]

Table 11 sets out the Matrix Test results for the S.T.U. sample (the original 200 was expanded to 400 for greater accuracy). They are arranged, for convenience of grading, into five groups. When the Tests were originally standardized on a sample Army population the scores were arranged in descending order of magnitude; Group I represented the range of scores covered by the top 10 per cent, Group II the next 20 per cent, Group III the next 40 per cent, Group IV the next 20 per cent and Group V the bottom 10 per cent. The main body of Army intake were obviously more intelligent

---

[1] See Burt, C., *Intelligence and Fertility*, appendix on 'The Meaning of Intelligence'. P. E. Vernon, 'Research on Personnel Selection in the Royal Navy and the British Army', in *The American Psychologist*, February 1947: 'the outstanding finding was the prominence of the general factor in representative adult populations.'

[2] The semi-illiterate (and a very large proportion of all delinquents are semi-illiterate) tends to be slower in his responses and less capable of showing to advantage in any sort of paper test. He may, therefore, be at a disadvantage in a non-verbal test because of his inexperience at handling symbols, even picture symbols. Though he may not be required to write or recognize words he tends to feel at a disadvantage in a situation which so closely resembles school work. Vernon, in 'Psychological Tests in the Royal Navy, Army and R.A.F.' (*Occupational Psychology*, April, 1947), says that the arithmetic and clerical tests are just as reliable as intelligence tests for measuring general intelligence in the Army population, since most soldiers were literate. With a delinquent population, the very wide differences between Intelligence (Matrix Test) results and those for the educational and clerical tests emphasize the need for non-verbal tests.

than the original sample, as the figures in the second line of the table show.   These Army norms, supplied by War Office, are for the Army intake of the same age during the corresponding period of recruitment.

TABLE 11

Percentage of delinquent and normal soldiers (aged 18 years) graded by the Matrix Test into Intelligence groups

	I Very bright	II Above average	III Average +	III Average −	IV Below average	V Dull
	%	%	%	%	%	%
S.T.U. population .	7	19	(21)	(26)	21	6
Normal Army population	11·5	22·4	(22·8)	(20·8)	17·3	5·2

The significant thing about these results, as Burt has pointed out,[1] is the great range of intelligence represented.   Even if it were true that the delinquent is rather duller than his normal neighbour—though these figures suggest that he is not greatly so—the fact remains that a large number of offenders are more intelligent than the normal.   In the case of the S.T.U. population, reading from the individual scores, as many as 47 per cent were above the mid-point of average intelligence (cf. 56·7 per cent in normal intake).

It should be noted that mental defectives are normally screened off before recruitment.   Most samples of civilian delinquents include a small proportion of mental defectives (roughly 5 per cent to 10 per cent) and had the Army admitted all applicants more defectives might have found their way to the S.T.U.   But it seems unlikely that their numbers would have been sufficient to affect the proportions above the average point by more than 2 or 3 per cent.

The differences between the two sets of figures in the table are possibly accounted for by two factors that influence intelligence levels in the population—size of family and social class.   Burt and Vernon have shown that intelligence is linked with the differential fertility rate, between one social group and another, and between individual families of varying size within each social group.   Since the great majority of the S.T.U. men came from large families (average number of children = 6·3) one would have expected the intelligence distribution of the group as a whole to have stood at

---

[1] Introduction to *Mental and Scholastic Tests*, C. Burt.

rather a lower level than the normal distribution. The extent of the correlation between intelligence and size of family is not great (Burt puts the coefficient of correlation at − 0·21)[1] but its effect should be noticeable in a group of several hundred. This factor alone, which Burt claims to be common to the entire population, may account for the slight inferiority in the offenders' intelligence test results.

Taking these various factors into consideration, the intelligence figures for delinquents may well prove little different, if at all, from those of normal men of similar background. This conclusion, however, does not support the findings of most investigators into problems of delinquency.

Estimates of Intelligence in Earlier Researches

Sir Cyril Burt—*The Young Delinquent*, p. 296—tested his cases and found them markedly dull—82 per cent technically dull and nearly 8 per cent definitely defective. The average mental ratio of his sample of offenders was 89 per cent though it is doubtful whether his control group, coming from the same social background, would have shown a mental ratio, on average, of 100 per cent (a mental ratio of 89 per cent is equivalent to a boy of 15 having a mental age of 13·4 years).

In J. H. Bagot's survey of delinquency in Liverpool (*Juvenile Delinquency*, Cape, 1940) the headmaster's assessments of the offenders' 'mental ability' was obtained, with separate assessments of a number of non-delinquents from the same schools. The results are as follows:

	Above Average	Average	Below Average (a)	Very much below Average (b)
	%	%	%	%
Delinquents, 1936	2·2	52·7	36·6	8·4
Non-delinquents	14·8	60·3	21·3	3·6

[1] So far as the individual families within the S.T.U. group are concerned there does appear to be a slight connexion between family size and intelligence. It was only possible to correlate family size with the coarse selection groups into which the intelligence test results were sorted, but the resulting coefficient of correlation was −·12, just significant. That is, as the size of the family increased, from one case to another, there was a slight tendency for intelligence to be lower. In a selected group like that of offenders, where family size was abnormal and varied less than in a normal sample of the population, one would expect this correlation to be lower than Burt's figure of −·21 for the population as a whole.

F

The percentages falling below the average groups here should obviously not be compared with the proportions given by Burt as falling below the average *point*. Bagot says: 'Making all necessary allowances for possibilities of error, it must be concluded that backwardness is strongly associated with delinquency; although in itself it does not make a child delinquent, the chance of delinquency is greater if he is mentally backward than if he is of average ability.' And later—'the influence which has been discerned is backwardness and not defectiveness.' The figures are interesting by comparison with those produced by Healy and Bronner (see below), but ability ratings by a number of headmasters, presumably working independently, are likely to be based upon different standards and may be misleading if simply summed. The boy's willingness to co-operate, his application to lessons, and his educational standard are likely to interfere with any individual estimate of 'mental ability', and Mr. Bagot, in his later remarks, suggests that he is discussing 'backwardness', which may include educational backwardness, and not 'defectiveness'.

Rudolf Pintner, in *Foundations of Experimental Psychology*, ed. Murchison (Clark University Press, 1929) says: 'among delinquent children one finds all degrees of intelligence, but there is a tendency for them as a group to be somewhat below normal.'

A further comparison may be made with Healy and Bronner's figures (in *New Light on Delinquency*). They write: 'Somewhat to our surprise . . . the mental age-levels of the two groups (delinquent and non-delinquent) prove to be only slightly contrasting. Skilful psychological testing shows that well within the limits of normal mental ability . . . were 93 per cent of the delinquents and 90 per cent controls.' Presumably the authors express surprise because some American surveys have shown very high proportions of dull and mentally deficient persons among delinquents. And in their own *Delinquents and Criminals* (New York, Macmillan, 1926) a study of 4,000 repeated delinquents, they mention a median I.Q. of about 90.

E. and S. Glueck, *One Thousand Juvenile Delinquents* (Cambridge, Harvard University Press, U.S.A., 1934) found only 41·6 per cent of normal intelligence or above, compared with 79 per cent of non-delinquent children at State schools. As the authors point out, the controls may include children from more fortunate homes, and the intelligence test itself may be culturally loaded so as to reflect educational standards as well as intelligence.

Healy and Bronner's test results are summarized as:

Intelligence Quotients

110+	90/110	80/90	72/80	69/71
above average	average	below average	much below	
%	%	%	%	%
11	53	27	7	2

This distribution is certainly more skewed towards the lower level than that for the S.T.U. population, though not as much as Burt's or Bagot's. Perhaps the differences between the assessments can best be shown by estimating the proportions below the median of average ability, as follows:

Burt's sample	82 per cent	
Bagot's sample	85 „ „	(estimated)
Healy & Bronner's sample	72 „ „	(estimated)
S.T.U. sample	53 „ „	(cf. 43 per cent normal)

So marked are the differences between the intelligence ratings of Army offenders (at the S.T.U.) and the various samples of civilian offenders that some explanation must be sought.

(1) Was the Army population as a whole abnormally dull? Some of the brighter recruits were filtered off into the R.A.F. and some into the Royal Navy. But the numbers concerned were relatively so small that they are unlikely to affect the proportions above and below the median by more than two or three per cent.

(2) Is it possible that the less intelligent civilian offenders kept out of trouble in the Army? From 1942 onwards there were fairly large scale transfers of the duller intake to the Royal Pioneer Corps where, employed at jobs within their competence, most of them settled down remarkably well, but it is doubtful whether this drainage would have been sufficient to have had much effect on S.T.U. intake as early as 1942/3.

(3) Perhaps the S.T.U. sample included a number of men who would not have been delinquents in civilian life, and the civilian delinquents among them may have been the duller members? To explore this possibility the test results have been broken down according to whether the man had previously been convicted of an offence in a civil court (36 per cent of the sample), and whether he had a large number (8 or more) Army offences recorded against him. The resulting distributions are:

TABLE 12

Intelligence distributions of civilian offenders and more
persistent Army offenders, arranged in selection groups

	I	II	III	IV	V
	Very bright	Above average	Average	Below average	Dull
	%	%	%	%	%
Civilian offenders	6	14	44	28	8
Persistent Army offenders	–	13	47	32	8
Whole S.T.U. sample	(7)	(19)	(47)	(21)	(6)
Normal Army intake	(11·5)	(22·4)	(43·6)	(17·3)	(5·2)

There is some suggestion of skewness towards the lower intelligence
groups amongst the civilian offenders, but the sample was rather
small and the differences are far from significant. In any case,
the distribution is very much nearer the normal than those suggested by earlier inquiries.

(4) Is it possible that earlier investigators have employed tests
that were partly dependent on verbal ability? If they have, then
a man's educational backwardness would hamper his efforts. The
extent of this backwardness was very great, as may be seen by comparing the proportions of the S.T.U. cases whose results fell below
the mean point—in Intelligence 53 per cent (cf. 43·3 per cent normal),
in Arithmetic 85 per cent (cf. 55 per cent normal), and in the Verbal
Test 78 per cent (cf. 51 per cent normal). This would seem to be
the most likely explanation.

Educational backwardness

The most striking feature about the mental state of these offenders
was their educational backwardness. It was apparent in any
written work or calculations they attempted, in the letters they
wrote and their answers to questionnaires, as many of the quotations in the following chapters will illustrate, and was amply confirmed by test results. One might have expected a large proportion
of gross illiterates amongst such men, considering their background,
yet the number seldom rose to 5 per cent of the total strength,
though the incidence of illiteracy in the Army as a whole only varied
between 0·5 and 1·0 per cent. The number of men in the Army
whose standard of education was very much below the school-
leaving standard in the elementary schools—according to the statement of the Secretary of State for War in the House of Commons

(13 Mar. '47)—was 26 per cent, yet as many as 44 per cent of the S.T.U. population fell within this category.[1] Unfortunately there is no common standard by which to determine where illiteracy ends and literacy begins, the one shades off into the other, and no useful comparison can be drawn between the S.T.U. figures and those for other delinquent samples.[2]

A man's educational standard can be fairly effectively measured by the Arithmetic and Verbal tests employed in Army Personnel Selection, and the S.T.U. sample's ratings in these tests are·set out in five groups below, with the corresponding proportions for normal Army intakes (drawn from two sample intakes, 4th March, 1948 and 3rd June, 1948, a total of 31,355 men of whom 56 per cent were 18 years of age and 38·29 per cent were 19.   The standard of education was probably lower in 1948 than in 1942 because so many of the later intake would have suffered from the effects of evacuation, their ages being 9 to 16 during the War years):

TABLE 13

Percentages of S.T.U. and normal young soldiers graded by Educational Tests into selection groups

	I Very good	II Above average	III + Average − high	III low	IV Below average	V Dull
(A) *Arithmetic*	%	%	%	%	%	%
Offenders	2	4	9	19	49	17
Normal[3]	6·75	17·79	20·16	20·28	23·18	11·76
(B) *Verbal*						
Offenders	1	7	14	26	33	19
Normal[4]	9·0	19·39	20·78	18·98	19·91	11·82

[1] The *Report of the Commissioners of Prisons* (1942–44) shows the proportions of illiterates and semi-illiterates ('read and write imperfectly') admitted to Borstal Institutions and prisons as between 2 and 3 per cent but the degrees of illiteracy are not defined.

[2] See Burt, C., 'Education of Illiterate Adults', *British Journal of Educational Psychology*, Feb. 1945, in which he estimates proportions for the entire population as 1·5 to 2 per cent illiterate, and 15 to 20 per cent semi-illiterate. P. E. Vernon, *Reading Ability* (H.M.S.O., 1950), puts the corresponding figures for Army National Service men (as measured by the new Watts-Vernon test) at 0.7 and 3.3 per cent respectively.   He defines an illiterate as one having a reading age of under 7.0 and a semi-illiterate 7.0 to 9.0.   Backward men (reading ages 9.0 to 12.0) totalled 15.8 per cent.

[3] Including 0·08 per cent unclassified.

[4] Including 0·12 per cent unclassified.

Reading from the original scores, 50 per cent of the offenders show an educational attainments lag of at least one whole group. Over 20 per cent have a lag of at least two groups—an astonishing degree of backwardness, tantamount to a child of 12 years having the educational standard of a child of 8.[1] The backwardness was certainly even more pronounced than is shown by this coarse grouping, because the scale was not fine enough—and was never intended—to show degrees of illiteracy at the bottom end. Further, a man whose intelligence was group V need not necessarily be expected to score group V marks in educational tests, but for the purpose of the following table such a state of affairs is taken as normal.·.'

Table 14 sets out the relation between intelligence test results and educational test results in terms of whole selection groups. Thus, for example, a man who was group 2 in intelligence and 3 minus in education would have a lag of 2 whole groups (or 40 per cent of the scale of the population as a whole). With normal populations, taken as a whole, the intelligence and educational test results should approximately balance though there would still be some advances and lags. The following figures from two different S.T.U.s show how closely the two populations compare in respect of backwardness.

TABLE 14

Relation of educational to intelligence test results
for two S.T.U. populations

	Advance in whole groups			Both equal	Lag in whole groups		
	3 60%	2 40%	1 20%	0[2]	1 20%	2 40%	60%
	%	%	%	%	%	%	%
Unit A	0	0	4	46	28	18	4
Unit B	0	0	8	47	25	15	5

The whole problem of educational backwardness was so serious

[1] See Burt, C., *Mental and Scholastic Tests* (P. S. King, 1922). One hundred juvenile delinquents were found to have an average chronological age of 13·2 years, an average mental age of 11·3, and an average scholastic age of 9·5. 'On an average the delinquents are retarded by nearly 2 years in general intelligence and by yet a further 2 years—4 years in all—in educational attainments.' It would be impractical and misleading to attach corresponding mental ages to an adult group.

[2] This column is made up of three combinations: (i) Intelligence and the two educational groups equal; (ii) Intelligence and one educational group equal and the other educational group one up or down; (iii) one educational group up one and the other down one.

a matter and was so prevalent among offenders[1] that a later chapter is devoted to it.

General Knowledge

The Verbal and Arithmetic tests measured the basic equipment, but it may be thought, and has often been suggested, that the offender has compensating powers. An allied theory, that backward children ought to be good at handwork (or in its cruder form, that backward children are not suited for anything better than handwork) has long been discarded. But one might well ask whether, as a compensation for his physical and educational deficiencies, the offender does not develop a quickness and a cunning, and a store of practical knowledge, like Tom Sawyer's, that help to see him through. A little observation of Army offenders at their daily activities suggests that there is little foundation for any such belief. Most of their offences were acts of defiance, some almost inviting punishment, and few of the calculated crimes were carried out by the brighter men. Their practical abilities, as reflected in their attempts at hobbies and handicrafts, were sadly deficient.[2] As for their general knowledge of everyday life and events, it was on a par with their educational development. The present writer drew up and applied a simple general knowledge test, with such questions as:

> 'A horse pulls a cart; what pulls a train?'
> 'Who is King of Great Britain?'
> 'What is wheat mainly used for?'

The questions, thirty-two in all, were graded by three independent judges so as to range very roughly from the general knowledge expected of a child of six or seven to that of an elementary school leaver. The average mark gained by the whole unit was 18 out of 32 —and this was after the majority had received lessons covering some of the questions. Normal groups at Day Release Institutes who have since completed the same test scored an average of 22·2 marks. A glance at a few of the answers reveals something of the gaps in the offenders' general knowledge. 'Who is King of Great Britain?' elicited the answers—Edward the Seventh, George the Fourth,

---

[1] S. and E. T. Glueck (op. cit.) found that over four-fifths of delinquent boys were retarded usually for two or more years, while they claim that only somewhat over one-third of the schoolboy population in general is retarded.

[2] Healy and Bronner (op. cit.) mention that it is sometimes said the delinquent shows more ability for manual tests. This, they found, was not substantiated by special tests, in which only 25 per cent showed any marked ability.

Fifth, Seventh and Eighth. Hollywood, Pearl Harbour and Spain were given as British Dominions, and Mexico, Buenos Aires and Brazil as British Colonies. A question that provoked some ingenious, and many fantastic, answers was 'Why doesn't an iron ship sink?' No exact scientific answer was expected, and any explanation that showed some elementary notion of displacement or of air being lighter than water was passed as correct. 'Because it balance and have hollow bottom', wrote one man. 'Because it is balanced by two large float tanks on each side', wrote another who may have been thinking of paddle steamers. 'Because a ship *isn't* made of iron', 'Because it has not got a whole to let the water out', 'Because it has a broad keel and the engine keep it up', 'Because water is continually being pumped out' (possibly a recollection of bilge water), and 'Because it has ballast and built up sides', were other attempts showing various degrees of observation. A request to name two members of Parliament brought suggestions of 'Wendy Willky', 'All-belesha', 'Lord Lou Mounblatten', and 'Mr. Asquith'.

They had little idea of the functioning of their bodies. To take only the examples that spring to mind, they did not know how babies are born (i.e. it was news to most of them that a baby normally emerges head first), where rain comes from, or weren't at all sure about the shape of the earth. One class was asked, during a map-reading lesson, whether rivers ran uphill or downhill. Several men claimed that they ran uphill, and gave as reasons that the pressure of the sea forced them up—perhaps having seen a tidal estuary—or suggested that the sun's heat drew them up. Others suggested that the pressure of springs forced the water along, or 'the earth's movement', or 'currents'.

Occasionally one would come across a man with some special ability highly developed: verbal ability, manual dexterity, or highly imaginative or artistic powers. Burt has described such types in great detail. They do not run to more than three or four per cent of any group and are probably not much more common among offenders than among normal people. But they are important because, combined with backwardness and a tendency to anti-social behaviour, such special abilities may turn into dangerous channels.

Manual Dexterity

Army tests were employed to measure general mechanical aptitude (the ability to put together a dismantled bicycle pump, electric lamp-holder or adjustable pliers) and agility (which included co-ordination of hand, foot and eye, by the changing of rings from one set of upright posts to another), but in these tests the S.T.U. men did not show to any advantage nor to any disadvantage, compared with most Army intake.

Manual dexterity is normally associated with mechanical ability but occasionally one came across an offender with unusual hand and finger skill, but without the intelligence or imagination to make any constructive use of it. One man who possessed this special aptitude was the Education Centre orderly for nearly a year. He was illiterate and never managed to learn to write more than a few painfully formed words (though he sent the author three or four undecipherable letters after he was posted away). He was dull and educationally backward, but scrupulously clean and hardworking. He was quite happy keeping the Centre scrubbed and tidy and, like so many backward people, was contented and well behaved so long as he was not called upon to do any work beyond his powers. In some ways he resembled a good-natured horse and was indeed passionately devoted to horses. He had remarkable manual dexterity, and scored very high marks indeed in the Assembly (mechanical aptitude) test. He was continually seeking out little repair jobs—a light switch, a punctured tyre, a broken lock, or a leaking fountain pen. Unfortunately, he had not the intelligence to direct his hands and many of his repairs were bodged. Doubly unfortunate was his propensity for using his fingers where they should not have been used. He could pick almost any lock—if ever one of the education staff came up to his room without a key he would be let in—and at one time there were suspicions of his good character precisely because he was so adept at opening locked doors. But he kept out of trouble and after posting made quite a satisfactory soldier until he was discharged with a duodenal ulcer.

Verbal Virtuosity

The three or four men of this type among the S.T.U. sample were glib talkers, but their voluble chatter was generally employed to cover up the gaps in their knowledge, or to impress the listener, or to ingratiate themselves with someone in authority. One little chap, an East End Jew, came into the education office one night and in the course of conversation tried to impress the writer with his knowledge of nine languages. His father, he explained, was a Russian Jew who had been driven out of what was later Poland and had taken to tailoring in the East End of London. 'I'm keen on soldiering,' he went on; 'I want to get into a fighting unit. I've got to avenge all my dad's people who have been killed, in the heroic state of Russia, I mean. There's plenty of fight in me', he chattered on. Looking down at him, a shrimp of a fellow with a pale, nervous face, one wondered whether the words really came from that body. It turned out that his Russian consisted of three or four words. He had taken a postal course in elementary German. His French was very elementary indeed and one suspected that his Polish, Czech and Dutch were even less extensive. His test results showed him much below average in intelligence, and, rather surprisingly, equally backward in the verbal and arithmetic tests. His verbal powers were therefore based on a small vocabulary and confined to speech. His ambitions as a soldier proved as groundless as his claims to be a linguist, for he was of very low combative temperament and was afraid of any military exercise. He was just a timid, undersized boy, chattering to convince himself by convincing others of a manliness that was only too obviously lacking.

Another talker, though a man of very different calibre, had unbounded ambition for the music halls. He liked to hear himself talk. He was backward mentally and educationally and, like the 'linguist', had only a small vocabulary, but he loved to pick up a new word, to sound and savour it and expected the hearer to laugh every time it was uttered. He thought himself a great wag and would prattle and caper in front of his mates for hours. His ambitions ranged to the highest reaches of variety fame, with his name blazing in lights from a West End theatre façade. But unlike the other verbalist this man had determination and some ability and though this may take him to a limited success it may also induce him to overreach himself. Both lived in a world of phantasy—the first spoke of 'hearing voices' after his mother died when he was eight years old, and his world was garish but quite unreal; the second was nearer reality and therefore more convincing as a verbalist. The first was discharged from the Army for mental deficiency; the second went overseas, took up entertainment work and was given an honourable release, but in civilian life has met furher misadventures (see pp. 176–8).

Romanticism

Another oddity is the man with strongly developed imaginative powers. An unusual case was that of a youngster who had been brought up in a Home where, to use his own words, they 'were led around like lost sheep'. It was soon discovered that he was very much afraid of the dark, and never went out alone at night. This was mainly because he frequently experienced material manifestations of his mother who had died when he was only seven years old. In earlier years, he told the staff, he used to hear her voice. He felt that these experiences made him unlike other men and thoughts of suicide had more than once taken strong hold of him. He had also been subject to fainting fits as long as he could remember. One night, during an air raid, he was found in a corner, shaking uncontrollably. He was later discharged as a psychopath. There were perhaps half a dozen men amongst the sample of two hundred who were subject to varying anxiety states but one or two managed to become fairly reconciled to Army life.

Quite a different case was an Irishman who had lost his parents a few years before. He had quite a pleasant tenor voice, soft and very high, and he would sit by the hour improvising tunes and verses and singing them over to himself. They were mostly about his mother or about suffering. The three examples that follow were taken down by the author while the man was actually singing them. They are interesting not only as an illustration of a remarkable romantic ability but because they show how strong was the link with the earlier home.

(1) Don't be afraid of me, little bird, little bird;
A pain, his heart was broken,
A bird can sing with a broken wing,
But not with a broken heart.
So I come your friend to be, little bird, little bird,
To ease your pains and your suffering.
So don't be afraid of me, little bird, little bird,
A pain in your heart which is broken.
A bird can sing with a broken wing,
But not with a broken heart.

(2) Just a plain old Irish mother,
Just with tears of gold in her eyes.
For the dew of Irish shamrock,
Which will sparkle in the night.
For just a plain old Irish mother,
With a kind and gentle heart,
For she always gave me a smile,
And she always gave me a kiss,
With those tears of gold in her eyes.
For just a plain old Irish mother,
Who was just like gold to me,
For she always thought of me dearly
As her boy with a golden voice.

(3) Just a silver haired old lady,
    Just a memory I sang.
    She always did teach me the right from the wrong,
    Just that silver-haired old lady of mine.
    When the church organ played,
    For her eyes there were sometimes tears,
    For she had only one lover,
    Who has gone far away from her,
    For just a silver-haired old lady
    Who's heart was broken and tired she went to sleep,
    And she went in peace to the only voice of the mighty organ,
    Which I always think of those memories.

A more common expression of strong imaginative powers was found in the highly romanticized versions of war stories. Little fabrications and vanities were common to most offenders, as to others. Many men improved on their war experiences or elaborated the hazards of their training ordeals, and they were not averse to putting up a chevron or two on their arms while on leave. Here, however, one is more concerned with the man who elaborated his phantasies and exaggerations to a point where he had constructed a complete and unreal background to his life. Two examples may be quoted.

One man's story began, by his own account, when he failed to get into the Royal Navy. He then volunteered for the Merchant Navy. He claimed over thirty sea trips on liners, in various capacities from cabin boy to deck hand. He said he had gone through Dunkirk and been blown up in the Channel on his way over from the French coast. He later served on board a liner which was torpedoed, and he spent several days at sea in an open boat before being rescued. He finally left the sea on his mother's plea, and did some factory work and then some farming. He then enlisted voluntarily for the Army. His desire to return to the Merchant Navy was strong, but was balanced by his respect for his mother's wishes that he should not return to sea. Shortly after he joined the S.T.U. he had a fit indicative of epilepsy and a letter was written to his parents about this. A reply from his mother stated that he had had fits as a child, but also revealed that his earlier adventures were confined to eighteen months' training on the *Arethusa* and one uneventful trip to South Africa.

The second case claimed to be Belgian by birth. He said he left school at ten, joined the Army at twelve, and was in a German concentration camp from November 1941. He was forced in

May 1944 to watch his parents being put to death. A month later he escaped to England, and got into the British Army by 'telling a pack of lies' as he put it. On another occasion he stated that he had been a steward on a cargo ship on the Russian and African convoys, and was captured off North Africa in November 1941. His later stories were inconsistent with his earlier accounts, and a large part of them proved to be imaginary. Three years after the War he was still masquerading, as an American soldier.

The promptings of such tale-spinning appear to derive from the all too common feelings of deprivation and inadequacy. Yet relatively few offenders possess the inventive powers to sustain such elaborate phantasies or have so urgent a need to escape.

The Creative Artist

The real artistic temperament is quite another matter. As educationists we were always looking out for the artist whatever his medium. Many hundreds of these offenders learned to draw or paint pictures and some produced very pleasing results. But the natural artist was very rare indeed. Amongst nearly a thousand offenders there appeared only one graphic artist, one writer with rather more sense but less talent, and no musician. These are possibly fewer than would be found among a normal sample of soldiers, but one must consider these men against the background of their social class where opportunities for artistic expression would be relatively few. The man who showed the gift for writing contributed regularly to the wall newspaper, and was a very rational, well-balanced fellow; he needed only an opportunity for expression and a fresh start. Subsequent records showed him well integrated into his new unit—the Royal Armoured Corps, earning promotion.

The artist's story was so exceptional that it might be thought undeserving of any further consideration but for the fact that it does illustrate how diverse are the emotional springs of delinquency. He was a Jew, intelligent, talkative and a very talented painter and draughtsman. Several of his paintings had been exhibited. But he was hostile to any authority, seemed unable to settle in any place for long, and was subject to fits of abject depression and self-pity in which he destroyed his paintings and often committed excesses of violence against himself or other people's belongings. At such times he invited punishment. He would walk into the guard-room and say: 'Arrest me. Lock me up. I'll only get into trouble if you don't. If you don't I'll throw something at you and then you'll have to.' Sometimes he refused to shave or to put on his uniform or obey any of the orders on parade. Punishment only made him more obstinate. He felt that there was a struggle going on between himself and the Army authorities and that he could not possibly admit defeat by conforming.

While he was with the Unit he had a good spell, in which he was excused parades and allowed to work in the Education Centre, painting or designing posters or doing odd jobs. He never became reconciled to the Army and was finally sent off to detention again. Just before he was due to leave there was the sound of a rifle shot from the guardroom. He had somehow obtained a round and shot it off but was apparently unhurt. The guards bundled him into the waiting lorry but at the station a pool of blood was noticed on the floor of the truck and a small hole was detected in the top and bottom of his boot. He explained later that he had intended cutting the main ligament in the top of his foot, which injury would probably have brought about his discharge from the Army. He knew something of anatomy from his life-study classes at the art school, but he had forgotten to make allowances for the jump of the rifle. 'That was where my neglect of Army training let me down,' he said with a rueful smile. The bullet grazed the inside of his big toe causing only a flesh wound, and after a fortnight in hospital he was well enough to go down for a long term of imprisonment. Here he went on hunger strikes, and wounded himself because, as he explained later, he had been weak enough to accept a mouthful of food. He was ultimately discharged as a psychopathic personality. His history since leaving the Army is not encouraging and he appears to be in need of special mental care. His emotional troubles were an obstacle to his talents and he is less and less able to express himself artistically. This man's case is, of course, in no way typical of the artist in service life who was frequently well integrated into his unit and generally managed to adapt himself, if not his environment, to suit his special needs.

CHAPTER X

EMOTIONAL TYPES

A FURTHER study would be needed to explore the many emotional conditions found amongst a delinquent population and the present inquiry makes no attempt to trespass on ground that properly belongs to the field of technical psychology. At the Special Training Unit some empirical classification of attitudes had to be made, not only for diagnostic purposes, but in order to have a rough working guide by which the training programme could be adapted to the men's peculiar needs.

Accordingly an attempt was made to sort the sample of two hundred offenders into groups according to their general emotional attitudes and their consistent, abnormal modes of behaviour, as they appeared to those of the staff who knew them intimately. A few of the men had been submitted to an Army psychiatrist who diagnosed mild psychopathic or anxiety states in several cases but recommended continued training at the S.T.U.[1] Two men were found to have serious mental disturbances and were discharged from the Army forthwith as psychotic.[2] The general classification was as follows:

	%
Aggressive, anti-social tendencies, very marked	4
Introspective, inhibited, despondent tendencies very marked	7·5
Immature types, mentally very backward, and generally childish in behaviour	20
Wanderers, escapists to a very marked degree	7·5
Drifters, apathetic, lethargic to a marked degree	2·5
Gross mental disturbance (discharged)	1
Not classified as a consistent type	57·5
	100

[1] Proportionately more (30 per cent) of the emotional 'types' were subsequently discharged from the Army as psychopathic personalities than of the unclassified men (13 per cent). The post S.T.U. records showing the manner of release or discharge were not seen until after the first draft of the present study had been completed. The classification of emotional types was therefore not influenced by any knowledge of subsequent diagnosis of psychopathic states.

[2] S. and E. T. Glueck (op. cit.) classify 3·1 per cent of 384 young-adult criminals as having major psychoses.

Apart from the 20 per cent who have been listed as emotionally very immature (a difficult definition to apply for the type does not always coincide with physical immaturity and shows a variety of sub-types), the remaining types comprise only small groups. And the isolation of such types should not obscure the tendency to aggressiveness, introspection, immaturity, wandering and apathy that was common to very many of these men.[1]

It should not be thought that the unclassified 57·5 per cent of the men were in any way normal people, with a balanced attitude to life. Nothing could be further from the truth. Further analysis would probably put a number of them into one of the five type groups or would possibly suggest quite different classification. Many of these unclassified men were generally unstable, ambivalent, full of anxieties, consumed by self-pity one minute, breaking loose the next, tied to their homes by the strongest feelings of dependence, yet resenting the deprivation of parental love that had obviously been their lot. Such emotional expressions appeared to be symptoms of an underlying disturbance which threw off feelings of deprivation, or of grievance, of being thwarted or frustrated.[2] And such feelings were as strong in the aggressive men as in the introspective, in the wanderers as in those who are not classified. A simple illustration of this sense of deprivation and grievance may be quoted in the words of a man whose feelings were probably milder than most (his post-S.T.U. history of military service was very satisfactory):

Well, my life has just been a bore. I was never spoiled. I lost my parents when I was quite young. I lived for a while with my very old grandparents. They couldn't do much for me as they were so old.

[1] After this present work was completed D. H. Stott published his interesting study *Delinquency and Human Nature* (The Carnegie U.K. Trust, 1950) in which he classified the 102 boys at an approved school according to behavioural reactions. Three such reactions—avoidance, demonstrative, and withdrawal, he describes as separate phases of a single process. Avoidance, Stott writes, is 'a situation in which the patient's emotional needs are thwarted without any seen possibility of their fulfilment. It is in fact an attempt at escape from an unbearable situation.' He describes the symptoms as 'need for an endless succession of amusements and excitements', 'unable to settle at any regular activity', 'feeling bored', 'day dreams'. The demonstrative reaction he defines as the 'phase of active retaliation and resentment . . . efforts to command the notice or test the affection of such parents. . . .' 'Withdrawal sets in', he says, when the child 'resigns itself to a state of lovelessness', the symptom being 'a sullen and melancholy reserve'. These three groupings bear some resemblance to our introspective, aggressive and drifter types.

[2] See Lydia Jackson, 'Emotional Attitudes of Delinquent Children,' *B. J. Psy.*, Vol. XLI, 3 and 4, Dec., 1950.

When I left school at 14 years of age I went into digs. Since then I have been very browned off with life. I have always wanted a break in life like other chaps but never had a chance till about a month before I was called up when I got a good job. Then I was brought into the Army to fight for what they will call a land fit for heroes to live in. If I get the breaks after the War like I got before, it won't be much of a life for me. That is why I am so bitter towards people who try and domineer over me. All I want is a chance in life which other chaps have had. Then I would be a bit more satisfied with life. The time I get out of the Army I shall be a bit too old to start making a break in life. It is while I am young I want it so my outlook on life is very poor. Up to now I have found that nine people out of ten are out for all they can get out of you, that is one reason why I am so bitter towards older people. I have never found any one who is willing to help you unless they are going to get something for it. I am afraid this is all about myself but I can't say much about the people who looked after me when I was young, because I have brought myself up from the age of 9 years, so that is all I can say about other people, only that if my Mother and Father were alive I would be better off in life and in understanding other people. I am the only one.

A man who could rationalize his problems to that extent had obviously a greater advantage than he knew.

The Aggressive Type

It might be thought that most offenders would show aggressive tendencies because in one sense their offences are encroachments on the rights of others. It is therefore all the more remarkable that only 4 per cent were noticeably aggressive in their general attitude to life.

Here, very much condensed, is an outline story of one man whose aggressive tendencies were very marked. He was perhaps more violent than most.

He had been sent to the S.T.U. after serving a sentence of detention for attempting to strike a N.C.O. He came from Ireland, a younger member of a large family. He agreed with neither parent and with few of his brothers and was often beaten, or so he said, by his father. When asked about his hobbies, he replied 'The simple reason why I had never had any hobbies or amusement was because my Father or Mother would not allow me to play'. That statement as it stands may well be doubted but it suggests the resentment that may have prompted it. His parents were ardent Roman Catholics but from their letters to him were not in the least concerned about him, except to get an allotment of his Army pay if possible. He had not been home since enlistment and showed no love for his

G

family except in so far as he felt it his duty to make them an allowance. He was a school truant and fought his masters on occasions. He had no friends at school, he said, because he was found too rough. He had some civil charges against him. He gave the following reason for volunteering for the Army: 'because I did not get on too well with my Parents, so I made up my mind, and ran away and joined the Army. I had to have two references and a birth certificate, so I forged my two references and got another fellow's birth certificate, so I joined the Army under a different name.' The last sentence is interesting because the change of name apparently gave him some satisfaction—and it may even have been construed as a repudiation of his parentage. He spoke with fair insight. He admitted his hot temper which was indeed flaming. In a normal mood he was not unattractive. He had a habit of holding his head on one side and was a chronic nail biter. He was then not eighteen years of age, having enlisted under age.

A psychiatrist's report on this man reads: 'Psychotic heredity—collateral. Below average intelligence. Aggressive in attitude. Evidence of vaso-motor instability. A poorly integrated personality of low intelligence and poorly controlled aggressive tendencies. Psychopathic personality with emotional abnormality, of doubtful value in military service.'

For three months while he was with the Unit he showed considerable restraint and seemed to be making a real effort to control himself. But the effort could not be sustained and he was later discharged from the Army. (His case is referred to as No. 13 in the table on p. 58.)

It was sometimes suggested during the War that Army training, with its inculcation of a combative spirit, was likely to induce a callous attitude to life, to breed aggressiveness and violence in the minds of impressionable young men. Such fears were much exaggerated,[1] for the greater part of infantry training was not concerned with killing at all, but with the handling of weapons and tactical movement. Bayonet practice was carried out on sandbags and was often treated jocularly, if the sweating soldier had time to stop and think at all about the significance of what he was doing. Commando training was a different matter and may have induced subsequent feelings of guilt, but that affected only a relatively small number of men. Battle itself was seldom a matter of the killing of

[1] J. R. Rees *The Shaping of Psychiatry by War* (Duckworth, 1947) argues that ill effects of this sort were slight.

individuals, and even when it was, the enemy was generally thought of as a target who would get you if you didn't get him. Indeed, if one were to assess the total influence of soldiering upon the character of a young man one would have to take into account the positive factors such as the communal life, the dependence on one's comrades, the sacrifice of personal liberty for a larger end. One would, therefore, hesitate to say that Army training is any more demoralizing an influence than, say, in civilian life, the tendency for tradesmen and customers to give or seek favourable treatment in the distribution of scarce goods, or the effect of insecurity in employment.

There were occasional outbreaks of sadistic violence at the camp, and animals were generally the unfortunate victims. One man was found toasting frogs on the combustion boiler in the basement of headquarters. Another snared birds with bird-lime to the interest and amusement of a circle of friends. The most regrettable lapse occurred on a day when the camp was open to relatives and friends. The men had given a splendid display of physical effort and skill. Late that evening one of the two fine swans which nested on a lake in the grounds was found dead on the bank. It had been stabbed to death, probably by a bayonet, with wounds in the breast, under the wing, in the leg and on the back. The same night two men went absent and were naturally suspected of the offence, and later one of them admitted it. Yet neither of them is listed among the aggressive types, and most of the similar offences of violence were attributable to immature youngsters.

There were very few cases of attacks on local inhabitants, and, on the whole, it would be true to say that neighbouring civilians were as safe with these men as they would have been with a boarding school on the same site.

Strongly aggressive tendencies were most often shown in the quarrels that were continually flaring up. Any little group, if unoccupied for a few moments, might be the scene of a bitter argument between two or more. Friends one moment, the next they would be shaking their fists in each other's faces, exchanging violent abuses, spitting and framing up for a fight. Yet they would seldom come to blows. 'If only you would save up some of that anger for your real enemies, the War would be over in six months!' was a frequent staff comment.

Only two of these eight men completed satisfactory military service up to the time of their release, as judged by the evidence in their records. Three were discharged as psychopathic personalities and the others continued their unauthorized absences and disciplinary offences until they were released.

The Introspective Type

The men who appear to have turned their emotions inwards,[1] who grieve and worry and are full of self-pity, often get a thin time of it from their companions. They are different, and on the defensive, and, like the ugly duckling, are inclined to be persecuted. One man who is mentioned again later (see p. 118) was incessantly 'chi-iked', as teasing of this sort was called. The introspective types are more unfortunate than the aggressive men in this respect. They are often accounted dull or stupid and the injustice of such misunderstandings only makes them feel more aggrieved than ever. Here is a brief outline of this same man's story:

He was sent to the S.T.U. as a man of 'indifferent character' after convictions for being drunk, insolent and absent without leave, and having made a sensational escape through the roof of a guard-room. He had several married brothers and sisters and one younger brother. His mother died in 1939 and his father in 1942. He spent his leaves with a married sister. He did not like school, did not mix. But as he had never had a job he liked he wished he were back at school. He was twice put on probation for larcenies. He had several labouring jobs that did not satisfy him, perhaps because he was found, through Army testing, to have high mechanical aptitude. He didn't care for games but quite liked P.T. His spare time he passed solitarily. He said he liked woodwork at school, so in an attempt to divert his efforts into channels that would be less frustrating he was found a job with the carpentry squad. In conversation one found him deeply introverted. His spoken responses were painfully slow and subdued, and he always appeared as though about to cry. Yet he had an honest smile at times. He was often twitted in class by the other men, and even accused of homosexuality though this charge was almost certainly groundless. He would only occasionally pop out of his shell, as on a memorable occasion when he spoke to a class for half an hour about his job.

Three months later it was possible to report that he was very much happier than when he came, though he had remained solitary.

---

[1] John Bowlby, *Forty-four Juvenile Thieves* (Bailliere Tindall & Cox, 1948) classified 9 of the 44 delinquents as 'depressive'. 'Such children are commonly "introverted" and might be called "shut-in",' he writes.

He was content to stand in the NAAFI canteen, never venturing to the town or the cinema. His main fear was a return to the infantry, not because of the dangers of active service, but because he lacked the confidence to carry out what was required of him. 'I was always doing the wrong thing', he would say. Writing of his Army troubles on another occasion, he said: 'When people go wrong in the Army I don't think it is their natural way; one reason may be on account of the change of life, another is because he has a different law from the Army's.' He was thoughtful and deliberate in his brief sentences, sensible and kindly in attitude. He was certainly not suited to the hurly-burly of life in wartime or of advanced infantry training. If he talked at all to any officer or visitor it was nothing but self-depreciation. Even the Welfare staff who were his constant friends and champions felt that the Army would be cutting a loss by discharging him.

Finally he was posted, not to the infantry, but to a unit where he would be regraded for normal work suited to him. The Welfare staff kept in touch with him by post and to everybody's surprise he began to gain confidence. He served overseas, without further troubles, and was eventually honourably released with a good testimonial. He gave the whole of his gratuity to the married sister who had befriended him and had recently been widowed.

Another man of this type was sent to the S.T.U. as 'shifty, with no sense of responsibility or duty'. His father was dead, his mother alive with a younger sister and two older brothers. His father had suffered from sleepy sickness and had been bedridden for ten years. His mother had to nurse the father which prevented her from going out to work. Their family income was thirty-six shillings a week, and sometimes, he said, 'we were half starved'. 'I never had any holidays at all,' he wrote. 'If the Government had given a family of four children and a bedridden invalid a little more I might have been like my pals and at least went for a day by the sea.'

After leaving school he had worked as an apprentice boiler furnaceman and when he was on piece-work he could earn up to five pounds a week. Later he was put back on a standard wage on account of his age, so he volunteered for the Army. He would often not talk at all and appeared very stubborn. 'I'm no good at games as I never took any interest in them', he told one of the staff. On another occasion he wrote:

'I only had one hobby and that was trying to tame wild birds. I succeeded in two cases. One was with a young crow which I took from a nest and by the time I had had it six months it used to fly to me when I clapped my hands and also perched on my cycle handlebars when I used to go delivering papers. I got a photograph of my crow perched on my cycle before it got roughly handled and KILLED. My second success was with a sparrow-hawk which I reared from being two weeks old till it was nearly ten months old. This hawk I reared on pieces of meat till it was able to fly and get its own food. It used to stay out in the trees all night and then come screeching during the morning at the front door to be brought in and fed.'

Writing of his other amusements he said: 'Walking was a favourite pastime of mine and I often used to slip school during the fine weather and go walking. I had no indoor amusements and spent the greater part of my own time rambling. I never played any instrument but when I listened to a violin I always imagined that if I had one at that moment I would be able to play it but later I knew that this was impossible.'

He looked worried and suffering, yet he was quite a good-looking fellow and on parade and at games he was of good example by his quiet efficiency. After being at the S.T.U. for some months he became more confident and was eventually attached to the unit police. His record after posting shows that he committed no further offences and was released with an excellent report.

The stories of these two men, though not representative of the 'introspective' types, for these were rather more pleasing than the others, may help to reveal the personalities of the type and indicate why it has been found necessary to consider their problems independently.

Seven of the fifteen men who fall within this category gave at least satisfactory service up to their release and their records show no significant variation from those of the whole S.T.U. group.

The Immature Type

Most of the men who have been grouped together as emotionally immature (20 per cent of the total) would have passed as ten-year-olds mentally. Their immaturity, physical and emotional, made them unduly homesick and often childish in behaviour. One would frequently come across them playing Cowboys and Indians, pointing imaginary guns at each other and shouting 'bang, bang'. One young fellow even asked if he could be moved back to the intake platoon because he had no friends in his new platoon to play shooting with. Another took an opportunity to punch small holes with a paper punch in the Quartermaster's hat! Their childishness was reflected in their dependence on their homes. Speaking of his home, one man wrote:

I think I was rather spoiled being the only boy and sometimes may have got out of hand and then my father has whacked me but my mother always sticks up for me. Although I am nearly a man now my mother always treats me the same. I also think my father is deeply fond of me but like all men he does not like sentiment. I would willingly die to right any wrongs I may have done to my parents in the past.

'Nearly a man now,' he wrote, yet he was over twenty years old at the time. 'I'm just very young. I can't grow up yet,' said another who was nineteen.

Several of these 'immature' men were putting up a show before their comrades, pretending to be tougher, or more experienced, or older than they really were. They maintained the bluff until, in some cases, it led them into a position that proved untenable. Then they fled home. One man was said by his mother to be only sixteen years of age. At her request an application for his discharge was initiated, but the boy himself was strongly opposed to it when the time came, though previously he had often expressed regret at joining up. He said that he did not want his comrades to find out that he was only sixteen as they would think he was a mere boy. Another man had made a special plea for a posting to the paratroops—a difficult transfer to effect. The application was finally granted and the man's name appeared on routine orders for posting the next day to a Paratroop Holding Battalion. When he read his name on the notice his resolution collapsed and he made a panic flight from the unit.

Tracing their service history after leaving the S.T.U., we find that about half of them became satisfactory soldiers, a quarter having very good records. In this respect they do not show any significant difference from the S.T.U. sample as a whole.

Wanderers

This type includes one or two nomads by birth and occupation, men of gipsy stock. It is not difficult to appreciate the feelings of the boy who was reared as a roamer, associating movement with his earliest memories, and even with such parental affection as he got. One man, a persistent absentee, wrote: 'My unit could do nothing

with me. I get terrible fits of depression. I just sit down some-
where and start thinking about something. You see I never lived
in one place more than three months before I came in the Army.'

Such men would naturally want a driving job or a seafaring life,
and nearly all of them did in fact ask for it. The numbers of
gipsies who came to the S.T.U. were so small, however, that there
appears to be no case for believing that an unusually large number
of offenders are drawn from this section of the community. It was,
incidentally, a gipsy who became the foreman of a party which
excavated a prehistoric site near the camp. He developed a keen
interest in archaeology, read up several books on the subject, and
would make solitary trips to cuttings and river gravels in the neighbourhood in search of early flints. Some months after he was
posted it was learned from the Curator of a county museum that
the same man had called in with a gift of a collection of neolithic
hand-axes he had uncovered in his spare-time wanderings.

Most of these wanderers were not gipsies, but were activated by
some emotional compulsion. A word that continually recurs in
descriptions of them is 'restless'. They seemed unable to settle,
as though some irritation were driving them to seek new fields where
they might find contentment. Behind them, in most instances, was
a lifetime of running away. It may have begun on the day they
toddled out of the front door to take refuge in the street from the
excesses of father or mother. So, through years of school truancy—
itself a practice necessitating deception and continual subterfuge
—and a job-changing adolescence, the early habits become ingrained.[1]
The escapist thus develops an eye for the easy way out. He can
generally spot an unguarded exit from a railway station. He knows
how to find his way into cinemas without paying. He finds it hard
to take criticism. If the foreman at work complained or if he
became unpopular with his workmates, he would walk out and find
another job. Several of these fellows had worked at between
thirty and forty jobs. It was, of course, easy enough in 1939 and
the early War years when labour was scarce and well paid. But
in the Army they found themselves confined for the first time. The
only way out seemed to be a driving job or transfer to a seafaring
life—preferably in the Merchant Navy where they thought discipline would be light. At times the discipline of the Army became
too much for them; the desire to escape came over them with

[1] Bowlby records that 16 of his 44 cases were guilty of truancy and wandering, compared with only 3 in the control group.

compelling force and almost before they knew what was happening their feet were treading the well-marked paths on the back way out of camp, to the main road and a hitch-hike for home.

A typical case came from Glasgow. Both parents were invalids, the father from the effects of the previous war. The lad was the eldest of nine children. A frequent school truant, he later had over thirty jobs, losing or leaving most through restlessness or quick temper; he had motor-driving jobs covering nearly two years. He was called up, reluctantly, and had remained averse to Army life. Shortly before coming to the S.T.U. he was acquitted of a charge of having a self-inflicted wound—the loss of his trigger finger. He looked pallid and unfit, and seemed of a fearful nature, ill-adapted to a robust Army life. He was worried about his home conditions. Investigation of these revealed that the mother had been telling untruths about her physical condition in letters to the son; actually she was still able to work and was earning £3 a week while the father received 26/– from the P.A.D. The home was dirty. There was little doubt that the mother was trying to engineer his discharge on compassionate grounds and the lad himself was conniving. An application was submitted to Army authorities for a special dependent's allowance so that his mother could give up work and he would feel that he was doing something for his family. The young man felt 'exposed' by this revelation, however, and needed a good deal of firmness and encouragement to prevent his going absent. A month later the mother was still exclaiming about her financial position but further inquiries revealed that she was receiving supplementary grants and there was no real hardship. The lad then got a few days 'confinement to barracks' for coming back a day late from leave, though it was something of a triumph to get him back at all. Three months later he was vastly improved. He had lost his disgruntled expression and was willing to accept his position as a serving soldier. He was therefore posted as a driver to an operational unit. He served overseas for two years with only one trifling entry on his conduct sheet and was eventually released as a fully competent soldier.

The urge to wander was a compulsion in these sixteen men. But, as with the other 'types', the same trait was present to some degree in perhaps a majority of the S.T.U. men, but was less compelling and combined with other, possibly conflicting, urges. In the large group of 700 men as many as one-third (33·5 per cent) expressed a strong desire for driving or for going to sea (including a number who were already drivers), surely a much larger proportion than would be found in any sample of the general public (23·1 per cent asked for driving and 12·3 per cent for the sea,[1] and some for both). In the smaller group 44·4 per cent were known to have expressed such a desire or were actually drivers, and this is probably nearer the true figure.

The subsequent military histories of these sixteen men reveal the encouraging fact that ten proved at least satisfactory soldiers including five whose records were very good. The case of one was doubtful and five could only be described as unsatisfactory, including two discharged as psychopaths and one discharged for misconduct.

Drifters

These were few (only 2·5 per cent) and were conspicuous by the absence, rather than the expression, of any strong emotional urge. Their apathy was so deeply rooted that they were resistant to all attempts to revive them; one of them was aptly described by the Welfare staff as 'needing sparking up'. One's first impression was that their trouble might be physiological, but those who were referred for medical treatment showed little improvement. Three were illiterate and hardly responded at all to individual teaching. They were of average or near-average intelligence. Several were untidy in dress, bodily dirty and babyish. They might have been classified as 'immature types' for they had many childish ways. Of all the different kinds of men passing through the Unit these were the most difficult to deal with. The hostility of the aggressor or the obstinate inwardness of the introspective man offered a challenge that one could sometimes meet. But the easy acquiescence and the lethargy of the drifter, propping his head on his hand, doodling instead of writing, sitting like a bag of dough that stayed in if you pushed it, almost defeated one.

Looking at the five men in turn, No. 1 was deaf in one ear. He was quite illiterate and made no progress that one could observe in his lessons. He did not attempt to answer any letters written to him after he had gone away from the Unit. The records show that he completed his war service but committed many further offences, mainly of absence.

No. 2 was sent to the Unit with the remark that he 'showed

[1] Leo Page (*The Young Lag*, Faber & Faber, 1950) mentions that 8 out of 23 young recidivists had attempted to go to sea.
        D. H. Stott (op. cit.) records a 'wish to go to sea' in 35 of his 102 approved school cases, in 15 of these to 'a fairly strong degree'.

no interest in Army life, or in anything much.   Untidy and loses kit continuously.   Colourless'.   His personality, when one got to know him, was indeed colourless.   He was apathetic about everything, like a man who sees the light but cannot be bothered to walk towards it.   The only time one ever saw him liven up was when he went on the excavation parties to the prehistoric mound.   He was so taken by this venture that he was put in charge of one of the parties, whereupon he followed the author around like a faithful dog for some time.   His military history after posting was satisfactory though not outstanding.

The three others also showed an interest in digging, so they were put on to gardening for a month or so.   No. 3 had previously driven a farm tractor for three years.   He said he 'didn't mind' the Army—a remark that characterized him.   He 'thought of marrying' a Welsh girl on his next leave.   He was lethargic and dirty to the day he left, but his subsequent reports were satisfactory. He was taken prisoner in France, the comment of one of his former comrades upon hearing this news being 'too much trouble for him to run'.

No. 4 was sent to the S.T.U. with the report—'Seems to have no interest in life.   Could be put on several charges for petty offences.   Drifts along.'   He made a poor impression on the psychiatrist who referred to him as 'a smooth, calculating type, his attitude suggesting a good deal of suppressed aggressiveness and resentment of authority.   He will evade as much of duty as possible.   He has anti-social tendencies and will require supervision but may respond to disciplinary measures'.   The psychiatrist recommended that the man be returned to his former unit, but the Commanding Officer decided to keep him on at the S.T.U. for another four months, during which time he settled down and gave little trouble.   He had lost interest in his home life though he spoke of happy memories of going away every year for a week's holiday to the seaside with his parents.   His mother died when he was still a boy.   'My first mother was very nice,' he wrote.   'Father has been married three times, a proper Henry the Eighth, as you might say.'   His later history was unsatisfactory.   He was a persistent absentee and a deserter and he was eventually discharged for mental deficiency (dullness), though his Intelligence Test result at the S.T.U. was average.

No. 5 was dirty and illiterate and the despair of the disciplinary staff.   He completed his military service but his final testimonial read: 'He could do well if he took more personal interest.'

Every one of these men was an habitual absentee, and after leaving the S.T.U. they averaged over four separate offences of unauthorized absence and some desertion between them. In the overall assessment none of them proved very satisfactory though two could be described as passable.

The Unclassified

There remain 114 men (more than half the sample) who could not be said to show any consistent attitudes. They include some of the worst offenders and they could certainly not be considered as emotionally stable or morally normal. Fifteen of them (13 per cent) were later discharged from the Army as psychopaths (cf. 25 amongst the 84 'types', or 30 per cent). In some a moral sense seemed almost completely lacking. Others were volatile, changing quickly from one mood to another.

CHAPTER XI

SOME GENERAL CHARACTERISTICS

Display

The S.T.U. men took a childish delight in any activity that brought them before the notice of other people. Taking advantage of this, the sergeant-major used to drill them in the main road where they usually put up a good show. The Unit was asked to take part in a local 'Salute the Soldier' Week by sending a contingent of fifty men to the march-past and presenting a guard-of-honour for Field-Marshal Ironside. For a fortnight the men worked with intense effort at their drill and there was keen competition to fill the place of any man who was compelled to drop out because of some misdemeanour. On the actual day they carried it off magnificently and gained high praise from the Field-Marshal. Yet many of these same men had only recently been exclaiming that they were 'browned off with the Army' and would like to get out of it. The soldiers who were being saluted were, of course, themselves.

It seemed as though they needed recognition all the time, and they were very sensitive to anything in the nature of a slight or an oversight. One fellow was deeply offended with a member of the staff for some time because he had passed him in the local town without recognizing him. It hurt them that the local civilians dubbed them the 'Borstal boys', which most of them were not.

Sometimes this display went beyond normal limits. They would wear badges of rank or decorations to which they were not entitled. Probably most of them had at some time or other put up an unauthorized stripe or two during leaves. One man (two years later he was convicted of the violent murder of a young WAAF and executed) had this vanity to excess. The present writer once had occasion to apprehend him at a London terminus when he was absent without leave. He was wearing a corporal's stripes, the shoulder flashes of a parachutist and several decorations. In his kitbag a spare battledress blouse bore a lieutenant-colonel's badges of rank and a pilot's 'wings'.

Though they were often careless about their personal hygiene they were much concerned with their appearance when walking out. One man was sent away from the unit for a spell of detention and when he came back it was noticed that his normally blonde hair was dark towards the roots. On mentioning this peculiarity to a friend of this man's it was learned that it had been his practice to bleach his hair with peroxide. In fact he made a habit of taking the friend to the cinema with him every Saturday night, and sitting in the back row so that his companion could apply the peroxide without being overlooked!

Tattooing

Tattooing was a popular practice. Every week-end, after pay day, a little group of men would come back from the local tattooist, covered with pictures of scrolls, naked ladies, daggers and tombstones inscribed with the initials of a friend and some such motto as 'faithful unto death' or 'death before dishonour'. The tattooist wisely advised against inscribing the names of girl friends, in case there were changes of fancy, but the favourite device was a scroll surrounding the word 'Mother'. Anchors were also fairly common, perhaps because so many of these men were interested in going to sea.[1]

Lying

A very different characteristic that often worried the staff a good deal was the offenders' practice of telling anything but the truth about themselves on first acquaintance. One could be quite certain that any man who was accused of some offence would straightway deny his guilt. Latecomers returning from leave were generally full of some pressing excuse. It was a rare occasion when a man frankly stated that he had just overstayed his leave. Even when a man was proved wrong he would sometimes still insist on his innocence, though it was quite common for a man to admit his fault privately but to defend his innocence at his trial. It does, of course, require moral strength publicly to confess one's faults, and these men did not possess such moral resources. It was

[1] Lombroso (*Homme Criminel*, Paris, 1895, I, p. 266) saw in tattooing evidence of the barbarism of the criminal! 'One of the most characteristic traits of primitive man', he wrote, 'or of the savage is the facility with which he submits himself to this operation, surgical rather than aesthetic, and of which the name even has been furnished to us by an Oceanic idiom. . . . It constitutes on account of its frequency, a specific and entirely new anatomico-legal characteristic.' Tattooing is probably just as common among non-delinquents in the social group to which these men belong.

almost impossible for some of them to admit to any charge that was likely to reflect unfavourably on them, especially in cases of theft.

The assertive youngster would sometimes go out of his way to prove his innocence against the most conclusive evidence. One man was charged with being absent from his 'lines' during the night. At reveille the orderly sergeant found his bed empty and several witnesses confirmed that he had been out all night. Yet he was so indignant at the accusation that the next night he made up his bed in the doorway so that, as he said, 'the orderly sergeant can make sure of seeing me this time'.

The inability to speak the truth, when it is inconvenient or difficult is probably an expression of the man's inner weakness, and is by no means confined to offenders. So too are those falsehoods that are told to impress the listener. At some stage of his development the delinquent is actuated by motives of self-assertion, by the need—by an imperative compulsion rather—to impress his listener in order to justify himself, perhaps to protect or preserve himself (for he is not strong enough to face the truth of his own inadequacies); therefore, he must fabricate a story.

It seems unreasonable to expect, as some who sit in judgment still do, to receive a completely honest statement and an open confession of fault from a man who has learned to protect himself from discovery and punishment by deceit. The delinquent has seen deception practised in his own home; poverty and discomfort have frequently been so acute that he has been conditioned to expediency as a means of physical and mental self-preservation; he has grown up in a social milieu where self-preservation is the first law of life and only the 'softie' exercises compunction. On trial, he finds his misdemeanours weighed in scales beyond his understanding, so he seeks to protect himself. His attitude towards society is like that of a fractious child towards a disapproving father. In dealing with delinquents, therefore, one should expect a lie the first, second and third time. The truth will only come with complete confidence.

Sex

Civilians in the neighbourhood of the Unit were sometimes anxious lest the men might prove themselves a nuisance with girls. The tendency of the popular Press to give undue prominence to crimes of a sexual character is no doubt largely responsible for such apprehension. The extraordinary fact was, however, that these men probably saw no more of the opposite sex than most troops; and very few sexual crimes came to the notice of the staff. Some of the men struck up friendships with local girls, and dances were held every Sunday night to try to foster open friendships. The dances were well attended; but one noticed that the majority of the soldiers were too diffident to step on to the dance floor and would stand around the hall enviously watching the few bolder spirits who were dancing. Dancing lessons were started, and some of the staff would try to bring the men out by introducing partners to them!

Nor was there any unusual traffic in pornographic photographs, nor sexual scribblings on walls of huts and lavatories. When the S.T.U. took over the camp from a coastal defence regiment the lavatory walls were covered with sexual and sadistic drawings. So one of the first jobs of the new unit was to paint over the scribblings, which never reappeared!

Homosexuality was thought possible, and the staff were always on the look-out for it, but only two cases of importance were ever established and there is no evidence that it was any more common amongst the S.T.U. men than among most troops. This fact surprised some of the visitors, and one cannot refrain from quoting the case of a distinguished visitor who asked, first the Commanding Officer, then the Second-in-Command, then the Adjutant, and finally the present writer, whether there was not really a good deal of sexual abnormality at the unit. From each separate inquiry he received the reply that there was practically none, but at the last he shook his head ruefully and murmured 'most extraordinary'.

One can only suppose that sexual impulses were either weak or unrepressed amongst these men. A possible explanation is that many of them were retarded in emotional development and were girl-shy or perhaps more concerned with themselves than the normally healthy young fellow of the same age would be.

Masturbation was certainly very common, a practice that would naturally be associated with feelings of guilt and a tendency to self-pity and self-love. The Education Instructor was once talking to a platoon of these men about sex and he mentioned that most youngsters go through this phase of masturbating but that they usually grow out of it soon after they leave school.

'Oh, no they don't,' contradicted a perky little Scotsman, 'there isn't one man here who hasn't ———— in the past week,' and he swept the audience with an accusing finger. There was silent acquiescence and several slowly and deliberately nodded their heads. Their ignorance of sex matters was pathetic. They were full of tales about babies being born with animals' heads or of modern examples of the immaculate conception, but in fact they knew practically nothing about the normal processes of birth and reproduction.

Religion

The figures below show the distribution of religious groups in the S.T.U. compared with the normal distribution for the Army.

	S.T.U. *population* %	*Normal Army* %
Church of England	70·7	70
Church of Scotland & Presbyt'n	5·3	10
Methodist	2·0	6
Baptist, Congregationalist, etc	1·0	3
Jew	1·0	1
Roman Catholic	20·0	10
	100·0	100

The most striking difference is the larger proportion of Roman Catholics (20 per cent compared with 10 per cent) amongst offenders. Other inquiries have noted unduly large proportions of Roman Catholics among delinquents,[1] especially in those parts of the country where Irish populations are concentrated. It would be a mistake to infer from these figures, however, that Roman Catholics are more prone to delinquency; it may be that Catholic priests are more successful as proselytizers amongst those sections of the population from which delinquents arise. In a later chapter ('The Home Town' and also Appendix A) it is suggested that Army offenders are mainly drawn from a lower stratum of the population, in which Roman Catholics are probably more numerous than elsewhere.[2]

[1] See Report of the L.C.C. Education Committee, 1925, *Juvenile Delinquency in London*. The 257 London children committeed to 'Industrial' (approved) schools in 1922/3 and the 233 in 1923/4 included 15 per cent and 16 per cent Roman Catholic children respectively. The peculiar social make-up of the London school population is shown in the proportion of Jewish children committed (5 per cent and 4 per cent, compared with 1 per cent in the total population).

[2] An interesting comment on the association of religion with crime is provided by Lombroso (*Crime, its causes and remedies*, Heinemann, 1911): 'The younger religions are, the greater is their moral power, because the letter has not yet encroached upon the spirit, because the enthusiasm for new ideas occupies the mind and draws it away from crime.' 'There are fewer criminals where atheists abound, than where, under equal conditions, either Catholics or Protestants dominate. This fact may proceed from their greater degree of education, the more so as in Europe atheists are especially numerous among the more highly educated.'

H

CHAPTER XII

ILLITERACY

BETWEEN a half and one per cent of the wartime Army were illiterate, that is to say, up to 50,000 troops were unable to make any practical use whatever of written words or to read consecutive words. Professor Burt has estimated that between 1·5 and 2 per cent of the total population are gross illiterates. These percentages, translated into whole numbers (over half a million) are disturbing enough to those who have tended hitherto to assume that with compulsory education we had ensured complete literacy. But it now seems that an even more pressing problem is that of the semi-illiterate, who can only read a printed sentence with difficulty, whose vocabulary is limited to a mere thousand words or so (the ordinary person needs 10,000 or more, and a BBC announcer may know 30,000), and who cannot write an intelligible letter.

The semi-illiterate is exceedingly numerous—Burt puts the number at 15 or 20 per cent at 21 years of age (as a proportion of the total adult population this would comprise about 6 millions)[1] Some 26 per cent of the Army intake had a standard of education very much below the school leaving standard in the elementary schools and probably a majority of these were semi-illiterates.

Among the S.T.U. offenders the gross illiterates never amounted to more than 3 to 5 per cent but they shade off into the semi-illiterates who were much more numerous. Some 19 per cent came within the lowest selection group (5) in the Verbal test, and more than half of these would be semi-illiterate.

---

[1] The semi-illiterate is difficult to define. Professor P. E. Vernon, in his investigation carried out for a Ministry of Education Committee (*Reading Ability*, H.M.S.O., 1950), defines a semi-illiterate as one having a reading age of 7 to 9 years He fixes 1·4 per cent illiterates and 4·3 per cent semi-illiterates at 15·0 years, and 0·7 per cent and 3·3 per cent respectively among Army National Service men. A further 15·8 per cent were 'Backward' (reading ages 9–12). The difference between Burt's and Vernon's estimates is considerable. The present writer would like to see the terms defined by reference to some practical test of the *use* of literacy by the subjects.

One reason why the problem of the semi-illiterate is so much more urgent than that of the illiterate is that literacy is not a fixed, permanent attribute. If we neglect to use words we eventually lose them altogether. One is constantly in the process of building up, maintaining or losing a vocabulary, according to the use one makes of literary forms. It would seem that there is an active and a passive vocabulary. The passive or latent has already passed into disuse but is not completely forgotten. It can be revived and brought into active use by practice in reading and writing. The young adult semi-illiterate with whom the S.T.U. was dealing possessed a passive vocabulary several times larger than his active vocabulary. The trouble was that since leaving school he had read little beyond the names of places and shops, public notices and occasional captions in the picture papers. His work was manual, and there was little call for reading and practically none for writing. His entertainment was the cinema. His conversation was restricted to a few stock expressions. Since leaving school he had been steadily losing his power of speech and his command of written words. If, for one reason or another he was already backward at school and was semi-illiterate when he left, his undeveloped literary powers would begin to shrink until within four or five years he would probably be a total illiterate.

It may be asked, concerning the illiterate, how it can come about that so many pass through nine years of schooling without learning the elements of their own language. Something of the causes may be traced from two sources which have been examined for this present study. One was the illiterate and very backward men amongst the group of Army offenders, and the other was a group of illiterate pupils numbering 130 at an Army Basic Education Centre with which the writer was associated.

The first cause is dullness. As many as 82 per cent of the Basic Education Centre cases were below the middle point of average intelligence, despite the fact that all the 130 men were selected as 'accidental' illiterates, of sufficient intelligence to offer hope of quick improvement (all those with group 5 intelligence test scores were excluded). In a random sample the proportion below the median of intelligence would therefore be at least 90 per cent, a figure which approaches Burt's estimate of 92 per cent among his cases. A second factor is that the great majority of these men had come from very poor homes where reading or cultural activities were extremely limited, and in at least 17 per cent of the cases there was already illiteracy in the family (very many more might have come to light if their backgrounds had been investigated). Another common factor was loss of school attendance between the ages of 5 and 10, in schools where large classes precluded individual teaching and where frequently the children were moved up from class to class by age instead of ability. Some 42 per cent of the cases had missed at least six months' schooling as a result of an illness or accident, and another 20 per cent through truancy. Between 40 and 50 per cent were moved up through the classes by age. An abnormally high proportion (41 per cent) attended schools other than urban council schools—11 per cent in village schools, 12 per cent special or open-air schools, and 16 per cent church schools.

The four links in the chain of causation are therefore—dullness of the subject; a poor, neglected or illiterate home; loss of education; and unsatisfactory school conditions and teaching methods. Various other causes were noted but they only affect relatively small numbers—gipsy, vagrant or bargee families; wartime evacuation; continual change of school; and unstable personality, were among such minor causes. An unusual reason was recounted to the writer by an illiterate offender:

'I was always in fights as a kid and was always getting my knuckles bashed, so I couldn't write with that hand. My teacher made me try and write with the left hand but I couldn't use it properly so I didn't learn much!'

The illiterate's situation bears a close resemblance to that of the blind but he seldom gets the sympathy the blind are accustomed to receive. He has to ask his way everywhere. If his train stops in a station he has to ask for its name. A journey by underground is a nightmare. If a form has to be filled in he must ask an official to do it for him. The few words he does get to know he often recognizes by the initial letter, though even there he is often wrong. 'I look for the letter C at the start of the word,' one man said, describing his way of reading 'Gentlemen' over the public convenience. He often tries to conceal his illiteracy. An orderly at the S.T.U. Education Centre was a total illiterate yet he used to arrange a writing desk for himself in a corner of one of the classrooms, with blotting-pad, several pens and pencils, and a little bowl of flowers (see description on p. 69).

Many who had worked out a reasonably tolerable *modus vivendi* in civil life found no such opportunity in the Army, which accentuated the unhappy consequences of their illiteracy. Inability to read and understand orders from the platoon detail board has resulted in many an unfortunate soldier being charged and punished for absence from parade. Then there is the constant problem of letters to and from home. The illiterate must depend on someone else to read the private correspondence he receives and to write out all the letters he sends. Whenever he moves to another unit he must seek out a new friend whom he has to ask to undertake this intimate service. Even with help and sympathy, this is hard to bear. One knew some cases of men in this position being exploited by practical jokers; coarse and offensive matter had been included in letters sent home. It is not surprising that, when given the chance, the illiterate man went all out to learn to read and write. Success produced a visible change in the man himself, more evidence of purpose and self-confidence, and less apathy and resentment in his life. Supine dependence on others, demanded by illiteracy, was no longer necessary and self-respect was relieved of at least one crippling bond.

During the early years of the war Army illiterates were given spare-time instruction wherever they happened to be stationed. This proved most unsatisfactory because very few of the men were receiving enough tuition to become fully literate. They learnt a little but the ultimate effect was to leave them feeling that they were unteachable. Moreover, there was no primer in the English language suitable for the adult illiterate. The Canadian Army, where illiteracy was a serious problem, had produced an excellent set of booklets early in the War, but educational instructors in the British Army were using Basic English or children's primers, which were not at all appropriate. It was seen by the Army authorities that even the semi-illiterate's ignorance was likely to be a danger to himself and his comrades. So two important decisions were taken. One was to set up a special committee from the Army Educational Corps to produce a primer—'English Parade.' The second was to establish special instruction centres where every illiterate soldier coming into the Army, and many of those already in, would receive full-time instruction for six weeks. This was little enough time in which to teach the rudiments of written language to grown men who had failed to learn in nine years of schooling, but it just sufficed.

At the S.T.U., an illiterates' class met for two hours every morning. Only a few of the men were completely without knowledge of the alphabet, and progress was usually rapid. When a newcomer was told that he would have the chance of attending a class to 'improve reading and writing' he was, in most cases, pleased enough at the prospect. The few who did make a show of indignation invariably thawed out when they realized that the offer was genuine. This class was recognized as the keenest and hardest working of all. Ability to write a letter was the primary ambition of the illiterate, but all available devices (newspapers, spelling games, gramophone, wireless, films, etc.) were used to maintain interest. The course was kept as comprehensive as possible; simple arithmetic was found to be a much-needed part of the work, and some elementary knowledge of history, geography and current happenings were caught up in the course of talks and discussions on the war and other subjects.

The results both at the S.T.U. and the Basic Education Centre were astonishing. Of the gross illiterates, 80 per cent became sufficiently literate to write a simple letter (stage 1); 8 per cent advanced further and were able to read a newspaper and write a fairly involved letter (stage 2); and 12 per cent failed to learn. Of the semi-illiterates, 80 per cent attained stage 2, 20 per cent became practically fully literate (stage 3); and there were practically no failures. The single instance of undesirable consequences known to the writer came from the local post office, where a member of the illiterates' class had drawn a sum of money by signing another man's name in a stolen post office savings book—a reminder that literacy brings its own temptations.

Thus for the first time in this country adult illiteracy had been attacked on a mass scale, and in such a way as to produce significant results in the shortest possible time. And this training was made available at a time when the Army was desperately hard pressed for manpower. It is sad to reflect that, with demobilization, much of this valuable experience has been dispersed and lost. The expert instructors have gone back to teaching their primary school classes or to their office jobs, and meanwhile the millions of backward men and women multiply, and the offenders, in civilian prison clothes, are put to their two or three hours a week of grinding and ultimately disheartening classwork in the three R's.

The beginning of literary comprehension, the writing of the first letter is thrilling enough for any illiterate adult; for the offender it has a double meaning. Not only is a whole universe of understanding opened up to him, but he has begun to find himself on equal terms with his fellows for the first time in his life. If he has been properly taught he will know, too, that he has achieved this mastery through his own efforts, after years of fear that he was incapable of it. Perhaps one of the most important steps in the teaching of illiterates is the initial convincing of the pupil of his capacity to learn. One of the most experienced instructors in the Army always opened a new illiterates' class by asking the men whether anyone was quite sure that he would *not* be able to learn. From the numerous responses he selected the most obstinate and, in front of the whole group, went over a simple sentence with him, word by word, until the man could recognize it and read 'I am a soldier. Jim is a soldier'. The effect of this achievement on the others can well be imagined. The clumsy hands would take up the pens, which at first may have felt as thick as broom handles, and the long laborious process would begin. The method of teaching suggested in 'English Parade' was expanded and revised by Educational instructors. Supplementary exercises, written and phrased to suit the emotional experiences of the average illiterate, were worked out, word games and aids to learning were evolved, and the curriculum was pruned and adjusted until the six weeks' course was as concentrated as an iron-ration pack.

Thus, in overcoming illiteracy the Army often overcame two of the offender's chief obstacles to redemption—the twin feelings of frustration and inadequacy.

CHAPTER XIII

EDUCATIONAL BACKWARDNESS

THE very desperation of the illiterate's case made him relatively easy to tackle. His misery was too urgent to permit pride or fear to stand in the way of escape. Provided he were educable (as most of them were) his immediate trouble could be eased. The trainees whose educational attainment was limited by ability to read simple instructions and write a letter of sorts set a more tricky problem. The prospect of meeting their educational needs by formal instruction in elementary subjects was obviously dim. The idea of virtually returning to school, to confront once more the despised tokens of childhood, was unlikely to appeal to youngsters in their position. Joining the Army had been a specific and dramatic putting away of childish things. The novelty of the status thus won made them particularly sensitive and resistant to any move seemingly calculated to push them back across the boundary between child and man. It was apparent from the beginning that the appeal and success of educational activities would be determined, in the first place, by informal and voluntary work rather than by conventional lessons or lectures held during parade hours.

With deliberate emphasis on voluntary interest, the 'Military Education Centre' developed as a club to which men came to work at hobbies, read, write or merely to sit round the fire smoking and chatting. The daytime lecture-room was the 'quiet room' in the evening, used mainly for letter writing. Art materials—paints, pastels, modelling clay, charcoal were available for those interested. They liked pastels because the colours were bright and they could get shading effects by smearing them with their fingers. The standard in drawing and painting varied from the immature sketch without sense of perspective to really promising work. The most gifted in this direction was one of the most unsettled of the trainees, who had pictures included in an art exhibition in London (see p. 73). They liked most to draw fantastic subjects, or battle scenes—mostly imaginary—or landscape. In the evening the handicrafts centre was full of men making toys, rugs, ornaments, bags, purses and such-like.

The making of petrol lighters maintained itself, amidst all the changes of fashion, as probably the most popular single hobby. Closely rivalling the attraction of petrol lighters was that of embroidery—of an imitative rather than artistic type. With the aid of transfers, supplied in packets with the other necessary materials, numerous regimental crests were, with varying degrees of skill, embroidered on cushion covers, table runners and the men's own underclothing. The fact that the trainees were so ready to bend their stubby fingers to so uncongenial a task was no small tribute to the strength of their pride of regiment. Few of the men had acquired a hobby before coming to the S.T.U. and the novel idea of making something appealed strongly to them, with the variety of articles made by their comrades as a constant stimulus. A local teacher, who gave instruction in woodwork during the evenings, found the trainees impatient pupils. The favourite models were those that satisfied their impatience with quick results. But the man who had completed a simple article was often willing to tackle something more ambitious. Wall displays were found to be an effective means of interesting the men in a great diversity of subjects. The unit wall newspaper, with the men's own contributions, was particularly popular. All wall material required regular and reasonably frequent renewing if interest was to be maintained. The great labour involved in collecting and making up displays, in typing wall newspaper articles and in arranging it all on the walls made it necessary to depend largely on the men's own efforts. The unit library was run, mainly by the men themselves, as an unofficial branch—complete with card index and individual tickets—of the local library, and was, for most of the trainees, the first they had patronized.

Keen eyes spotted the true nature of a mound in the neighbouring wood, that had till then escaped notice. It was a bronze age barrow, probably the site of a burial. The arduous work of excavation was done by volunteers working during summer evenings and week-ends. One of the trainees was sufficiently interested and knowledgeable to take charge of operations and to give talks on this particular project. On one occasion he caught the imagination of a group of newcomers with a glowing account of the excavation of Troy. They all volunteered to assist in what they assumed to be a comparable exploit at the S.T.U. Their first visit to the site, with its dull heaps of clay and its waterlogged holes and ditches, brought cruel anticlimax to the anticipated scenes of ancient splendour! Hope of finding the burial chamber was, however, sufficient inducement to persevere. The work, unfortunately, was not completed when the unit disbanded. A large collection of medieval fragments was at least partial recompense for the heavy work. Those discoveries were frequent and spurred the workers on to greater efforts.

The men were very fond of organized visits to local places of interest—more so, perhaps, than maturer men more capable of finding their own leisure interests. Visits to a nearby cathedral city, to shipbuilding yards and to a shoe factory (with a large staff of very attractive girls) were in such demand that they were made regular events. Arrangements were made with the naval authorities to send men for four days' stay on board mine-sweepers working off the East coast. The rest were keen to read or hear the stories brought back by the lucky ones, and keener still for their chance to come.

The educational staff were not tied to a precise number of subjects or departments in their attempt to cater for the men's leisure, as these disconnected glimpses at some of the major interests might suggest. The object was, as far as possible, to provide each individual with the opportunity of a congenial activity during his spare time. The intention was not to organize a limited number of alternative activities but to encourage and help the individual to go ahead with his ideas. The few men who did come to the educational instructors with clear ideas about doing something could usually be helped to whatever was needed by way of advice, books, tools or materials. Some were distressed beyond measure over situations that the normal person would naturally dismiss as absurd. One memorable case was that of a North-country lad who came along in desperate anxiety. He had received a valuable trombone from his mother, but pleasure at so handsome a gift was more than offset by the obsession that she would expect him to learn to play it. The other men in his hut, who had been interested enough at the appearance of the instrument in their midst, had refused to tolerate his untuneful practising. He had been the round of all the unoccupied corners in the camp, but had been turned out of each. His last sanctuary had been in a civilian home—and now 'they' would not let him go even there. It was afterwards learned that he had become undesirably entangled with a married woman, and that 'they' were discouraging his visits. His ardour for the lady did not, however, bear comparison with his passion for the trombone. He was at last given a place where he practised long enough to get fed up with the whole business and to decide to send the instrument home.

Occasionally someone would find conditions at the S.T.U. conducive to resuming a hobby practised in civilian life. One man brought his nine-mm. cinema projector and entertained his friends. Those who came with any clear ideas of things that they would like to do were, however, in a small minority. It was necessary to suggest activities to most of them and to help and encourage them through their initial awkwardness.

Education in the S.T.U. was closely associated with the important welfare work done there, and had a largely remedial function. The majority of the trainees were deplorably barren in initiative and interest, with powers of self-expression—verbal and otherwise—poor and incapable, for the most part, of benefiting substantially from normal class-room instruction. More weight had to be given to the mental state of the trainees than to the logical sequence of a syllabus. Like infants in the nursery, they required education. Facilities for activity and relaxation, like those already mentioned, were designed to further the general policy of making the S.T.U. itself a community providing each member with reasonable incentive and opportunity to develop normal personal interests. Few who came to the unit could boast even the beginning of such development. They had habitually attended cinemas and football matches or had roamed the streets in the hope of some fortuitous distraction, but few of them had used their initiative to develop their own aptitudes. Any initiative shown had been displayed too often in mischief and crime. Unpretentious as were the facilities available at the S.T.U., they did seem to meet certain needs of the trainees. The centre was consistently busy, despite the fact that there were no restrictions on going out in the evening—not even the usual turn on sentry duty—and the town was only a couple of miles away. All types, from the noisy extravert to the timid, neurotic youth, found something to hold their interest.

The more specific educational needs of the men still required attention. They were not with the unit more than a few months and during this time one had to teach them something of the military studies like map-reading and message work, to impart a little rudimentary knowledge about themselves and their environment, and, one hoped, to give them a taste of the higher pursuits—music, reading, natural history and art. The military subjects, like map-reading, were taught in two ways. One was through practical work —making contour models or constructing a compass or going on outdoor competitions—and the other was by papering their walls with what one wanted them to learn. The surroundings of a room are important to a man whose attention is inclined to wander. So bright wall displays were put up, telling their own story without much written explanation. The staff made up little diagrams and pictures that demonstrated the simple principles of mapwork. In the same way the stories of the fighting fronts and of industries or social life at home were told in pictures. Over the whole ceiling of the class-room hut the men had painted a large circular blue back-ground to represent the sky, and pasted on silver stars to show the principal star constellations. It seemed such a pity that the social offender, who is forced by his semi-illiteracy, his lack of concentra-tion and his paucity of hobbies or mental resources, to turn his attention to his environment perhaps much more than most people, should so often have been expected to mend his ways in bare and ugly surroundings.

A permanent place in the curriculum was set aside for the teach-ing of simple science. Talks and discussions, always illustrated by a small display or by colourful diagrams, on such subjects as the human body, reproduction, animals, vegetation, the soil and rocks, the stars, the sea, weather, metals, raw materials, food and so on, would, one hoped, fill up some of the gaps in general knowledge. But whatever the subject, one had to start from some point within their own limited experience. That was a very obvious, but a terribly necessary first principle. They themselves would soon make that point clear if for a moment one got above their heads, for they would fidget, giggle or go into a day-dream. Most of them clearly needed to improve their standard of English and arithmetic before they could meet with confidence the modest demands of everyday life. Although not illiterate, they still suffered quite practical difficulties from educational backwardness. They could write a letter, but the process was an ordeal and the result gave little satisfaction. They could read simple passages, but not always with understanding—the meaning of the written passage was often obscured by unfamiliar words—and they were baffled by the simplest arithmetical calculation. Instruction in these elementary subjects was closely associated with the voluntary work done in the Education

Centre. This contact with the men's leisure preoccupations provided a community of interest that made possible a smooth approach to compulsory education.

The improvement of English was regarded as primarily a question of encouraging expression, in writing and speech, on any subject. This resolved itself into the problem of either drawing out existing interests or giving the men new ones—the voluntary activities helping in this latter way. As with the illiterates, however, letter writing was the main inducement. Before entering the Army, many of the trainees had seldom written a letter; now it was the link with home and friends, and here the consequences of weakness were most keenly felt. One hour of compulsory education time per week was devoted to letter writing. Help was given, when asked, in spelling and composition, and common mistakes in grammar, etc., pointed out. A surprising number had not been writing to anyone; some of these said that there was no one to whom they might write, but, in most cases, were, in fact, able to think of someone. This had the effect of increasing letter writing by making regular correspondents of those who, previously, had been writing only spasmodically, or not at all.

Nearly all their letters were the same, just a collection of stock phrases. The typical letter home began: 'Dear Mum, Just a line to let you know that I am in the pink. Thanks for the letter and cigs received today.' And always concluded with the words 'hoping this finds you as it leaves me at present, etc.' Perhaps four out of every five letters were of this sort, and since their parents' communications were often little better, the exchanges were merely token greetings. The trainees were perfectly normal in the value they attached to the letters that they received. When these did not arrive they grumbled. The weekly letter-writing period naturally increased the intake as well as the output of letters. However reluctant they may have been to set about writing, the increase in mail received was always greeted as well worth the trouble. Many who did not worry over the standard achieved in letters sent home were more sensitive when the occasion arose to write to their girl friends, and would commonly come for coaching in this delicate matter. Censoring of mail proved a severely cramping blow. The stereotyped pattern was badly hashed by the limitations on what could be written. Even the inevitable allusion to the weather was officially discouraged! Some fell in the dilemma of either offending the Censor or not writing anything. They welcomed hints on what might be written and gradually evolved a new pattern to suit the new circumstances.

The wall newspaper provided a strong attraction. It was confined, almost entirely, to unit affairs. Camp sport news, a gossip corner, correspondence, reviews of library books and letters from men posted to other units were typical features. 'My most exciting experience' was a very popular series, for which there was keen competition. One trainee produced a sequence of entertaining articles on the 'crime does not pay' motif—each instalment being an incident in his civilian career of shopbreaking! They were very proud to see their contributions (complete with name and platoon) on the sheet. These were nearly all written in their own time but, occasionally, an education period would be given over to writing for the wall newspaper. This brought in many who would, otherwise, have been content to slide along passively. Some would in this way begin articles which they would take away to complete in their spare time.

The film is a powerful aid to learning with backward men. It was a medium to which they were already attracted and they could never have too much of it. Even the silent film is not unsuitable. It allows the instructor to fit his own commentary to the story, in words that will be intelligible to the audience. It intersperses passages of script that can be read aloud so that the backward pupil is helped over the difficult words. It can, on occasions, be taken slowly so that the men can appreciate some subtler point, or be stopped and re-run, to test their observation. Sometimes, with a documentary film, the writers used to set them a competition and offer a prize of half a dozen cigarettes for the winner. If it was a film about a part of England the competition might be to try and guess where it was by following such clues as the name of the railway, the name of the brewers on public-house signs, building materials, style of churches, the shape of the ground, walls, hedges and so on. In the evenings more varied film shows were given, including one of the early silent films like *The Lost World*, *Metropolis* or the early Charlie Chaplins. The room was large but it was always crowded out on these occasions; it reeked of cheap tobacco smoke and sweat, it was overheated, and the shows were continually interrupted to change the reel or repair a break in the film strip, but they never had enough.

The men were backward also in oral expression—more so than first impressions indicated. Men who could maintain themselves in conversation with disconnected shots of wisecracks, wit and cliché, would often make a poor showing at a coherent description or account. Newcomers were very diffident about speaking to the class. With one platoon, the ice was broken by an ex-miner. He was interested in a wall display on mining and offered to explain the thing to his mates. His talk was very interesting and well received and, thereafter, civilian occupations became a favourite line of exposition, with other themes developing later. Performance improved noticeably with practice in speaking and writing. The habit of sober and coherent discussion in speech or in writing (apart from letters) was new to the great majority of the men— and, for many of them, letter writing began only with Army life.

Weakness in arithmetic is not as readily observed as the case of the other two 'R's', and so tends to receive less attention. It was found that the general standard in this subject was even lower than that of reading and writing, bad enough to be a handicap in practical affairs. The approach to arithmetic was similar to that to English, but the appeal to the men's interests was more restricted. One had to make sure that new intakes particularly were led gently. Schooling was a childish business, and it was foolish to offend susceptibilities on that point. Map-reading required the brushing up of some simple points in mathematics. A long incursion into arithmetic was once started with the rash suggestion that every man should be able to calculate his balance of pay (the soldier normally uses his paymaster as his banker also, and the state of his balance is often a matter of vague conjecture). Once the subject had been introduced, the men were keen to revise the elementary rules with all kinds of problems, the brighter ones assisting the more backward.

The writers had long been impressed by the contrast between the men's actual state of ignorance and the very satisfactory progress made, with practice, in both English and arithmetic. This anomaly was clearly revealed by the standardized tests that were given to S.T.U. personnel. The average level of intelligence in the S.T.U. was nearly normal (see pp. 60). As the figures on p. 66 show, about half the men were backward, therefore, not merely in relation to the normal population, but in relation to their own ability to understand and learn. The men whose educational attainments (as shown on the rather coarse grouping of Army tests) lagged furthest behind their innate ability, were naturally those whose intelligence was rated above the average level. The distribution of intelligence scores for the 49 men (a quarter of the whole S.T.U. sample) whose verbal and arithmetic results were retarded by at least two whole selection groups was:

Intelligence Selection groups:	I	II	III+	III−	IV	V
Backward men (49):	4	16	20	9	—	—

Thus, to the frustration of being undeveloped was added the irritation of sensing that they were more intelligent than most of their comrades. This fact accounts largely for the rapid improvement effected by many of them during their stay at the S.T.U. With opportunity to read and write under satisfying conditions, progress was sometimes astonishingly rapid. One man, who began as a virtual illiterate, was writing letters unaided within a few weeks. He developed a passion for writing, and was soon producing, in an attractive style, accounts of his experiences. This is, no doubt, partly explained by the possibility that he was to some extent recovering lost ground. But, even so, such men ought not to have been either illiterate or backward. Their condition was not justified by corresponding lack of ability, but was rather the result of peculiar circumstances that will presently be examined. Working on material well within their mental grasp, they were able to race ahead. There were also, of course, the few dullards whose intellectual horizon did not extend nearly as far as normal. Their progress soon declined as the limits of their cognitive ability were reached; they were backward only in relation to the normal individual. The gross illiterates, too, were below average in intelligence though seldom dull. But, in the case of the others—about half of the trainees—the lag of attainment behind ability was of a more disturbing character, a lack of balance between inherent ability and actual performance. The individual of low intelligence who finds congenial work and pastimes need not be haunted with any sense of inferiority. That sensation is more typical of the man who has not been able to develop fully his real powers, who, consequently, does not receive the recognition merited by his true self and is continually disturbed by the knowledge that he cannot raise himself to his full stature.

There were strong indications that much of the restlessness and emotional instability of the men was associated with this state of under-education. They were conscious of their backwardness and extremely sensitive about it. Bitter references were occasionally made to their inability to read and write properly. When asked, in the course of a questionnaire, if they had learned a foreign language at school, one reply was: 'I did not even learn my own properly,' and another, 'I can't speak my own language very well.' One can see that remarks like the above expressed the men's concern at their backwardness and point to this condition as a disturbing factor in their lives. It is not surprising that the individual who is abnormally deficient in his power to understand and use the common language should suffer frustrating handicaps in practical affairs and severe affront to his feelings of self-respect. Backwardness in arithmetic and in English nearly always occurred together, resulting in difficulties of a practical nature and in an apparent sense of inferiority.

In the circumstances, it seems reasonable to infer that the practical and psychological consequences of under-education were potent causes of much though, as later chapters will suggest, by no means all of the men's troubles. The normal person, who takes his elementary knowledge for granted, may not see any obvious association between educational backwardness and crime or delinquency. But the acute shame and the constantly irritating obstacles to normal activities experienced by the under-educated man produce special circumstances, compelling a logic very different from that of a normal individual. Practical difficulties apart, the mere sensation of being separate from and inferior to one's fellows prevents that assimilation with the group that makes army discipline (and, indeed, all social discipline) tolerable.

The men who began with resentment at the idea of education often became the keenest to learn. This was true of Pte. Mac——, a small, high-spirited Glaswegian, whose 'real' age was little over seventeen years ('Army age' was always above the minimum for enlistment). His chief trouble seems to have been his habit of yielding to spasmodic urges to speak his mind, quite irrespective of the dignity or other circumstances of his immediate surroundings. On his first day at the unit he arrived with his platoon in the classroom and, as the instructor began, gradually realized that he was on an education parade. He took the opportunity to express, emphatically, but without malice, his disgust at the situation. He had learned very little at school, most of that he had forgotten, and he was certainly not going to have any of 'that kind of stuff in the army'—army life was bad enough without that. Having expressed his feelings, he sat down and gave no trouble. Next day, the same platoon were discussing regulations concerning the percentage of a unit's strength permitted on leave at the same time. Mac took a

I

prominent part in discussing the implications of this in the S.T.U., and in establishing just what the percentage referred to meant. He virtually pushed class and instructor through the subject of percentages and, when the period ended, was wrestling resolutely with the mysteries of vulgar fractions. Resentment at having to take part in education was an unfailing indication that the man was sensitive about his backwardness—an understandable reaction to the prospect of the public probing of a private sore. When the dubious newcomer was satisfied that there was a real chance of learning the things he needed so badly, and that he was not going to be ridiculed, he was usually eager to take part in the work of the class. The really difficult case, refusing to co-operate, was very exceptional. An extremely youthful Irishman was one of the most intransigeant (see also pp. 77–8). He seemed to wish to get into trouble, and lost no opportunity of displaying his defiance. The work of the platoon was regularly interrupted with his uncomplimentary (and unprintable) remarks, delivered in a thick Irish brogue. On one occasion, as the platoon were settling down to a lesson on map-reading, the instructor, acting on a momentary impulse, quietly approached 'Paddy' and asked him if he would be kind enough to make a copy of part of a local map for use on a map-reading exercise. He worked assiduously at this task for the whole period, handed it in as he left and, next day, offered to continue the job.

PART THREE: THE OFFENDER IN CONFLICT WITH THE ARMY

CHAPTER XIV

REACTIONS TO ARMY LIFE

Enlistment

One of the paradoxes arising from this study of Army offenders is that whereas a large majority did not like the Army and as many as 69 per cent stated that they would take their discharge if they could do so without disgrace, almost as many (64 per cent) had originally volunteered to join, and many had joined before they were eighteen years old.[1] One man, for instance, had been a miner and therefore in a reserved occupation; he had left the pits and attached himself to a travelling fair in order to qualify for enlistment. A few months later he was under sentence for refusing to obey orders and for being absent while under technical arrest.

Of the one-third who were called up, about half said they did not mind being conscripted. The addition of these two groups gives 82 per cent of the men coming into the Army voluntarily or without reluctance.

Many reasons for volunteering were given, from pique to a desire for travel, or one as casual as:

'It was raining. I was on my way to the pictures, and I was passing the Labour Exchange when I saw a queue standing under shelter. I thought I would join in as I was curious, and when I got up to the counter I found it was the nineteen-year-olds signing on. So I put my age on a bit and thought I might as well go in with them. I was 17 then.' (This man, it is not surprising to learn, was later discharged as a psychopath.)

[1] At the time when most of these young men were coming into the Army, in 1941, 1942 and 1943 the percentages of volunteers (enlisting for the duration of the emergency) were 15·4, 13·7 and 18·9 respectively for each year's intake. The contrast between these figures and the proportion (64 per cent) of volunteers amongst the S.T.U. intake is indeed striking.

J. C. Penton, in a study of 2000 Army deserters undertaken for the War Office writes: 'The number of young volunteers amongst deserters is double that in the control group.'

The most common motive was discontent. Some 27 per cent said they were discontented with civilian life generally, and 15 per cent mentioned troubles at home:

'I had a row at home so I joined up,' said one. 'I joined up', said another, 'because I did not get on too well with my Parents, so I made up my mind, and ran away and joined the Army.' (This case is quoted more fully in Chapter X, p. 78.) A second Playboy of the Western World wrote: 'I joined up when I ran away from home after hitting my brother over the head with a crowbar.'

Another common motive for volunteering, mentioned by 26 per cent of the men, was the wish to join friends or relatives in the Army—an older brother or cronies from a snooker club. The suggestion does imply, however, a certain discontent: it infers that the man could not be happy without his friends, that life without them was so unsatisfying as to cause him to take steps to join them:

'I volunteered for the Army because all my mates had joined and I did not want to be the only one left.' Or another variant:

'My mates went and I didn't want to be left. I resented volunteering.'

A further reason for joining up, common to about 10 per cent of the men, was the desire to travel or to seek adventure. This, too, suggests a restlessness and a discontent that has already been noted as a common characteristic amongst offenders.

Under the more rational motives of duty or of interest in Army life are grouped about 18 per cent of the men, and these were noticeably the more balanced and normal in their attitude to other matters. The remaining 4 per cent mentioned their wish to revenge the loss in air raids of parents or brothers.

The main reasons for volunteering may be summarized as follows:

	%
Discontent with civilian life	27
Trouble at home	15
Wish to join friends	26
Desire for travel	10
Duty or interest in Army life	18
Revenge	4
	100

Combatant Temperament

On admission to the Army, recruits are medically examined, tested for ability and attainment, and interviewed by a Personnel Selection Officer who assesses their suitability for various jobs, and makes recommendations for training. He also estimates their 'combatant temperament' (or, more vulgarly, 'guts'). This is rated on a three-point scale—high, average, and low, and the distribution of ratings amongst the S.T.U. men is shown in the following table alongside those for normal intake of approximately the same age at the same time:

Combatant temperament rating	Offenders %	Normal %
High	5·4	4·9
Average	94·2	92·3
Low	0·4	2·8

The size of the S.T.U. sample (200) does not permit any conclusions to be drawn from the figures beyond the fact that the two groups are not significantly different. One should take into account the abnormally large proportion of volunteers amongst the offenders. The recruit would be interviewed within a few days of his enlistment, and the first flush of enthusiasm, or hope of something better ahead, that had prompted so many to join, would not yet have been dispersed by the stern realities of Army training. A second scrutiny a few weeks later might have told a different story, though the S.T.U. men were lacking not so much 'guts' as its application to the business of soldiering, as their subsequent and generally satisfactory overseas service confirms. The following remark illustrates the change of attitude that came over so many:

'I volunteered to go abroad and fight for King and Country and all that tommy rot, but I have been taught different since I came into the Army.'

In the course of the present inquiry, the offenders were asked: 'What are you personally fighting for?' Naturally only an odd man or two saw anything ironical about the question. The largest group (29 per cent) were fighting for their families or their homes; 26 per cent said 'for freedom'; 11 per cent said they didn't know; 7 per cent for themselves; and the rest, apart from the few who were fighting for 'revenge', put forward various reasons from 'because I'm mad', to 'God knows'.

A further question was put: 'Why is the country at war?' As many as two-thirds (perhaps a tribute to the successful influence of ABCA) gave a political answer concerning German expansion, broken treaties, or national defence. The remaining third either could think of no reason at all (20 per cent), or attributed the war to the wickedness or the greed of their rulers (12 per cent). There was more than a trace of defeatism in some of the views of this disgruntled 12 per cent, for example:

'Because we kept the Germans down after the last War and as they are a great nation they think they can rule the world.' A number had been associated with fascist or extremist activity in this country or in Ireland. They were fond of quoting 'Lord Haw-Haw's' prophecies including the usual story about the clock in the market square having stopped at two o'clock. They tuned in to the German news broadcasts regularly until we were compelled to forbid it.

Integration into the Army Group

The first few weeks of Army life are bound to be unsettling even for the most normal individual. The loss of one's friends, the discomfort of wearing a uniform and heavy boots, the restriction of freedom, the continual criticism of untidy, irresponsible ways, the feeling of impotence beneath an omnipotent, impersonal authority —the power that commands 'Private Atkins *will*' do this or that —the rigour of the training, and the doubt as to one's future: all these factors bear heavily for a time on any impressionable young man. They are especially heavy for one without the moral backing that can only be given by the affection of a good home, without friends who can write him a satisfactory letter and without the ability to write one himself, without a hobby to occupy his spare hours, and without the social manners to recommend him to the friendship of the more resourceful men in the unit. It needs only a sharp word or two, or a slight misunderstanding to strain such a man to breaking point and to provoke him to hostility, or, more generally, to flight.

The present inquiry arises from the fact that many thousands of young men failed to integrate themselves into their Army groups. The comradeship of soldiers, belonging to a 'good mob' as the troops termed it, was one of the most powerful factors in the Army's morale. Most of the S.T.U. men did not 'belong'; they were out of step with 'the mob', and they thought all the others were out of step with them.

The normal young recruit quickly gets adjusted to the new life and feels part of it. With the S.T.U. men that did not happen. Within a few months of joining, their reactions ranged from a grudging acceptance to total rejection of the Army. They have been classified according to their attitude to the Army, as follows:

(1) *The totally disaffected class*, numbering about 15 per cent. These are divided into two groups:

(*a*) The most extreme group (about 8 per cent) had no use for the Army whatsoever and were only concerned to get out of it by any means within their power, honourable or otherwise. They had mostly absented themselves from their units on numerous occasions, and had an average of over eight offences recorded against them including several of absence without leave. As might have been expected, all but one of this group said they found the Army 'too strict' and not one had found the Army authorities 'sympathetic'. They included several aggressive, restless types—described by the psychiatrist as mildly psychopathic. It is doubtful whether many of these men ever had much interest in the Army and their subsequent histories show that two-thirds of them proved unsatisfactory soldiers. That any at all adapted themselves to Army life is a wonder.[1] An example of the bitterness and strength of feeling expressed by this group is the following:

My first unpleasant recollection was when I was sent to —— (name of unit) of which to put in writing man to man I hate the very sight and word whenever it is talked about. I have never hated a place as much in my life. I have felt nothing but down hearted ever since I came. their is one or two reasons for feeling like this is you can try your damned hardest but it gets you nowhere at all. I would do almost anything to get away, but all I can do is just keep carrying on and hope for the best but I hope for my Familys sake I can get out of it all.

(*b*) A subsidiary group, also totally opposed to the Army but rather less bitter and desperate because they had some purpose in their discontent, were those (about 7 per cent) who were trying to get transferred into the Royal Navy or Merchant Navy. This group were fairly evenly divided in their replies to questions whether the Army was too strict or the authorities sympathetic. In many cases the desire to go to sea preceded their Army service. Nearly half had been called up but rather more had volunteered for the Army either because they were too young for the Navy, or they couldn't find £12 that was apparently required before admission to the Merchant Navy, or, as one man put it: 'I wanted the Merchant Navy but lost patience with waiting.' Another alleged that 'I was told that when I had done 6 months to a year in the Army my brother could claim me into the Royal Navy but I have been twisted'.

[1] This classification of attitude to the Army was made before the post-S.T.U. histories were known.

The more difficult Army training became, the more rosy grew the mental picture of life at sea—'I would never have gone absent or stolen things if I had been in the Navy,' wrote one man. There were also a number of men who had tried to get into the Royal Navy before enlisting but were later reconciled to the Army, and others who only wanted the Navy among several alternatives. These have not been included in the present group. Subsequent records show that half of this whole group became reconciled to the Army and completed their service as satisfactory soldiers.

(2) A less radical class, though still very disgruntled were those (36 per cent) who *wanted to get out of the Infantry but not necessarily out of the Army* for one reason or another. The large majority of the S.T.U. intake were from Infantry Regiments. It is felt by some people in the Army that the infantryman has such a hard and thankless job that it is little wonder so large a preponderance of absentees and deserters come from this arm of the service. Nowadays the infantryman must be skilled in the use of many weapons; he is constantly putting his physical powers to the test, and is much exposed to the elements. Where others ride he must walk, as some of the S.T.U. men quickly noticed. If the infantryman's job does impose particularly heavy strains on the individual it seems only fair that he should receive compensations, and he now receives something in the shape of proficiency and trade pay, but the job is by nature plodding, arduous and unspectacular and nothing can fully compensate for that. But it does not seem that the reason for the breakdown of morale in the offender (assuming it ever existed) lies in the nature of his Army job. The discontent seems deeply rooted in the man himself and most of such men would have been in trouble wherever they were. It is true that the majority of those who had been in infantry units and were posted from S.T.U. to technical or other arms of the service became useful soldiers, but then so did those posted back to the infantry.

(*a*) A number of the men in this class, wanting to get out of the infantry, sought driving, mostly in the Royal Army Service Corps. They generally claimed that they had asked for a driving job on enlistment and felt let down because they had not got it. Altogether about 13 per cent of all intake came into this category. The Personnel Selection Officer who interviews recruits might ask a man what sort of a job he wanted to do, but he could only make recommendations and would certainly not promise anything, particularly in a job like driving that was already too much in demand. It is just possible that some of the men had been told that a recommendation would be made, and they were quite capable of misunderstanding the meaning of the word 'recommend'. An examination of the mechanical (Assembly) test results shows that few of them were really suited to a mechanical job, nor were those who had in fact become Army drivers especially skilful at the job. This urge for driving can, therefore, only come from some inner compulsion; perhaps it is an expression of that restlessness already noted, demanding a continual change of environment. A further attraction must also be the driver's relative freedom from continual supervision, and the feeling, voiced by a small fellow as 'I'd sooner ride than walk'.

The contrast between the lot of the driver and that of the private soldier is more keenly felt by the man who saw both jobs in the wrong order:

My worst moment was when I left a lovely happy entertaining Drivers I.T.C. and came into the b———y battery. The Company commander was a Major, 25 years of age, and he didn't treat young lads like men but like hooligans. Although I got on well at times, I just done as much spit and polish as I do here, but one day I told him to look at what he talks at and not growl, and now, I am the same old lad now that I'm here, although I'm certainly not proud to be here . . .'

(b) Amongst those who were dissatisfied with the infantry, a second group (13 per cent) wanted to be transferred to a technical corps or to a special corps like Commandos or Recce where they thought life would be more adventurous.

(c) A third group (10 per cent) just wanted to leave the infantry because it was not to their liking though they had no very clear idea where they wanted to go. Some wanted to get out of the light infantry because it marched with a very quick step, about 120 paces to a minute. Others, especially the immature youths, found the 'foot-slogging' too heavy going. Others just hoped to find a more comfortable 'billet' elsewhere. One of these men described his predicament as:

'I don't like the infantry. It has turned me from a good citizen into a dog.' (The 'dog' had ten Army convictions; the 'good citizen' was a Glasgow delinquent!)

(3) A third class (about 18 per cent) *wanted to change their regiment, though not necessarily their arm of the service*, generally because they had not made friends and hoped that by getting into their own County regiment or joining friends or relatives all would

be well. Here again, though to a lesser extent than in the first two classes, there was evidence of a failure to achieve integration into the group life of the unit. They had sometimes avoided trouble in one unit but had got into scrapes in another. They always blamed the unit, and at first glance it seems odd that they should have avoided trouble in one unit and not in the other. But a study of the individual generally showed that he was far from normal, and that he had never been far from trouble even when his record suggested that he had been clear of it. The following explanation from an offender who was introspective and emotionally starved (see a reference to the same man on p. 80), illustrates the point:

> When I joined the Army I was completely ignorant as to how it was run and I thought that all you had to do was drill and go on route marches and I was disappointed when it came to scrubbing floors and peeling potatoes. After I got used to these things everything ran smoothly. I took everything in my stride during training. When I went to my first unit, the 70th ——— I thought I was in a pre-war Battn. with the NCOs and Officers wearing peaked caps. I soon got used to it and it was the best Battn. I have ever been in. The C.O. of this Battn. seemed to understand you and when you went to see him you came away relieved. The next Battn. I went into was the 17th ———. I did not like this Battn. because everybody pushed you around, and the N.C.O.s picked on you and didn't give you a chance, and I just couldn't soldier there.

(4) Lastly, some 31 per cent *did not want to change their regiments* (including 13 per cent who were already drivers), or had no quarrel with the Army as such, or in those cases where there had been disagreement, were more concerned with particular N.C.O.s and officers, than the whole group.

Exactly half of the drivers were conscripts, as were one-third of the others in this class. Altogether, 38 per cent of this 'satisfied' class were conscripts compared with 35 per cent amongst the rest of the sample—suggesting that the conscript was probably at least as reliable as the volunteer in a group of this sort.

The following table sets out the various reactions in the whole sample:

TABLE 15

Reactions of S.T.U. sample to the Army.

(1) Totally dissatisfied with Army	%	%
a. No alternative wanted	8	
b. Wanting Royal Navy or M. Navy	7	
	—	15

(2) Dissatisfied with arm of service (infantry)
    a. Wanting driving   13
    b. Wanting technical or Commando 13
    c. Wanting change of arm, finding
        infantry uncongenial   10
                                          36

(3) Dissatisfied with particular regiment or
      unit (mostly infantry)
    a. Simply disliking former unit   8
    b. Wanting to join friend or relatives 10
                                         18

(4) Reasonably satisfied with Army
    a. Drivers   13
    b. Others   18
                                       31
                                      100

Pride of Regiment

It was quite common for the men at the S.T.U. to assert the superior claims of their own regiments, against all others. They would frequently engage in furious arguments as to which was the oldest or the best regiment, taking the caps off their heads and pointing to the battle honours listed on the badge or snatching their antagonist's cap and grinding it in the dirt. The cap badge was a favourite subject for drawing, embroidering, carving or mounting on a belt. If one asked them how it was possible for them to be so bitter against the Army and yet so fanatically proud of their regiment, no logical answer could be given. The anomaly was that they rejected identification with both the small practical group (platoon, etc.) and the Army in general, but clung with pride and spirit to the regiment, the latter free apparently from both the practical objections to the platoon and the idealization—as in 'the Army', of those practical objections.

Pride of regiment was for them an expression of their need to belong to a group, just as their attachment to home reflected their yearning for what they had mostly been deprived of. There was also a feeling that, if the Regiment could be established as something distinguished and superlative, they themselves would share in its distinction—one further indication of their inadequacy. One could, however, turn this interest to account by recounting some of the true stories in military history, promoting a sense of responsibility and an understanding of the sacrifice and achievement that lie behind every regimental tradition.

CHAPTER XV

ARMY OFFENCES

OFFENDERS, whether in or out of the Army, are commonly regarded as black sheep among a spotless flock. During wartime, minor evasions of regulations were widespread and there was a general lowering of moral standards which was felt at every level. In the Army, for instance, men would frequently proceed beyond prescribed bounds without authority. They were generally given local leave at week-ends, if stationed at home, and they could pass freely within a short distance of their camp without a special pass. Some, however, took the opportunity to travel home, and for this purpose 'communal' passes were sometimes circulated round a unit, for use in any encounters with military police. Men would occasionally write out their own passes. They would often travel back by train without buying a railway ticket. Such evasions were not considered abnormal. 'Red-caps' and railway companies were 'fair game'. All this was not only practised but commonly known. It suggested that in wartime the soldier had largely transferred his allegiance from civilian authority, not to the Army, but to the individual regimental unit (in most cases the company of a hundred or so men).

The Army unit was now the important group and its laws had to be obeyed. Thus, social morality in the services tended to be split up into small self-contained units. Outside, you might scrounge or evade the rules as much as you could get away with. There were limits, of course, and most men knew when they were in danger of exceeding them. Hope of promotion might curb a man's ventures, but hardly affected the S.T.U. type. They had few moral standards to begin with, and there was often little at home to inspire or restrain them. They would, indeed, often point to what was going on and ask 'why pick on me?' Where they had failed, so far as their officers and fellow-soldiers were concerned, was in getting out of step with their own unit and consistently breaking its rules.

First Offences

A man's first conviction might be expected to make a deeper impression on him than the subsequent ones. It was, in fact, alleged by a few of the men that harsh or unfair treatment on the occasion of the first slip in the Army had been the 'cause' of their subsequent wrongdoing. There were odd cases where, according to the record on the conduct sheet, a man had received the unusual award of twenty-one days' detention for a first offence of having a dirty rifle whilst on sentry duty, but even stray instances of this sort cannot be assessed from the conduct sheet record alone; there may have been other circumstances not recorded or the offender may have been giving continual cause for offence, and these factors would certainly not be shown on the brief written statement recording the technical offence and the punishment.

The allegation of initial unfairness setting off a sequence of offences is not borne out even by the men's own testimony. In a questionnaire dealing with their first offence in the Army they were asked 'Do you think you were treated fairly then?' As many as 58 per cent stated that they were treated fairly, rather a surprising number considering how bitter and disgruntled many of them were over their offences and punishments. An examination of the records of the 42 per cent who considered that they were treated unfairly shows that in a majority of the cases (27 per cent of the whole sample) the offence was sufficiently serious to warrant the punishment. In three instances the punishment awarded was particularly light, and in three others no punishment at all was given. In about a quarter of the cases claiming unfair treatment discrepancies were observed between the men's own accounts of their first offences and the records. One or two spoke of absence or lateness when it should have been the much more serious offence of improper possession; one or two had received so many convictions that a little confusion is perhaps excusable, but in a number of cases the man was obviously preoccupied with a particular offence that actually occurred later in his record but obscured the earlier charges from his mind. Altogether, about 85 per cent of the men correctly recalled their initial offences. Yet the punishments were almost invariably light (only 10 per cent of the first awards were for detention—but still too large a proportion for young soldiers—and most of those were for more serious offences like improper possession or prolonged absence). Considering that, on average, seven other offences followed with more severe sentences, the fact that so many recollected the first charge accurately suggests that it did in fact make a deep impression on them.

A majority (55 per cent) of the first offences (as indeed of all subsequent offences) were of absence from the unit or from parade, and they occurred on average within three months of enlistment. This sets a limit to the time taken for the volunteers' enthusiasm to burn out. The next largest group of first offences were infringements of disciplinary orders. These comprise 21 per cent of the total and occur on average six months after enlistment. The third largest were offences of personal neglect, numbering 19 per cent of the total and occurring five months after enlistment. The longer interval between enlistment and the recording of convictions for disciplinary matters partly reflects the latitude usually given to a new recruit before he is 'put on a charge' for misbehaviour. If he goes absent without leave he must be charged.

Two other types of first offence—criminal (including the Army charge of improper possession and indictable offences under civil law), and desertion—only affected 4 per cent and 1 per cent respectively. Of the total number, 31 per cent of the first offences occurred within one month of joining the Army.

Considered in terms of the men's subsequent attitude to the Army (as shown in the table at the conclusion of the preceding chapter) the average time intervals between enlistment and the first offence are:

For men totally dissatisfied with the Army	2·7 months
„ „ dissatisfied with arm of service	4·1 „
„ „ dissatisfied with unit	5·5 „
„ „ tolerably satisfied	4·0 „

There is thus a tendency for those whose dissatisfaction with the Army is greater to begin their offences sooner after enlistment. The average number of offences per person, registered on their conduct sheets prior to coming to the Special Training Unit, was 7·4. About 17 per cent had three convictions or less, and 9 per cent had 15 or more. The highest score was 44.

Absence without leave

The urge to escape from a situation that proved difficult was deeply ingrained in many of these men. Truancy at school and, later, in many cases, frequent job-changing, had evidently established a habit that Army discipline alone could not break.

Some idea of the extent of this offence in the Army as a whole may be gathered from an investigation[1] carried out in 1941 amongst 6,177 other ranks in anti-aircraft regiments, an infantry brigade, and a training centre; 23 per cent of all the men were absent at least once, but only 4·5 per cent were absent three or more times. Thus about 4 per cent of the men accounted for 45 per cent of the absences. About half of the S.T.U. men would have come into this 4 per cent, having three or more absences on their records; 74 per cent of the S.T.U. intake had been convicted of absence at least once, and if absence from parades and desertion are included the percentage is 83. The average number of absences per man was 2·6 (see Table 5 on p. 23). Only 2 per cent of the men had been convicted of desertion, which is a much more serious offence than absence without leave. To establish a case of desertion it is necessary to prove the soldier's intention not to return to military service, or to avoid some important military duty. The length of time during which a soldier is absent without leave may establish technical desertion in Army records affecting a man's documents, but it is immaterial to establishing the legal offence of desertion except in so far as prolonged absence adds weight to other evidence.

Many absentees were 'picked up' before they had been away more than a few days so that one could only guess at their intentions. Most absentees probably had no clearly worked out plan. The decision to walk out of camp or not to catch the last train back was the crucial step. After that had been taken, they tended to drift, hoping to have at least a few days' 'fling' before being apprehended.

It was quite common for a man to come up to one of the staff and say that he felt he would be going off soon, just as one might say one has caught a cold. He might talk about it to his friends and it would soon be common knowledge that so-and-so was thinking of going absent. On such occasions some of the more experienced young soldiers who had been made N.C.O.s and taken on to the staff could plead with the men more effectively than the older staff. In a few cases going absent appeared to be an irresistible impulse and it seemed that the act of escape had a special

[1] *Report of an Expert Committee on the Work of Psychologists and Psychiatrists in the Services*, page 56 (H.M.S.O., 1947).

emotional meaning for such men quite apart from putting them temporarily outside the reach of Army discipline.[1]

To explore the absentees' motives for taking the initial step into their offence and to see what precautions against detection they took and what excuses they chose to offer, the S.T.U. sample were invited to write at some length on the subject. The results showed that the man's home and his unit formed, as it were, the positive and negative poles of his life. He would run away from his unit because he could not stand Army life; if he was home on leave he found it exceedingly difficult to return to his unit. Most of the absences were therefore extensions of privilege leave. But in all the accounts the vital point of the action—the moment of decision to overstay leave —was dismissed in a word or glossed over completely. Many were tempted to stay by the prospect of a 'good time', by companions or a girl friend, though several mentioned that their parents or their girl had urged them to return. Some had delayed their departure from home until the last minute, had then missed the train and decided to make another day of it; and so a process of indefinite delays was set off. Once the decision had been taken a number, perhaps most, just waited for the 'red-caps' to come and fetch them, and made little attempt at evasion. Others, however, went 'on the run', 'joined the Trotters' Union', as they termed it, holding out as long as they could against want or detection. The two reactions are perhaps best illustrated in the men's own words:

(1) On the 24th of January I was on my way to catch the 8.30 train to Crewe to return to my unit off privilege leave, when I met one of my best pals, just coming on leave. I was browned off at the time and it did not take long to change my mind. My mate tried to make me come back but I had missed the train and I said I would go back on the 1.15, but when we were down the town I met another mate and then I decided to stop another day, but when the next day came I could not make up my mind and when I was trying to come back I had missed the last train and so it went on like that for five days and at last I came back on the sixth day and arrived at my unit seven days overdue.

[1] The emotional satisfaction of the delinquent act is a matter on which psychological investigators have written much. Healy and Bronner quote a case as saying: 'I got going just for the fun of it; it wasn't for the money because my mother always used to give us plenty.' 'I was the slipperiest, they patted me for it and it made me feel good and I wanted to do it again.' An interesting description was given by a notorious bag-snatcher to the writer. He said: 'When I took the bag from the woman and got it in my hand it made me feel wonderful. I can't describe it. It wasn't what was in the bag for I often threw it away without opening it.' In some cases, the act obviously has an emotional significance connected with the man's earlier life which psychological research has gone far to explain.

(2) I was on the run not so long ago and the way I did it was very good. You go walking along the road and you see a red-cap and get out of his way. You get a lot of fun out of it but it ends some time. (The level of intelligence of this man is apparent.)

In many cases the duller men were unable to take precautions to safeguard themselves against detection or even to think up a plausible excuse, much as they tried. They were asked to write a description of their best excuse for returning late from leave. The results were examined for evidence of imagination, originality and feasibility, and each paper was marked on a six-point scale corresponding as closely as an individual assessment could, to the six selection groups of the Army tests. These markings (made without reference to the intelligence records) were then compared with the men's intelligence test ratings. The results showed a striking resemblance (the coefficient of correlation between the two sets of figures being $+\cdot91$). Here, then, is further evidence of what is well known to police and prison authorities, that the intelligent offender may think of the most plausible excuses, but the dullard can usually think of none, and that although offenders may display unusual skill in actually committing a crime, they usually show little ingenuity in protecting themselves.

Several times this question of absence without leave was openly debated at educational sessions and there was nearly always a slight majority who defended the absentee. They saw the absentee as a sort of Charlie Chaplin, a lonely, unfortunate, persecuted figure in a hostile world.

In writing of this subject about one in four offered no excuse to justify absence without leave. Just over half cited domestic troubles as ample justification:

'If a man goes absent because of home troubles I think he is in the right if he cannot get leave to go home.'

A more subtle argument was:

Some people really have family troubles at home which the Army don't see in the same light. And as those people in the Army are only human, then their own families come before anything to them. But the Army argument is always 'What would happen if everybody was of the same mind'. Well, there is an answer to that as its foolish to look at it in that light. If it were true, there would be no Army except when it was inevitable, such as when we had to guard our own shores. So everybody can't be of the same mind.

Nearly all the rest (about 15 per cent) laid the blame for unauthorized absence upon the Army's injustice, or niggardliness

K

with pay, or the monotony of training, echoing the remark of one
who said: 'I say good luck to him if he goes absent. If the Army
was fair he would never have got into trouble.'

The same distribution of opinion is shown inversely in the
answers to the question 'What steps could be taken to cut down
absence?'—26 per cent advocated punishment or deprivation of
privileges, whereas 70 per cent wanted to make Army life less
onerous and called for more privileges, better treatment or compassionate postings.

The records of all those men with convictions for three or more
unauthorized absences shown on their field conduct sheets have been
scrutinized to see whether they differ from the sample as a whole
in intelligence, in education, in their emotional make-up, their
attitude to the Army, in having urgent domestic troubles, or in being
unsuitably employed.

(1) The persistent absentees are generally no less intelligent
than others in the group. (The recidivists, those with a large number
of offences of all kinds recorded against them, are more backward
[see p. 64] in intelligence and much below standard in educational
attainment.) The proportions of men with intelligence below the
average point (as measured by the Matrix test) are:

	%
Persistent absentees	54
All S.T.U. offenders	53
Normal Army sample	43

(2) The corresponding figures for educational attainments (as
measured by the Verbal and Arithmetic tests) show a similar correspondence, though here, as has already been stated, there is a striking
difference between offenders and the norm:

	%
Persistent absentees	84
All S.T.U. offenders	82
Normal Army sample	53

(3) The persistent absentees were also examined to see whether
they included any undue proportion of emotionally abnormal types
(as classified in Chapter X). Again the proportions were almost
identical, except that, as might be expected, a larger proportion
of 'wanderers' are included amongst the absentees.

(4) It might be thought that the persistent absentees would
include a disproportionately large number of conscripts. But 68
per cent of the absentees were volunteers, compared with 64 per

cent in the entire group, and 61 per cent amongst those who were not persistent absentees. Though slight, this difference tends to confirm the tendency, noted in Chapter XIV, for volunteers in an unstable group to be less reliable than conscripts.

(5) Another line of inquiry was to examine the persistent absentees' reactions to their Army units and jobs, in case any were serious misfits. Once again, there was no great difference, though the absentees did include rather smaller proportions of men who were fairly satisfied with their Army units. Misfits, men who were grossly unsuited by intelligence or aptitudes for the job they were doing, were very few indeed. In considering this factor one must distinguish between a man's inclination for a job (like driving) and his suitability as measured by tests. Very many wanted jobs that they had not been given; very few were really suited for those jobs. So the apparent misfitting was not, for the overwhelming majority, the cause of their trouble; it was merely a symptom of it.

(6) Finally, the absentees' home conditions have been examined in case they had special compassionate reasons for wanting to go home. Only an odd man or so (2 per cent) was found to have really strong grounds for wanting to be with his parents. One man, for instance, whose case is listed as No. 11 in the table at the end of Chapter VIII, had five unauthorized absences to his debit, and came to the Unit suffering from chronic pharyngitis. He had spent six months in a sanatorium for chest trouble and had been detained in three Army hospitals for blood spitting. His father had been dead some years and his mother lived with his married brother. The mother was delicate and had had to give up work on munitions. She had also adopted a small child. Three months after the man had been at the S.T.U. an appeal for his presence arrived from the mother; the married brother, who was unfit for military service and who had been her chief means of support, had been given three months' imprisonment. She claimed to be suffering from phlebitis and in desperate straits. The man's privilege leave was brought forward and he was sent straight home, but he returned four days late. He had wired for an extension but inquiries by the police revealed that apparently his mother was not dying as he had suggested. Two months later, however, came an urgent appeal from the workhouse infirmary and he was granted compassionate leave. He arrived to witness his mother's death. From that leave, too, he was two days overdue but the astonishing thing is that he did return. But such cases were not common.

A further 9 per cent had domestic troubles which were likely to cause them considerable concern, and which must have influenced their absences.   One or two men went absent in order to join their girl friends or wives, and two had over-anxious mothers who distressed them by sending alarming and unnecessary letters about conditions at home.   The Commanding Officer's difficulty was sorting out the cases of genuine need from the spurious, though the compulsions in the minds of both might be equally strong and their stories equally moving.   But apart from these 20 per cent or so with serious home troubles or unsettling conditions at home, the S.T.U. men had no more grounds for unwarranted absence than the many soldiers with ailing parents or young families of their own. Indeed, in many cases, their homes were more likely to repel than to attract a young man.   That the large majority wanted desperately to be home was only too plain, but they were driven by inward compulsions rather than drawn by urgent home troubles.

The results of these six inquiries show only insignificant or slight differences between the persistent absentees and the whole group of offenders (where differences were suspected, those who were not persistent absentees were compared).   Unauthorized absence would, therefore, appear to be merely one further expression of the delinquent state which in other individuals manifests itself as indiscipline, larceny or some other anti-social form of behaviour.   Unauthorized absence, to the offenders, was considered solely as an issue between themselves and the Army authorities.   There was a deep-seated grudge against the Army (which the psychologist might regard as symbolic of father-rejection) and they felt fully entitled to take French leave if they could get away with it.   Considerations of loyalty, of patriotism, of national expenditure, of letting friends and comrades down, or personal integrity, did not enter into it.   The only factors that weighed with them at all were the disapproval of the mother or loss of pay which might indirectly affect her (through the dependents' allowance).   The whole situation was irrational and could not be met by argument or normal Army punishments.

Disciplinary Offences

These varied in severity from making 'Donald Duck' noises while on parade to throwing a bucket of whitewash over the Regimental Sergeant-Major.   As many as 77 per cent of the men had disciplinary offences recorded against them, and the average number of entries was 2·1.   In very few cases did these offences amount to a deliberate flaunting of Army authority. The minor troubles usually arose from childish and irresponsible behaviour. A man would be warned by his platoon sergeant that if he continued to chatter and fidget and act the fool on parade he would get into trouble. The incident that finally provoked a charge might have been trivial but it had to be seen as part of a chain of misdemeanours.

But the offender did not see it that way. 'A man can't help making a silly little mistake,' wrote one. 'The Army hits you below the belt.' Or again, 'Some men don't like the Army life and they get nothing else but keep being put on charges for the least little thing.' Or, more emphatically, 'Such small, bloody, miserable, petty, childish charges for nothing at all. Its all a big black market, stopping lads pay etc. Its a big waist of time and a hinderance to the war effort.'

The more violent breaches of discipline were usually the result of temper and may have been occasioned by an imagined injustice. Unfortunately offenders had not learned to swallow small injustices —'no one will stand lip of anyone,' as a hot-tempered Glasgow youth put it.

Personal Neglect

It is said by farmers that dirty pigs are bred from the litters of dirty sows. If that is equally true of human families one can only suppose that the S.T.U. men came from dirty and untidy homes. Though they liked to look smart on public occasions they were generally loath to keep themselves clean and tidy. They were equally careless over their weapons, so it is not surprising to find a large number of entries of 'dirty rifle' on the conduct sheets. Half of them had one or more convictions of this sort and the average number of entries among this 50 per cent was 2·4.

The Offender's View

Some of the young soldiers applied themselves to the problem of their Army troubles and put forward some general statements like:

'After all, we're all strangers', or 'Some men have never been away from home before', or 'Some are born that way but the reason for others is that they have not got confidence in themselves'.

A few of the more intelligent suggested that the error might be in the man and not in the Army:

(*a*) 'Some get browned off feelings and just don't care and get their selves in trouble and we call them "bad".'

(*b*) 'No, I do not think people who go wrong in the Army are bad. It is only when they are in a crowd that they want to show off, or when they are browned off.'

One or two, in considering the problem, were surprisingly objective in their views:

(*a*) 'When people go wrong in the Army I don't think it is their natural way; one reason may be on account of the change of life, another is because the army has a different law from civvy street.'

(*b*) 'I think there is a certain type of man who had a free and easy life in civvy street and who finds Army life too strict, and so commits offences.

(*c*) 'Some people stick out wherever they go or whatever they do and therefore are always checked up on if anything goes rong and are nealy always blamed even (if) it was (not) them that commited the offence. But this happens in every walk of life wich is so rong.'

The majority, however, could not think of the question disinterestedly. It was the Army or the Unit or the N.C.O.s who were at fault, and often they would answer the general question by some reference to their own misfortunes. One man, in reply to the question about responsibility for offences, could only refer to a difference of opinion the day before:

'Yesterday the sergeant asked me how far we were off the camp, and I said "f— off, I'm not in the infintry". He said "We can stop here all night its or right with me." Then I said "f— the map", just put it down and walked off. You see I have forgot all about map-reading.'

They were asked in the questionnaire: 'Do you think that people who go wrong in the Army are simply made that way?' Some (14 per cent) thought they were, and others (15 per cent) thought that only some were, and a few (7 per cent) attributed the blame to their upbringing, or (6 per cent) to separation from their home, but the majority (56 per cent) said that the Army was at fault. Another question was: 'Is it a clever man or a stupid man who commits offences?' A number refused to be caught by this question and answered 'He is stupid if he is caught', but 57 per cent answered 'stupid', and only 5 per cent 'clever'. It might be thought that those who considered the offender a clever man—or clever if he were not detected—would be more, or less, intelligent than the rest.

Their intelligence test results, however, show no appreciable difference. The fact that a majority considered offenders 'stupid' does suggest that they did not look upon themselves as professional criminals, beating the world at its own game; they felt they were more to be pitied than admired.

The same problem of responsibility for offences was approached in another way by the questions: 'Would you say that you yourself have been unlucky if you have got into trouble in the Army?' and 'When have you felt that you deserved all the punishment you got?' The questions are slightly equivocal, for a man might interpret his answer as meaning that he was only unlucky in being found out.[1] About half of them felt that they had deserved some of their punishments; the others considered themselves the unfortunate victims of circumstance, having fallen foul of a particularly vicious N.C.O. or a bad unit. As many as 37 per cent gave details of how they had been 'picked on'. 'Nine times out of ten', wrote one, 'I've been victimised owing to the fact that N.C.O.s take a dislike to me for no apparent reason.'

'My reason for being sent to this camp where I am being Victimised every day is because I tried to Soldier, they would not let me fire the Gun nor they would not let me do anything, they always put me in the Guard Room for Refusing to do Something I wasn't told to do.' (After posting this same man wrote letters back from India describing further persecutions; he completed his military service through to Class A release, but is only counted as a 'doubtful' case in Chap. III.)

Some 40 per cent considered that they were unlucky in getting into trouble, and these were mostly the more persistent offenders, their average number of convictions per man being nine. It is interesting that the majority felt that at least some of the responsibility was theirs.

Lastly, they were asked whether they thought people 'were treated as fairly by the Army as by civilian authorities when they got into trouble'. Here again the question is open to some misinterpretation because in wartime Army justice has often to be meted

[1] The drafting of questions that cannot be misconstrued and are likely to produce answers of equal value is one of the most difficult undertakings, as Sir Francis Galton once pointed out. The present inquiry was concerned with men whose vocabulary was very restricted, and therefore a first consideration was that the meaning of the words should be clearly understood, and that the meaning should be the same for all. Hence one chose 'defend' instead of 'justify', 'picked on' instead of 'victimized', and so on.

out in the field, and the prisoner does not have the same opportunities for legal defence as he would in civilian life. Furthermore, in the Army it is the same authority that arrests, tries and punishes a man whereas in civilian life the offender is dealt with by at least four different authorities, the police, the Courts, the prisons or reformatories, and the after-care organizations.

Commanding officers hear first charges and can deal summarily with the less serious offences. They are roughly equivalent to the magistrates' courts, but there is no trained clerk or lawyer or probation officer present. It may, therefore, be argued that Army justice cannot be administered as fairly as civilian. One particular practice that often distressed offenders was marching the prisoner before the Commanding Officer with a Sergeant-Major shouting 'left-right-left-right', and 'left turn, right turn', through passages and doors until he was marking-time before the officer's desk. This formality was certainly unnecessary and only served to intimidate the prisoner.

So it is not altogether surprising that 60 per cent of the men considered Army justice less fair than civilian; it is perhaps much more remarkable that nearly 40 per cent considered it was as fair and is a tribute to the justice of most commanding officers. One of the chief sources of irritation was the inevitable inequality of awards from one case to another and from one unit to another for the same type of offence. Army justice, like civilian, embodies a scale of awards that can be adjusted to fit the circumstances of each particular case. But these men, perhaps because of their general backwardness, could not see the point of this and were especially aggrieved when they heard of someone receiving a lighter sentence than their own for the same offence.

Punishment

The more common forms of punishment in the Army are extra duties, confinement to barracks and detention. C.B. is applied in the unit and during his sentence the soldier carries out normal duties, except that before breakfast, during morning break, in the dinner hour and in the evening he must report to the guard-room to answer roll-call, and is given fatigue duties like scrubbing floors, peeling potaoes, shovelling coke, etc. During the period of his 'confinement' he is not allowed out of camp, nor can he normally visit a canteen or recreation room. Detention may be served in the unit cells for short sentences, or away at a military prison.

The prisoner loses pay and privileges, is under the supervision of provost staff all the time and does not (or rather did not, for changes are taking place) carry out normal training. He is confined in a cell when not working or exercising.

The S.T.U. men had received an average of 4·5 sentences of C.B. per person, and 1·3 sentences of detention. There were three times as many awards of C.B. as detention. They were questioned in some detail as to their reactions to these punishments. Those who had experienced both were almost equally divided as to which they preferred. The arguments in favour of detention were that it was 'cushier' and that one did not work such long hours there. C.B. was preferred by others because it did not affect pay, as detention did, one could receive letters and the food was better. Detention in the unit was much preferred to military prisons, because 'your mates in the unit can pass you in cigarettes', among other reasons!

Their opinion of life in detention barracks was unanimously unfavourable, though it was obviously never the intention of the Army that detention should be pleasant. The best that could be said for it by about a dozen was that it was 'easy' or 'not bad', or 'better now' or 'alright if you're tough'. The rest spoke of it as 'horrible', 'a dog's life', 'awful', 'couldn't stick it again; I'd rather commit suicide', etc. They were also asked whether 'detention prevents a man from repeating his offence'. A few (9 per cent) thought it did but the great majority felt that it made him worse. Several echoed the man who said, 'Once you have had detention you know what it is like. When you have not, the word detention frightens you more than you think.' Although a few had become inured to institutional punishment, the majority hated it and were embittered by it, and a few dreaded the prospect of returning there. Two men even attempted to poison themselves by swallowing phosphorous anti-gas ointment on being sentenced to spells of detention. The purpose of these remarks is not to criticize military detention or to say whether it is good or bad. It is merely to state what effects sentences of detention have produced on a sample of young Army offenders.

Habitual Offenders

Just over a quarter of the S.T.U. sample had more than eight offences recorded on their Field Conduct Sheets. Their cases have been scrutinized in the same way as the persistent absentees' to see whether they differed significantly from the rest of the group. Although the number was small a clear distinction emerges in the intelligence and educational standard of this recidivist group, as the following table shows:

Proportions of habitual offenders with test results
below average point:

	Intelligence %	Education %
Persistent offenders	67	97
All offenders	53	82
Normal Army sample	43	53

The habitual offender had, at least, remained behind or returned to his unit, to answer for his crimes. Others, with fewer entries on their conduct sheets, may have deserted or been absent for very long periods. His backwardness may, of course, account for this. One cannot escape the conclusion that normal methods of punishment had no beneficial effect upon such habitual delinquents, and any authority, if it wishes to redeem a man of this sort, should consider whether alternative methods would not produce better results. The Special Training Units were, after all, set up for such a purpose and their successes only prove how wasteful the older methods were. It is all the more significant that 46 per cent of these habitual offenders had satisfactory records after leaving the S.T.U.

CHAPTER XVI

CIVILIAN EMPLOYMENT

IN attempting to explore the earlier and formative years of the lives of these young soldiers, one must pass beyond the compass of one's own observations and depend largely upon the statements of the men themselves. Apart from the normal imperfections of memory it is possible that the subjects deliberately distorted their accounts in order to put themselves in a more favourable light; or their recollections may have been influenced by the violent emotional situations that had often played a large part in their early years. It was felt by the authors of this inquiry that they had the men's confidence and knew them well enough to be assured of their intention to co-operate fully and fairly. And where one could check the information given against earlier statements made to Personnel Selection Officers or to other members of the staff, or by letters received from Probation Officers and civilian institutions, or from the men's own parents, in nearly every case the truth of their testimony was confirmed.

Their civilian employment was fairly fresh in their memories. Even so, some of them found it quite an effort to recall details of all the jobs they had held, because there had been so many. It was especially difficult with building workers for whom each new contract of their employer's was a new 'job', and as, in such cases, one could not be sure whether a man was speaking of a change of employer or a change of building job, all doubtful cases of building work have been counted as a single job. For this reason, and also because the men sometimes recorded the trades instead of the separate jobs they had worked in, the figures may be taken as minimal. When they are compared with corresponding proportions in other inquiries it should not be forgotten that the S.T.U. men were mostly working during the early years of the War when unemployment was almost unknown and labour in essential work was directed and therefore immobile.

In the following table the proportions of the men working in the various occupations are set out alongside an abstract of the 1931 census figures,[1] the latest available material suitable for comparison. The offenders were working between 1938 and 1942, a period which, compared with 1931, would include much larger proportions in the permanent defence services, more in labouring jobs in the construction of aerodromes and defence works, and fewer in the commercial, personal service and unoccupied groups. A limitation of the 1931 proportions is that they do not represent the choice of occupations that, in fact, lay before the particular social class from which the S.T.U. men came. To some extent the differences would have been common to all the members of that social class, and this factor can only roughly be estimated.

As each man had held a number of jobs, the first problem was to decide how to make the count of occupations for comparative purposes. The most satisfactory method would have been to fix a date on which the greatest number were working and to reckon up the occupations as shown at that time. But one was working retrospectively and the men could not be certain of the dates of their employment. The job named by them as their favourite has, therefore, been counted in each case, as having the advantage of showing the drift of their inclinations though there are statistical objections to the method. The results are shown in column one of the table. The figures in column two show the frequency of each occupation in the various jobs listed. They are expressed as percentages of the total number of men concerned, so that, for example, 40 per cent had worked as drivers at some time or other. The third column sets out the fathers' occupations so far as they could be estimated from the cases where the information was given. The groupings suggest functions but they convey only an imperfect impression of actual occupations. The majority were employed at menial or unskilled work because of their youth and backwardness. Even apprentices to a skilled trade were relatively few (14 per cent). The total number claiming some sort of apprenticeship or skilled training was 36 per cent compared with 57 per cent in the control groups. For 'transport worker' one could therefore generally read driver's mate; for 'clerical', office boy; for 'commercial', shop messenger or counter hand; for 'building', builder's labourer.

[1] Quoted by H. Frankel 'The Industrial Distribution of the Population of Great Britain in July, 1939', *Journal of the Royal Statistical Society*, Vol. CVIII, Parts III–IV, 1945.

TABLE 16

Civilian occupations of S.T.U. offenders (190 cases)
and of their fathers (131 cases)

	Favourite job	All jobs	Father's job	Normal (1931 census)
	%	%	%	%
Production, Repair and Maintenance	30	53	30	20·6
Mining and Quarrying	2	3	4	6·6
Commerce, finance, retail distribution	7	14	7	10·0
Transport (road, rail and water)	20	40	15	10·7
Agriculture and fishing	6	8	4	7·8
Clerical	2	6	—	5·4
Labouring, storehouse, etc. warehousemen	20	42	17	11·6
Building, painting, decorating, wood'rs	7	14	10	9·7
Professional and administrative	—	—	—	3·1
Personal service	1	2	1	3·2
Unoccupied and retired, Entertainment, sport and unclassified	3	4	8	10·1
Defence	2	2	4	1·2
	100	188	100	100·0

The figures for the offenders show unduly large concentrations in transport and labouring though a normal sample of the same social class would probably show similarly high proportions of labourers. The 1931 census numbers in transport (10·7 per cent) include very many men engaged on the railways, for example, who were not driving. The number of commercial A, B and C vehicle licences issued in 1938 was 513,147 (or 3 per cent of the adult male population) and this figure affords a better comparison, since the number of commercial drivers was certainly smaller than the number of licensed vehicles. The disproportion is emphasized by the figure of 40 per cent in column two. By comparison, the control groups produced only 9 per cent who had been or wanted to be drivers. There is a suggestion of the same tendency in the fathers' occupations which include a number of hawkers, coal deliverers and van drivers. Some 59 per cent of the S.T.U. sample claimed to have taken up a different job from their fathers', compared with 88 per cent who made the same claim among the control groups.

The average number of jobs per person was 4·5 (cf. 2·3 among the controls). Not only had many changed their jobs frequently but they had drifted from one trade to another. One man, for instance, had been an office boy, a casement-maker's errand boy, a fitter's improver, a chippy's mate, a builder's labourer, a furrier's cleaner, a milk sterilizer, bench hand, paint miller, driver, etc. The authors of *Young Offenders* [1] record an average of 3·8 jobs for sixteen-year-old offenders in London, and 3·1 in provincial towns (compared with 2·0 and 2·1 for the control groups). [2] With another two years of free employment the same offenders might have shown an average of five or more jobs per man, and the immobility of labour in wartime would tend to reduce the figure in a group like that from the S.T.U., which was, on average, fifteen years of age in 1939. Rhodes, in *Young Offenders*, suggests that the tendency to job-changing in the offenders may be due to 'restlessness or to unsuitability of the jobs found'. The delinquents, he argues, may obtain less suitable jobs because of their lower social standing and correspondingly lessened parental influence in securing a good initial job. A third possibility, which probably comes back to the same cause in the end, is that the delinquents' inferior school attainments, which would militate against finding a more responsible job, may derive from an initial restlessness. These lines of inquiry have been examined from the evidence of the S.T.U. case histories, working on the assumption that any such factor would operate differentially, so that it would be more apparent in the men who held more than, say, four jobs (44 per cent of the whole group) than in those who held fewer jobs.

If excessive job-changing has a deeply-rooted emotional cause, [3] expressed in the offender's restlessness, one would expect to find

[1] op. cit. [2] cf. also the 1949 Westfield College, Birmingham, inquiry '80,000 Adolescents', which reported that the average number of jobs held by 19-year-old boys who had left school at 14 was 2·62. S. and E. T. Glueck (op. cit.) report that four-fifths of juvenile delinquents changed their jobs frequently.

[3] The abnormality is indicated by the answers to a question: 'Do you feel you have settled into a job for life?' to which 41 per cent of the S.T.U. group answered 'no', compared with 18 per cent of the controls.

Kate Friedlander, in *The Psycho-Analytical Approach to Juvenile Delinquency* (Kegan Paul, 1947), p. 109, has an interesting observation on this point: '(The boy with anti-social character formation) must have satisfaction at once, and this desire will be strengthened by the fact that in an unsuitable job none of his instinctive energy will find a way into socially accepted channels. He will most probably get out of the job, try another one, find it equally unsatisfactory, and with this history will find it more and more difficult to secure a satisfactory position.'

evidence of it in other spheres of activity, at school or in the Army. The job-changers (those with four or more jobs) have been compared with the others to see whether they show a greater tendency to absence without leave, or to general Army offences, but the differences are not significant. They have also been compared in terms of the emotional types into which the whole group has been classified (Chapter X). The job-changers include more wanderers, as might be expected, but otherwise they are hardly distinguishable from the rest of the sample. Their school records, however, show a really significant difference: 81 per cent of the job-changers admitted to truancy compared with only 38 per cent of the others.[1] This establishes a link, though whether the truancy produces a backwardness that, in turn, causes a man to be dissatisfied with any job that is not suited to his undeveloped powers, or whether both derive from some primary restlessness is not clear from this evidence alone. Probably both factors are at work. What appears to happen is that a man will go for a job that seems likely to satisfy his emotional craving, as a driver or a sailor,[2] but is not necessarily suited to his innate ability. His backwardness is still there and in fact jobs of that type do nothing to remove it, and his emotional need is still unsatisfied. He therefore suffers from a double frustration.

It is curious that the job-changers did not show to any disadvantage in the Army, beside the other offenders. They certainly continued their escaping to the extent of an average of three absences per man, but they were not worse in this respect than most of the other offenders. Perhaps it is that unauthorized absence from the Army is the result of an emotional compulsion different from that of truancy or job-changing. In the one case the offender is cut off from his home; in the others he is not. The job-changers included more civilian delinquents than the rest of the group (55 per cent compared with 27 per cent). The inference is that job-changing is an important factor in the background of any abnormal group.

The degree of social standing of the offenders' families is not a factor that can be gauged from the present records with any exact-

---

[1] C. Lummis 'School Attendance, Employment and Army Records' (*British Journal of Educational Psychology*, Feb. 1946) writes: 'Truancy from school tends to foreshadow an indifferent civilian employment record.' 70 per cent of his truants among unfit men at an Army Selection Centre had been job-changers or repeatedly unemployed.

[2] D. H. Stott (op. cit.) writes: 'Among the very few types of employment which an acure "avoider" can tolerate is that of van-boy. With the constant jumping on and off the van, the bumping and jogging and the change of scene, it provides a ready-made restlessness.'

ness.   But the case histories do shed some light on the educational qualifications of the job-changers.   Here they prove to be even more backward than the rest of the offenders, 10 per cent more falling below the middle line of average attainment in the educational tests.   Perhaps a more important consideration is the extent to which their educational development lagged behind their capacity for learning, as measured by the intelligence test.   The job-changers do not show to any disadvantage alongside the others in intelligence, 52 per cent (against 53 per cent) falling below the mid-point of average ability.   But when one measures the lag of education behind intelligence (as expressed rather crudely in the six selection groups employed in Army ratings) and relates this to the number of jobs held, the result suggests that there is a positive correlation (the coefficient of correlation being $+ \cdot 28$).

Thus, to sum up from this evidence, there is a clear connexion between the tendency to truancy and the tendency to excessive job-changing, and between job-changing and civilian delinquencies, but job-changers do not appear to indulge in noticeably more unauthorized absence from the Army than other Army delinquents. There is also a tendency for the job-changing of a man to increase as the gap between his innate capacity for learning and his actual attainments widens.   This very backwardness is possibly connected with the boy's school truancies.

CHAPTER XVII

THE HOME TOWN

POVERTY has been held responsible for nearly all our social ills, including delinquency. J. H. Bagot in a Liverpool survey [1] concluded that juvenile delinquency is concentrated in a 'subnormal group of the working classes, one which is characterized above all by poverty'. To examine the homes and living conditions of two hundred young men and to assess the extent of poverty they endure would be a considerable undertaking in itself and is beyond the scope of the present inquiry, although contact was made with many of the homes. Sufficient is known of the men's home background to enable one to say that they came, almost without exception, from poor, sometimes the poorest homes (the men from middle-class homes number between 1 and 2 per cent). But since poverty is not confined to offenders' families, or so one is given to understand, it cannot be a sole cause (though see Appendix A for an estimate of the probable extent of delinquency among the lower social groups). One can but note it as a factor that must, at the very least, act as an irritant upon all the other background conditions, physical and mental.

The shock of first-hand acquaintance with slum conditions has prompted some social investigators to inquire how the inmates of such houses manage to retain any social morality at all. A visit to the home of one S.T.U. offender in the East End of London may be mentioned as an illustration.

The entrance to the house was through a broken door in a wall, across a yard littered with rubbish and dust and up to an open iron staircase which led to 'the flats'. On each level there was more rubbish, broken chairs and old boxes. One lavatory on the top floor served the whole of this tenement. It opened on to the iron landing; it was appallingly filthy and had to be flushed by pouring a bucket of water down the pan. The young soldier's home was near the top. The door opened into the living-room. The floors

[1] op. cit.

L

were uncovered boards. The wooden table in the middle of the room was covered with newspapers in readiness for the meal. There were two beds against the walls and much of the remaining floor space was taken up with wooden boxes of clothes and oddments. On the mantelpiece a cheap alarm clock was ticking. There were two brass candlesticks on either side of it with a little Union Jack flag sticking in each. On the wall was a large clock, such as are seen in shops, with an old enlarged photograph of the father in the uniform of a private of the first World War underneath the dial. In the only other room, the bedroom, was a large iron bedstead and two single beds. In this apartment dwelt a family of eight, the mother and father, two girls, one of them fourteen years old at that time, three boys and the S.T.U. man when he was on leave.

A home of this sort was admittedly not typical, though the size of the family was average for the group, but it was not at all exceptional judging by the homes which were visited by various members of the staff.

The authors of the *New Survey of London Life and Labour*[1] have considered the links between poverty and crime. They write (page 363, Vol. IX):

'A distinction was drawn in Volume III between "static" poverty arising from a low level of income, and "dynamic" poverty caused by a decreasing income, such, for example, as results from unemployment. The concurrent increases of unemployment and of crime in recent years are consistent with the view that it is with vicissitudes of employment, rather than of poverty, that the movement of crime is related.'

The *New Survey* undertook a five-fold classification of all London streets according to the social class of the residents, as follows:

(1) 'the lowest class of degraded or semi-criminal population',
(2) 'those living below Charles Booth's poverty line',
(3) 'the mass of unskilled labourers' (above the poverty line),
(4) 'skilled workers',
(5) the 'middle class' and above.

Street maps showing these classifications are published in the *New Survey*, and those S.T.U. offenders whose homes were in London have been grouped accordingly. The *New Survey* also shows the distribution of all arrests for indictable offences in 1929 in London streets and the proportions borne by this number to the populations

[1] Pub. P. S. King.

of the streets. Half the arrested persons came from unskilled, labouring or lower class streets. Only 8 per cent lived in middle class districts. Nearly a quarter came from the groups below the poverty line. Similar proportions were found amongst the S.T.U. offenders. When the arrests were represented as proportions of the population living in each class of street, the indices increased steadily from 6 per 10,000 in middle class streets to 41 per 10,000 in the lowest class streets.

The *New Survey* classification shows the social grouping of whole streets or parts of streets, but two factors must affect the relative poverty of the offenders' homes. One is the size of their families which are so much larger (an average of six children per family) than the average for all but the lowest class represented in the *New Survey* maps. This would naturally produce serious overcrowding, even in the average lower middle class home. The other factor was the large number of offenders who came from homes where the father was an invalid or dead or separated (40 per cent of the total) or frequently unemployed (16 per cent). This factor, too, would tend to add to the relative poverty of their homes. It is therefore probably no exaggeration to say that a majority of the offenders' families were living near the poverty line and that a very great majority were living in overcrowded and unsatisfactory homes. If unemployment is related to the incidence of crime, then the overcrowding that results from large families and the chronic illness of the breadwinner must be equally related.

There is a link between the size of the family and the truancies and job-changing habits of the S.T.U. men. It is not very marked but it is a factor in the causation of delinquency. When the records of those men coming from families of more than eight persons were compared with those of men from families of less than eight, they show to slight disadvantage in the proportions of truants, jobchangers, and civilian offenders. It seems likely that these factors are the outcome of a condition which was generated in a poor and overcrowded home.

E. C. Rhodes[1] has demonstrated that 'the extent of crime, juvenile and adult, appears to be associated with urbanization', and 'that the incidence of juvenile delinquency is greater in places where there is a larger proportion of juveniles in the population'. The tables he presents, taking the factual data from the annual

[1] E. C. Rhodes, 'Juvenile Delinquency', *Journal of the Royal Statistical Society*, Part III, 1939.

Criminal Statistics prepared by the Home Office, compare the incidence of crime in England and Wales under three physical divisions: (1) London (the Metropolitan and City Police areas), (2) all 'towns' of more than 40,000 inhabitants with separate police forces (unfortunately these exclude some of the large towns in one or two industrial counties, Durham for instance), and (3) small towns and the remainder of the country, under the heading of 'counties'.

The figures show that detected crime is more prevalent in the larger towns, and also in those counties, like Glamorgan and Durham, where the urban population is relatively greater.

The Army offenders have been grouped under the same three headings to see how far they correspond in proportions. Forty-two of the 86 'towns' are represented among the homes, and 25 of the 53 'counties'. Of the 227 men concerned in the count, 35 came from Scotland or Northern Ireland. The remainder were divided up as follows:

	London	*Towns*	*Counties*
	%	%	%
S.T.U. Offenders	26	41	33
All Juvenile Offenders[1]	19·4	41·3	39·3

It would require a total sample of several thousands to disclose reliable variations between separate towns and counties. The distribution of the figures for the S.T.U. men between London, Towns and Counties, however, follows the same general pattern as those for all juvenile offenders.

The S.T.U. men were asked to make maps of their home neighbourhoods, and small prizes of cigarettes were offered for the clearest and most detailed drawings. In nearly every case the most intelligent men produced the best maps. The dullards were often pathetically incapable of understanding the principles of a sketch in plan, or of proportions in diagrammatic representation. Their efforts consisted generally of a few lines for roads, coloured shading for houses or open spaces, and perhaps a building sketched in elevation. The slum dwellers were faced with the problem of reproducing continuous rows of houses with few other features to relieve the monotony. It was surprising how much of the local detail some of them were able to remember and many maps showed intricate mazes of streets and alleys, all named and marked with 'pubs',

---

[1] Number of persons under 17 years of age found guilty of indictable offences in courts of summary jurisdiction in England and Wales during 1936.

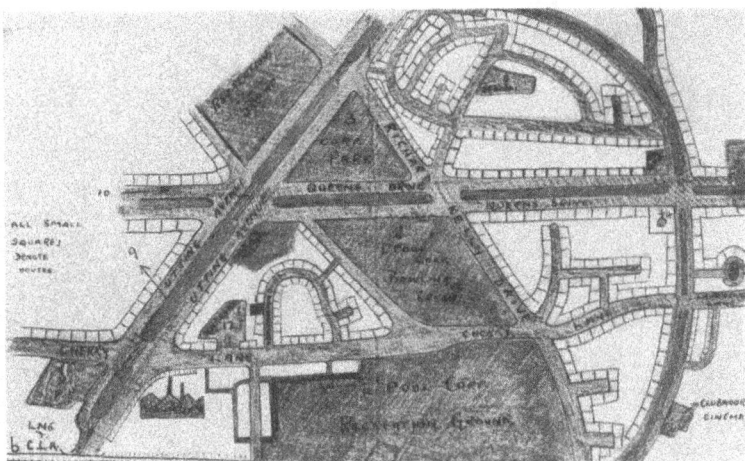

Drawn by man of high intelligence—good sense of plan, accurate spatial proportions; post–S.T.U. record unsatisfactory—11 convictions of absence without leave.

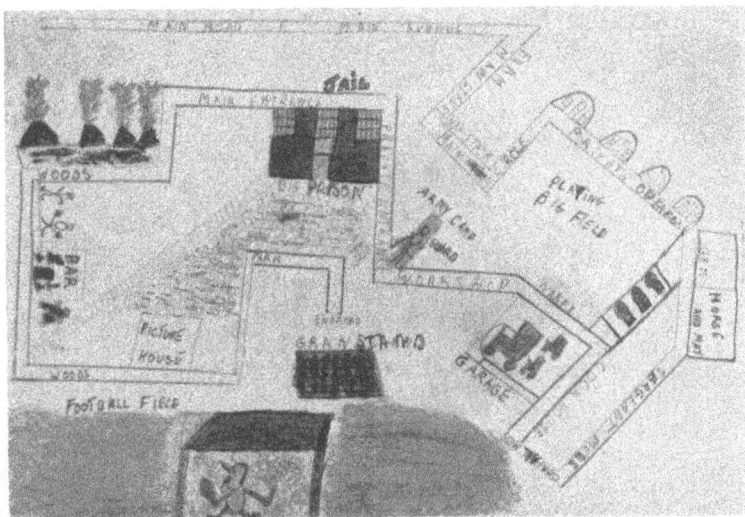

Drawn by man of low intelligence—plan and elevation confused, childish representation of footballer, trees, motors; he served sentence in jail so prominently depicted; criminal heredity; discharged from Army on receiving further sentence by civilian court.

'copper stations', schools, factories and shops. The open spaces were almost always remembered and clearly marked even when they were situated a long way from home, suggesting that they were much frequented and played an important part in their earlier lives.

Holidays

Holidays sometimes took these men, as youngsters, out of their gloomy surroundings. Very few could ever, during their childhood, look forward to an annual holiday at the seaside or in the country with parents or relations.[1] Some did not know what it was to see open fields until they were grown up:

'I never had no holidays. When I was at school, on my holidays I used to go to work every day with a milkman. I got up at 5 in the morning, and worked till 3 every day, 7 days a week, for five shillings a week. When I was finish work every day I would go home and scrub the house out. When the week end came round, on Sunday morning I got my pay, five shillings, I would give it to my mother and she would give me a tanner back. That's how I spent my holidays.'

Some were able to look back on a single trip to the seaside, the memory of which still shone brightly, so that even those who would stumble and halt in writing a letter home were able to describe that journey with excited words:

'It is August and we are all excited because tomorrow morning we are going on our first holiday. Well, there is no sleep that night and we are all up early in the morning and dont eat our breakfast, that is somethin unusual. Well, there are about 300 of us, all boys between 12 and 16. This is my first time and our destination is Dymchurch on the coast of Kent. . . .'

Some of the bolder spirits spent their time with gangs of lads, occasionally making expeditions into the surrounding country, 'scrumping' orchards, and raiding farms, but more often roaming the streets or frequenting a corner of waste ground. Sometimes, even if the home was poor, the children would get an annual holiday by saving through a school fund:

'As far back as I can remember my first happy memory was when

[1] The authors of *Our Towns—a Close-up* (Oxford University Press) write: 'His playground is the street; it is there that he spends his holidays to judge from the fact that two out of three of the 400 children in the same sample had not been away from home for as much as a week in the past 12 months. . . . he is in surroundings where all pleasures cost money; theft offers adventures where no other adventure is.'

I went on holiday to Blackpool with the school. Before we could go we each had to pay our fare to the school teacher. This cost I think about 4/11. It was fun doing this, saving our Friday six-pences and odd halfpennies, and so on. Well, on the great day we all tripped down to the station with our parents who came to see us off. We all got on the train after a lot of bustling about and shouting, where's Billy and where's Joan and so on. Well, I think most of us got the nearest seat to the window and I for myself was looking through all the way to Blackpool. It was only a three hour run from where I live but I thought I was going to the end of the world. I think the reason for that was that the farthest I had ever been before was a 1d bus ride.'

A number of the Londoners went hop-picking with their parents. Some of their happiest recollections were of a day or a brief holiday spent away with one or other of their parents. To have Dad in a holiday mood, without the cares and fatigue and the bad temper and the rowings, and to be taken for a special treat, that was an occasion always to be remembered. It did not matter whether the objective was a Cup-Final match, or a trip on the river steamer to Southend, or an excursion to Blackpool. The immediate response of the child shows only too clearly how different might have been some of their subsequent stories had something of the holiday mood entered occasionally into their daily lives. On holiday everything was new and wonderful to the child's eyes. And when the scene was indeed beautiful and the youngster un-usually observant, the resulting picture was something rare:

On the day fixed for my visit we set off for Harlech in the early afternoon. On the way over I noticed particularly the absence of trees and hedges, but as we drew nearer the outskirts of the town we felt a strange silence over us, and on entering the town itself we were aston-ished to find that nearly everyone in the town lived as simply as it was possible. There was not a sign of a pretentious building to be seen for a good way. On asking the way to the castle we were directed down a very old-fashioned street with its cobbles dating back several hundred years. When we actually saw the castle we were not disappointed because after all it has dignity and charm about it. It stood by itself with green fields on the right side of it, the Irish Sea at the back of it, and the town of Harlech itself at the front and on the left hand side. We did not go into the castle as the day was drawing to a close, and it was with a small pang of regret we left this simple community where everything was peaceful and quiet to return to my own home which is in Middlesbrough among the roar and bustle of the traffic and the smoke and grime from the factories.

CHAPTER XVIII

CIVILIAN TROUBLES

ONE-THIRD (36 per cent) of the Special Training Unit sample had been convicted of indictable offences before coming into the Army. Rather less than half of these had been bound over, put on probation or fined for a first offence, and had kept fairly clear of further trouble. The rest had been persistent offenders. Altogether, the records showed that 12 per cent (10·5 per cent in the larger sample of 700) had been sent to approved schools, and 3·3 per cent to Borstal (4·3 per cent in the larger sample) for repeated offences. Some had been to both, and the proportion of men who had been to one or other institution is 14·3 per cent. These are minimal figures but it is unlikely that more than 15 per cent had been to one or other place.

Local civilians dubbed the S.T.U. men 'the Borstal boys', but it is perhaps a tribute to the work of Borstal institutions that so few of their old boys found their way to Special Training Units. There is no record of the number of ex-Borstal men entering the Army. There were mass discharges from Borstal institutions in 1939, and making rough calculations from the numbers discharged over the previous years in various age-groups, and from the fact that 72 per cent of those on licence were in the Forces in 1944, it is estimated that about 3,000 ex-Borstal men between 18 and 20 years of age (corresponding to the group of S.T.U. offenders) may have been in the Army at the time of this inquiry. Some would have been serving sentences of detention, but the total number of young soldiers (under 21 years) in detention at this date was between 500 and 700, though they were mostly serving short sentences of 28 days or less. But even assuming that the proportion of ex-Borstal men in detention barracks was three or even four times as great as at special training units, the great majority must have remained clear of serious trouble.

Gangs

Many offenders come before the courts in company with other youngsters, and when two or more are involved it is usual to refer to the offence as a 'gang' crime. The Home Office inquiry[1] finds that nearly three-quarters of recorded juvenile offences are committed with others, and the same source quotes a Metropolitan Police District return[2] for 1938 showing 65·8 per cent of the offences committed in gangs. Other inquiries[3] show large proportions. From these rather startling facts investigators have concluded that gangs are responsible for much of the crime, and Bagot speaks of 'group influence . . . which most frequently results in wrongdoing'.

The S.T.U. men were questioned about their youthful associations. Two out of every three (65 per cent) had regularly played or gone on expeditions with groups of boys; 24 per cent had associated with gangs of boys to the exclusion of girls. If gangs are responsible for wrongdoing one would expect the men concerned to show to disadvantage in their records of offences. Yet when their records of school truancy, civilian offences and numbers of Army offences are compared with those of the others in the group, the gang-associates show a similar proportion of truancy, but a clear advantage in the incidence of civilian offences and also in Army offences; 37 per cent of the gang-associates were truants compared with 35 per cent amongst those without gang associations; civilian delinquents number 35 per cent among them, compared with 44 per cent, and persistent Army offenders 27 per cent compared with 39 per cent. Further analysis of the cases who associated with boys to the exclusion of girls shows about the same proportion of civilian offenders as those without gang associations, but much fewer persistent Army offenders. Perhaps the gang-associates found it easier to grow into an Army group than the others and so were less inclined to rebel against it. One can only argue from these findings that the S.T.U. offenders who associated with gangs were no worse and perhaps a little better than the others.

It seems that the temporary associations young men form in committing offences like shop-breaking, house-breaking, thefts of bicycles, etc., are often only alliances of convenience, and are not necessarily the same groupings as the gangs or 'clicks' (as they are

[1] op. cit.

[2] 'Metropolitan Police District, Arrests for Indictable Offences in 1938, with particular reference to persons under 21 years of age, S.2 Branch, 21 Feb. 1939.'

[3] *Report of the London County Council's School Medical Officer* (1930, Vol. II, Part II) speaks of 50 per cent of the thefts by boys being committed in gangs. J. H. Bagot, *Juvenile Delinquency in Liverpool* (Cape 1941), quotes similar proportions amongst boys in Liverpool.

called in London) formed by youngsters in the streets and waste grounds of our cities. These gangs often got into mischief but they were not formed for wrongdoing and may even absorb in harmless activities some of the adolescent stirrings that would otherwise lead to wrongdoing. Judging by the descriptions of some of the men, the gang seemed to satisfy some deep emotional need. It had the elements of a club and of a secret society. The youngster would often become attached to his mate or to the gang because of his starved emotional condition. Within the gang opportunities arose for adventure and accomplishments that could not be tackled single-handed. One lad might prove a foil to another. Deft fingers in one could be employed by a clever head on another. The leader would find opportunities for leadership. And most would find substitutions for the disappointments and bitterness of home life. The attachments were strong, as the following sad story suggests:

'This was my first unpleasant recollection, and I can remember it as if it appened yesterday. Just befor I left school I was looking forward to going for a bick ride with my brother and my mates and I had just gon down the street for my mother and they went and left me and I spent all that day by myself.'

One typical London 'click' consisted of five youngsters, aged 12 to 17. They usually met in the evenings in a small piece of waste ground surrounded by high advertisement hoardings. They had made an entrance by pulling out a loose board, which they carefully replaced after they had gone into the ground. The little triangle of waste land was strewn with rubbish and fouled with human and animal excrement. In one corner, the boys had constructed a lean-to shelter of pieces of wood covered with sheets of poster paper, many layers thick, peeled off the hoardings near-by. In the shelter they would pass round cigarettes and smoke and chat. Sometimes they would bring girls in, some of them as young as eight, but that would only happen when one or two of them were around. From the full 'click' girls were excluded. On Saturdays they went over to watch the local football team. Two or three nights a week they went to the pictures together. Days, weeks might pass and they would commit no worse offence than trespass. Then, if they got bored, they might suddenly appear in a street and play practical jokes on the residents—tying up door-knockers, throwing pebbles through letter-boxes, putting low trip strings across gateways, or the favourite trick of booby-trapping passers-by by putting a paper parcel in the middle of the pavement and pulling it away with a string when the victim bent down to pick it up. They might seize a cat and tie a bag on its head or cans to its tail. In their own street they played games together—street cricket, using a piece of flat board for a bat and the base of the lamp-post for a wicket, or street football, with a tennis ball and two stones in the roadway to mark the goal.

'Billy-Billy-Horney' was a favourite game. This is a vaulting game played with at least three a side. The leaders toss for turns and the losing team make a 'crocodile' at right angles to the wall. Each man bends over double and holds the haunches of the man in front; the first man holds on to the wall or fence. The boys on the other side then run up in turn, vaulting on to the back of the 'crocodile', leaping as far forward as they can. When the whole side is mounted they cry out 'Billy-Billy-Horney one-two-three, all o-o-o-ver', to the following tune:

Billy-Billy Horney one-two-three all o--ver

If the 'crocodile' collapsed under the strain, or any of the vaulting side fell off or touched the ground their side lost the game.

The gangs' practical jokes sometimes got them into trouble, and they would naturally become objects of suspicion to local residents and to the police. Here, for instance, is an account of a practical joke that went too far:

'I never hardly went away from home for my holiday. With living in a big town I was always satisfied and me and a few of the lads used to have a good time in our way but it used to sometimes lead into a lot of trouble such as going into a corner shop and seeing a stack of biscuit tins, pushing them all down and make a run for it. I remember one Sunday night about four of us walked into a shop and we never bothered to knock on the counter in case the shop keeper came out and there was lots of different kinds of chocolate and sweets on the counter. Anyway we started to fill our pockets with them and decided to go. We got outside and just ready to go on our way when one of the lads decided to go back and take some more. Well, we waited at the corner of the street and he wasnt satisfied with a couple of blocks of chocolate he had to take the lot and knock a big glass case over, so you can see how much we run.' The choice of shop is interesting, a corner shop obviously being more isolated. The mixture of facetiousness ('we never bothered to knock on the counter'), fear ('how much we run') and destructiveness ('knock a big glass case over') is typical.

Several of the gangs made excursions outside the towns:

I used to look forward to the holidays because I used to go out with a gang of boys, and we used to go swimming, cycling, walking and many other things, and I enjoyed myself a lot. In summer we always used to go swimming in what we nicknamed the Blue Waters, because the water looked a deep blue, it was surrounded by fields which are filled with ferns, and in the summer months we used to get a lot of fun out of setting fire to the grass, no one used to bother about it, I dont know why, but the farmers never used to bother at all and they used to watch us do it. On Good Fridays we used to go up the Pike, there was an old castle there, and there also used to be a fair there and we used to have a smashing time on this day. As I got older I was getting worse and worse. I started boozing and I got into stealing and when I was. 17 I was punished for it.

Many of their activities were harmless enough:

We went to the beaches every day and played football on the sands, bathed in the water and the best about it we had a tent on the beach and we used to sleep in it for a few days. When we finished our grub we used to go home for some more and some money as well. All of the lads and I had a good time. We cooked all of our own stuff and we went for our suppers to the cafe on the prominard. We did that every holiday until the war started and they took our tent off the beach but we will get it back after the war and I hope we can do the same again.

Some of the Glasgow and Liverpool gangs were quite different. Many of these men still felt that they owed an allegiance to their gang. They had an alert awareness of things, derived from life on the street corners, and they were inclined to strike before they thought. One fellow, for example, explained his absences by saying:

If I go home on leave and get with my pals I don't come back. I am out every night with the boys and our greatest fun is street fighting. I run about with an organised gang named the Bath Boys and we all have very good times, if we have no money we all stay at the corner and sing songs and they are all party songs, and if we get fed up we all got together and went down to some other mob and had a good battle with pint pots and bayonets, and if any of us got hurt it was just a laughing matter.

The 'Bath Boys' were Orangemen and no doubt their songs lauded William III and were intended to incite the opposing Catholic gangs. Loyalty to some of the gangs was enforced and if any man betrayed or stole from another member of the gang he had good reason to be afraid. One such young Glaswegian came to the Education Staff room one evening and told a long story of the theft of several thousand clothing coupons from a member of his father's gang. He greatly feared going home on leave, yet had nowhere else to go. The next morning his mind was quite unbalanced and he had to be removed to a mental hospital. His mental disorder was probably long-standing and derived from some much earlier source, but he was not alone in fearing the gang's displeasure and his concern was real.

To sum up, the gang may vary from a harmless holiday group to a fanatical secret society exacting lifetime loyalties. Though it usually led to pranks and mischief, and sometimes to serious trouble, it also offered the disgruntled youngster an outlet for his energies, a rudimentary social discipline, a sense of comradeship, and a substitute for a defective home.

CHAPTER XIX

LEISURE ACTIVITIES

A CASUAL visitor to the Education Centre at the Special Training Unit might have seen, almost any evening, a number of young men working at rug-making, carpentry, leatherwork, sketching, embroidering their regimental badge designs, and a great many other crafts. What industrious, resourceful fellows they are, he might declare. He would be somewhat misled, for such activities as were in progress were the result of much inducement. They had no idea how to occupy their spare time; they needed constant help and encouragement to start anything, and could not stick at it for long. We tried to stimulate their interest in hobbies by putting out handicraft displays, bringing in professional instructors, and having a panel of staff helpers who came in every evening to help with practical work. Once a week during duty hours they were encouraged to start up some recreational activity in the hope that they would carry on in their spare time. Many started but few finished anything.

Handicraft materials were sold to the men on credit at cost price. They paid by small instalments on pay days. Nearly every man in the unit bought something. Whenever a new consignment of leather, for instance, came in they would crowd round the office and buy sometimes whole skins. But when it was found that so much of the material was being wasted, indiscriminate buying was discouraged. A typical conversation was:

'Are you sure that you want a whole sheepskin?' the educational instructor would inquire.

'Yes, of course. I'll pay for it.'

'We're not worrying about that, but have you made anything in leather before?'

'No, but I want to make a handbag—like that one you showed us.'

'Well, don't you think it would be better to let us help you make something smaller to begin with, like a purse, and then if you manage that all right you can go on to the bag?'

'No, I want to make the handbag now.'

'All right, but you only need half a skin for one bag.'

'I'll take the whole skin. I might make another bag after this one.' So the skin would be bought on a wave of good intentions, and one would have to suggest a pattern, mark it out, cut it out and begin the stitching or thonging. The man would probably then ask the instructor to keep it safely for him, and it would be labelled and stacked away with the many others on the shelves. There it would probably remain, unclaimed and forgotten, until we sought out the purchaser or released him from his contract.

The men were questioned about their hobbies as youngsters. As many as 68 per cent said they had no pastime of any sort (compared with only 20 per cent of the control groups). They watched or played games on Saturday afternoons, and went to the pictures two or three times a week, but they had no private hobby with which to occupy their leisure hours after school or work. One might speculate on the reasons—the lack of facilities in poor homes, discouragement by the parents, a preference for going out into the street or open space to play with other boys, or a condition of mind that prevented their settling to any activity for long. Whatever the initial cause, the result was still painfully evident in the Army. One man described the general attitude when he wrote:

'I was a fellow in civvy life that did not have any particular sort of hobby, as I was always looking for something new with which to occupy my mind.'

The hobbies that were mentioned by the 32 per cent were mostly carpentry or some other handwork for which few would have had the tools or benches in their homes, and it is doubtful whether more than a handful of the whole sample had any regular, serious hobby.

Looking over the histories of the men without hobbies one finds that civilian offenders were twice as common among them as among those with hobbies. Persistent Army offenders, too, were nearly twice as numerous among them. Thus, there is a link between delinquency and the want of hobbies, though its direction is not easy to determine. It may be that the restlessness already associated with delinquency prevents a man settling to any pastime; or, less likely, the boredom that comes from inactivity may induce him to find outlets for his pent-up energies in unlawful behaviour; or both factors may operate.

Sports

The offenders watched and played games. They played much

more than they watched. Every other man played football; one in four played cricket. Next in popularity was swimming (16 per cent), then boxing, and one or two mentioned cycling and hockey. They watched the same sports, and in the same order of preference, except that visits to 'the dogs' occupied the Saturday afternoons of about 8 per cent. A relatively large proportion (43 per cent, cf. 31 per cent of the controls) said that they used to place bets on dogs or horses.

Social Clubs

It is often suggested that boys' clubs and social organizations like the Boy Scouts and the Boys' Brigade keep youngsters out of trouble by occupying their spare time, and positively, by moral training and precept. That being so, one would expect to find fewer offenders among club members. On the other hand, youth groups and clubs may appeal most strongly to those who are unable to find satisfactory occupation in their own homes and to that extent offenders might be attracted to such organizations. That is particularly true of the homeless boys who are numerous among offenders. The evidence of earlier surveys is wildly contradictory,[1] but the findings of the Home Office Inquiry of 1942 suggest that nearly half the young offenders (from 'normal' homes; the method employed limits the sample for purposes of reference) have been

[1] The *Report on Juvenile Delinquency*, 1920, produced by a Committee appointed by the Home Secretary, found that only 4.46 per cent of the offenders were members of a club at the time of the inquiry. Club facilities have obviously been considerably extended since that time, but the figure still seems extraordinarily low compared with those in more recent inquiries. W. L. Chinn, 'A Brief Survey of Nearly One Thousand Juvenile Delinquents' in Birmingham, *British Journal of Educational Psychology*, Vol. VIII, Pt. I (Feb. 1938) states that 61·2 per cent of delinquents compared with 31·2 per cent among non-delinquents belonged to social clubs.

J. H. Bagot, op. cit., finds that 1 per cent of the Liverpool offenders in 1936 were club members when the count was taken, compared with 24 per cent amongst the general population of 8–16 years.

In the Home Office inquiry, op. cit., Rhodes has distinguished between regular and nominal, and previous and present membership of clubs, an important distinction, because it had been claimed that offenders did not stay in clubs. Thus Healy and Bronner, op. cit., say that delinquents have irregular and short-lived membership because they are 'more outgoing and active', and they quote 'prior club membership' among 47 out of a delinquent sample of 105, compared with 28 in the controls.

Rhodes finds, in London and provincial towns combined, 31 per cent delinquents with regular or nominal club membership at the time of the count (cf. 35 per cent in the controls) and 13 per cent with previous membership (cf. 12 per cent) totalling 44 per cent (cf. 47 per cent). Unfortunately, these figures only refer to men from 'normal' homes (only 40 per cent of the total group).

members of social organizations at some time or other, and their non-delinquent coevals only slightly more. Just under half the S.T.U. sample (49 per cent) claimed to have belonged to a social organization at some time or other, and the more commonly named were:

Percentages of whole group claiming membership of:

	%
Boy Scouts	19
Boys' Clubs	14
Boys' Brigade	9
Snooker and billiard clubs	9

There was a little duplication of membership, so that these figures are not quite exclusive. One man had belonged to five organizations and several had attended two or three. Snooker and billards clubs have been counted as social clubs because many of them do offer facilities for other social activities. Boxing and football clubs have not been counted as clubs in this sense. In cases where the length of membership was known it would appear that nearly half the men belonged to a club for less than a year. At the age of, say, 15 it is doubtful whether more than 25 per cent of our offenders belonged to a club, and those who did would not have been members for long. The corresponding estimated figure for the general youth population is 44 per cent.

The Cinema

In contrast to the sordidness of home life, the exposure of the street corner and the boredom of leisure hours, the cinema offered a world of warmth, shielding darkness and make-believe. Is it any wonder that the offenders visited the cinema frequently and, once inside, usually stayed there as long as they could? The average attendance for all the men was 2·7 times a week (cf. average of 1·1 visits per week among the controls), and nearly one-third went more often, some as many as seven times a week.[1]

[1] Healy and Bronner, op. cit., find 88 delinquents (out of 105) with regular cinema attendance, against 42 in the control group, and 33 with excessive attendance, against 10. The terms 'regular' and 'excessive' are not defined, so comparisons are impossible, but the figures show the general tendency. A recent study of the leisure interests of 500 A.T.S., for instance (J. W. Reeves and Patrick Slater, *Occupational Psychology*, July 1947) showed 28 per cent of the girls as having a definite interest in the cinema.

The figures quoted by Albert Royds ('Report on an Enquiry into the Relationship of Juvenile Delinquency and Environment in an Industrial Town', 1936) relating to Oldham, are rather mystifying, for only 17 per cent of the offenders and 20 per cent of the control cases visited the cinema twice a week or more.

(*Continued opposite*)

So strong was the urge to go to 'the pictures' that some of the men would take on a spare-time job to pay for their admission:

'I remember from when I was nine years of age when I was working at a butcher's shop every week end to get my pocket money to go to the pictures with.'

As with many of the other questions on the questionnaires, the answers to the inquiry about visits to the cinema were checked by means of private interviews with some of the men, and discussions in class meetings. They were asked, for example, how they managed to find the money to go to the cinema three times a week. The answers were varied and interesting. Some worked at odd jobs; some got the money from their parents; some made money by fantastic schemes—like tearing up marble slabs from graves in the cemeteries and selling them to monumental masons; some knew the usherettes or bribed them; and some simply went in by one of the emergency exits. Evidence of the influence the film exerted on these men is afforded by the attendances at the S.T.U. exhibitions of films, and the men's reactions. There was only a silent projector available, and the films were early Charlie Chaplins and early romances like *Metropolis* or *The Lost World*, but the shows were always packed and were the subject of much discussion.

Reading and Study

With so many semi-illiterates amongst them one would hardly expect to find the habit of reading for pleasure very widespread. It is rather surprising that 31 per cent claimed to have belonged to a local lending library at some time or other (the proportion in the adult population is 25 per cent at any one time, but over several years many more would have been members). In their earlier youth, three-quarters (74 per cent) said they had read books and of these two-thirds mentioned their reading matter as 'Westerns', murder stories or thrillers. These proportions bear no relation to the numbers of men who read books at the unit—for though the Education Centre had a branch of the County Library for ticket issues, and several cases of varied books accessible to all in the recreation rooms, only a minority attempted to borrow a book. Many must have lost the habit of reading after leaving school (see Chapter XIII).

Various youth surveys ('Eighty Thousand Adolescents', Birmingham, 1950; Midlothian Education Committee, 'Survey of the Sixteens', 1942; 'A Youth Inquiry', BBC, 1951) and the *Board of Trade Journal*, 25 Nov. 1950, have shown that on average the younger generation attend the cinema between 1·1 and 1·3 times per week.

M

Systematic study of any subject was even less common. Only 14 per cent (cf. 40 per cent controls) had attended evening school or followed up any favourite line of instruction through private reading. Yet it could not be said that they disliked education as such. In the education sessions at the S.T.U. they were willing and active co-operators, and when they were asked, in a questionnaire, what form of training they preferred at the unit, education was named most often. The cynic might retort that they simply preferred sitting on their behinds to marching or drilling. Fortunately there is evidence to the contrary.

Other Activities

If these men were so devoid of resources, so inactive, how did they fill in their spare time, one might inquire, apart from their visits to the cinema? Many did not manage to fill it in at all and were bored and restless. 'Did you have too much spare time?' they were asked; exactly half said 'yes'. 'And did it get you into trouble?' ran the next question, and nearly a third answered that it did.

It is not generally realized how few opportunities there are for the poor city lad to meet his girl friend in privacy and comfort. Even if he were not too shy to ask the girl into his home, there would in most cases be no facility for conversation and certainly no privacy. They may try to find a park bench or risk a chill by sitting on damp grass, but most of the public parks are closed at dusk except where—one of the benefits of the War—park railings have been removed. So, apart from indiscriminate flirting on the street corner, young people can only seek each other's company in the dance hall, and for intimacy they must find a dark doorway or a cul-de-sac.

Dancing occupied the time of some 44 per cent of the S.T.U. men (compared with 51 per cent of the controls). On analysis, the dancers showed almost exactly the same incidence of civilian and persistent Army offenders as those who could not dance.

Sunday is a grey, comfortless day in big towns. Shops and funfairs are closed and often shuttered. Few cafés are open and the streets are often deserted. There are no street traders or hawkers, except an occasional vendor of shell-fish or muffins for Sunday tea; no markets, and the dirt and waste paper of Saturday's trading only add to the impression of dreariness. It seems that time passed slowly for the S.T.U. men on Sundays. A few of them (5 per cent) were working at paper rounds or milk deliveries, one or two went out with their girl friends; rather more (11 per cent) played football or cricket. Some (17 per cent) spent most of the day in bed, getting up about mid-afternoon. Others went to the cinema and nearly half (42 per cent) went to church.[1] The greatest number (59 per cent) spent much of the day out of doors, in parks or open spaces, often with friends, roaming, exploring and getting 'up to larks'. One man protested aptly:

'I played in the Park. They should have had some place for us to play for we had a long walk to the park and when we played in the streets we would have got into trouble.'

Rhodes has constructed an interesting table in *Young Offenders*, showing the proportions of offences committed during the hours in 'which, by all reasonable standards, a boy should be within the control of his parents or guardians'. The 'curfew' hours vary according to age and to the time of year, from 5 p.m. for the younger boys in January to 10 o'clock for older boys in June. The Metropolitan Police records disclose that about one-third of the offences occurred within this restricted period. There are no exactly comparable figures for the S.T.U. sample showing how their hours of play varied with the seasons, but they were asked to state how late they usually stayed out at night. If one measures these times against the extreme limit of Dr. Rhodes' 'curfew', 10 p.m., it is found that 71 per cent of the S.T.U. men stayed out later (cf. 30 per cent among the control groups), some to 12 o'clock and even beyond. Only about one-quarter said that their parents raised any objection to their late hours. This suggests strongly that many of the parents were indifferent to their children's needs or were unable to exercise sufficient control over them.

The greatest number of youthful offences are petty larcenies and many of these take place in shops that display their goods within reach of young people. Those who argue that lack of pocket money is a cause of delinquency might paint a touching picture of pinched and hungry faces peering over the brightly lighted counters, or of noses pressed against sweet-shop windows. Yet when the S.T.U. men were questioned about the amount of pocket money they received as children, it appeared that the big majority (86 per cent)

[1] The authors of *Young Offenders* give 50 per cent regular, nominal or previous church attendance in London, and 67 per cent in provincial towns, but again these only represent the offenders in 'normal' homes. Healy and Bronner (op. cit.) found 44 per cent attending church (61 per cent among the controls).

had been given some regular sum of money to spend, and in half the cases it amounted to more than 1/6 a week. Perhaps a majority of these, however, earned the money by work on paper or milk rounds, handing over most of it to their parents.[1] Surely, in pre-War days when sweets were unrationed and cost only fourpence a quarter-pound, this was a reasonable sum for a youngster? The 28 cases who did not get pocket money deserve attention. Four or five were orphanage boys; one or two were evidently treated harshly at home and in their cases pocket money was withheld. In the rest of these cases, dire need was an apparent cause. It can be no coincidence that in every case of hardship except three the home was also defective because of the separation of parents, or gross neglect of the child.

After leaving school they seemed to have more money to spend, and only 4 per cent said that they did not keep enough of their earnings to pay for their amusements.

A question that produced some surprising replies was: 'What was your greatest fun or thrill?' 'Diving into the Victoria Canal and discovering a corpse', wrote one. 'Being suspended sixty feet up in the air on a crane hook for half an hour', or 'Going to sea on a raft', were other obvious thrills. Apart from such novelties, there were a number of socially interesting stories. 'Fighting with gangs with weapons', 'murder games', or 'watching drunk men fighting', to mention only a few. One man who showed very little apparent abnormality replied: 'clouting girls with a regimental cane', and a cockney who later came to no good said 'riding on a street trader's horse collecting jamjars'. A number mentioned their associations with women, but the most common thrills were those connected with competitive sports.

There are sadistic touches in these stories and recollections of wild encounters with police or rival gangs, but most were harmless enough. And one is left with an impression only of inactivity and boredom alternating with fits of restlessness and wild adventure, a mode of behaviour that we have already seen repeated in the spheres of employment and military service.

---

[1] Rhodes, op. cit., finds 7·3 per cent of the cases receiving no pocket money, compared with 6·7 per cent among the controls. 'There is certainly no evidence suggesting that delinquents as a group suffer from lack of pocket money, nor is there evidence that they enjoy an abundance,' he writes.

CHAPTER XX

SCHOOL DAYS

A QUESTIONNAIRE on school days was answered by the group of S.T.U. men and by the control group.

Comparison of the figures for the two groups reveals a distinct and consistent difference between their school experiences. The answers to the first question, 'Did you like school?' show that more of the S.T.U. (29 per cent) than of the control group (18 per cent) had unhappy memories of school. This general impression is supported with remarkable uniformity in the answers to all the more detailed queries with a relevant bearing. More of S.T.U. than of control group men (27 per cent cf. 8 per cent) did not like their lessons and similar proportions (26 per cent cf. 11 per cent) disliked their teachers. The answers to the questions on school work confirm the general dislike expressed in the replies to the first three, and, indeed, give a good reason for this dislike. The proportion of the S.T.U. group who found school work (or some of it) hard is three times that of the other group (43 per cent cf. 13 per cent). The corresponding results for the two questions dealing specifically with any difficulties found in arithmetic and writing maintain the same tendency (48 per cent of the offenders, cf. 27 per cent of controls, found arithmetic difficult to pick up, and 34 per cent cf. 13 per cent of controls, had trouble with their writing). There is, however, agreement between the two groups that arithmetic holds more terrors than does writing for the human young. This is probably explained by the fact that, in writing you do achieve your own standard—however poor—but, in arithmetic, you are confronted with an array of hurdles that must be either cleared or failed.[1]

The question 'How many classes from the top were you on leaving school?' may be a little confusing, as some attended only primary while others went on to secondary schools, but the figures, showing a relatively higher proportion of the S.T.U. group leaving

[1] D. H. Stott (op. cit.) found several cases of dislike of arithmetic among his sample of boys in an approved school and suggests that it may be symptomatic of the delinquent state.

in the lower classes (55 per cent cf. 26 per cent among the controls), agree with the general impression from the other questions.

The consistency of the difference between the two groups maintained in the answers to those six questions—all associated with school progress—places their general significance beyond reasonable doubt. The S.T.U. men were abnormally backward at school. It was natural that fewer than normal of them should have pleasant impressions from school days; the life of the class dunce is seldom joyful. This account, by the men themselves, of their performance at school is, of course, only what one might have expected from their backwardness at the S.T.U.

Backwardness at school may be due either to poor attendance or to some defect, such as low intelligence, deafness or bad eyesight, preventing the child benefiting from instruction. If one consults the questionnaire for some light on the cause of the relative backwardness of the S.T.U. men, the figures for absence stand out conspicuously. The percentage (46)[1] of the S.T.U. group admitting frequent absence due to ill health is three times as big as that of the control (13), and the former can boast a four to one superiority in the relative number of truants (57 per cent to 15 per cent).[2] This amount of absence must have constituted a major cause of backwardness. The irregular attender loses the continuity of learning and usually fails to keep up with the work of the class. The teacher of a large class of uneven attainment finds it impossible, without neglecting the main body, to meet the needs of either extreme. The bright ones chafe at the slowness of the pace, 'too easy, time was wasted waiting for the rest to catch up', one man writes. At the same time, the backward pupils give up the struggle (if, indeed, they do struggle) in despair. Mac, already introduced, writes, 'I did not like school because I do not know much. I was always in trouble with the teachers so I did not take much interest. The day just would not go quick enough.' Most of the men described school life as boring or monotonous; 'it was monotonous', 'Very boring, the same thing every day' and 'it was too boring being in a

---

[1] Cf. C. Lummis, 'The Relation of School Attendance to Employment Records, Etc.' (*British Journal of Educational Psychology*, Feb. 1946); 19 per cent of his 1,000 cases from an Army Selection Centre (to which men who were unfit in one way or another, or of very poor quality generally, were sent) had irregular school attendances through illness.

[2] Lummis records 8 per cent only, but his standard of 'irregularity' is: missing 20 per cent of possible school attendances. S. and E. T. Glueck (op. cit.) say that two-thirds of their young offenders had been truants from school.

classroom all day', were typical remarks, all expressing the plight of children who have fallen behind and lost interest in the lessons. And Mac's '—always in trouble—' describes the certain fate of the bored child in school.

The backward child who is put back into a younger class does (despite some disadvantages) gain another opportunity to make good. But, when movement is by age alone, the effect of a temporary lapse may be cumulative, with the chance of recovery diminishing as the pupil gets more and more out of his depth. Some of the most backward men had this experience of tailing along hopelessly for the greater part of their school lives. It is not difficult to imagine the development of a vicious spiral of backwardness and truancy. One man writes that he was 'away from school on every opportunity', another played truant because 'the school was too strict'. Some replies showed the importance of the parents' attitude: 'I didn't like going but was forced to', and 'I did not like school but the old man would not like me staying at home, so I had to go'.

Interest is given to the unusually high proportion of school-time truants among the S.T.U. group by the fact that, in the Army, absence was their commonest offence. It was possible to obtain figures for the investigation of the army absences of nearly all those admitting frequent truancy at school. One-third of them had become persistent absentees, and most of the rest had been absent occasionally.[1] Although these figures are very much higher than one would expect in a normal unit, they are almost identical with the corresponding proportions for those who were not truants at school. So that, while the S.T.U. had abnormally high records of both truancy and army absence, the truants themselves did not show an incidence of army absence higher than their fellows.

We have seen how the S.T.U. men fared with the heavier subjects in the curriculum. The figures for participation in handicrafts and games show close agreement between the two groups. Although as many as 85 per cent of the S.T.U. group claim to have learned some form of handicrafts, few of them developed a hobby after leaving school. They nearly all liked their school handicrafts: 'There was not enough woodwork for the boys', expressed a common feeling. 'The best thing I ever learned was the handicrafts'

[1] C. Lummis concludes (op. cit.) that 'truancy from school tends to foreshadow a much worse Army Conduct Record than is shown by men with good school attendance.'

—from a man who was a keen worker in the handicrafts centre and who had developed hobbies from the stimulus of school.

About ninety per cent of both groups took part in their school games, and enjoyed them. One man replied: 'I liked them but thought it clever to dodge.' There are probably few schools without a few such uncompromising young souls—despising the sacrifice of principle to pleasure.

Both groups agreed very closely in their answers to the question: 'Was your school building pleasant inside?' The answers did, however, reveal that the pupils were by no means indifferent to either the comfort or the appearance of the school. The figures (20 per cent unpleasant) suggest that criticism was by no means harsh. 'Very grim', 'The school was falling to pieces', 'Too crowded', '—— cold in winter' and 'a shambles', are some of the descriptions given by the minority who thought that the school buildings were not what they might have been.

The question on distance of school from home brought out a considerable divergence between the two groups, but one cannot attach weight to these figures, as part of the control group were living in a small town and probably were not representative. The answers, however, yield the usual crop of interesting individual cases. One boy had the daily distraction of an intriguing brick kiln on his way to school; he writes:

Well we had a long way to go to school and there was a quarry near the school and we used to spend all our time watching the men on the machine that put the clay in one end and the bricks came out the other end then they would mark on one of the bricks that had just come out of the kiln how many they had made during the day. And we used to wait five minutes before the bell rang and then set off to school we would just be in time because we knew there was the stick waiting for us if we were a minute late.

(The standard of composition in this quotation is, incidentally, typical of that of the men who were not among the more backward. The flow of ideas is obviously hampered by lack of a working knowledge of the principles of punctuation and of composition generally.) A long journey to school, with correspondingly greater likelihood of such distractions, may, indeed, conduce to unpunctuality or truancy among the susceptible. Might not a Friday afternoon excursion to the kiln have gone some way to overcome this particular distraction from school, by bringing it within the scope of school interests?

The question on evening school attendance was framed to exclude those who might have enrolled without attending for an appreciable length of time. The figures for the two groups are, as one would expect, significantly different, 14 per cent of the offenders attended and 40 per cent of the controls. Some 'couldn't be bothered', and others started but 'soon got fed up with it'. Others again confessed their feelings of inferiority in all matters of education: 'I was not clever enough.' A good number were prevented by evening work: 'I would have liked to have kept on attending, but when I was sixteen I had to start working overtime'. Delivering of newspapers was frequently cited as an obstacle.

Answers to the question 'Was yours a church school?' show that, according to the control (15 per cent), the S.T.U. group contained three times as many (48 per cent) former pupils of church schools as one might have expected. Of the 48 per cent of the S.T.U. men who had attended church schools rather more than half (27 per cent of the total group) came from Roman Catholic schools.

The figures for the two questions concerned with relations with schoolmates appear to conflict. Rather fewer (but not significantly so) of the S.T.U. than of the control group claim to have liked their schoolfellows (81 per cent cf. 85·5 per cent) but, on the other hand, a higher proportion of the S.T.U. group than of the others (21 per cent cf. 11 per cent) stated that they had been picked on by their mates. They were, possibly, thinking of only their friends in the first of these two questions. A variety of reasons were given for the bullying that they experienced. The small or weak boys were commonly victimized: 'Yes, by the bigger boys', '— because I couldn't defend myself', 'They called me "Tich".' Some of the other reasons given were: 'Yes, when I was a new boy', '— because I couldn't dress up like the rest of them', 'because I was quiet' and 'We orphans were picked on' (this boy lived in an orphanage and attended the local council school). Others claimed to have settled would-be bullies: 'Some tried but did not succeed', 'Yes, but they didn't come back again (I was a big guy at school)', '— cured by hitting back' and 'I used to go around with about ten chaps'. Children tend, like animals, to fix aggressively on any indication of weakness. It seems reasonable to assume that, as children, the S.T.U. men had more than their fair share of the diverse disabilities that draw unfriendly attention (see Chapter VIII).

It is understandable that the backward child in a normal class should find school discipline irksome or even terrifying. His mind, unable to grapple with the lesson, drifts to pleasanter things and, like Mac, he is ' — always in trouble with the teachers'. Of the S.T.U. group, three times as high a proportion (45 per cent) as of the control (15 per cent) found school too strict. The men's attitude to school discipline had, therefore, been similar to that displayed in their units. Intolerance of discipline seemed part of their general restlessness. It is arguable that, in both cases, their state of under-education was militating against assimilation with the school class and, later, with the platoon. Whatever the true explanation may be, the S.T.U. men did show an extraordinary state of restlessness. It was easy to interest them in something new, but difficult to keep them at it once they had started. This is also true to some extent of normal men cut off, in the Forces, from their former habits and interests, but was much more conspicuous in the young soldiers at the S.T.U. Their willingness to volunteer for new jobs or for other branches of the Service, irrespective of their fitness for the work, suggested that calls for volunteers for particular duties must require careful scrutiny of the responses.

The S.T.U. men almost certainly suffered more frequent punishment than does the normal child. More of them (94 per cent cf. 81 per cent) answered 'Yes' to the question, 'Were you ever caned or punished much?' though the true difference is probably obscured by the framing of the question, as even a few instances of punishment in a whole school life would justify an affirmative answer. Many of the S.T.U. men add telling remarks to their answers: 'I used to be caned nearly every morning', 'Yes, every ruddy day', 'I was caned and never given a real chance', and 'Physical punishment ought to be washed out altogether as we used to be living in fear all the time'. Another form of punishment was commonly mentioned, 'I was kept in four nights out of five for not paying attention'. Most of their answers contained some such reference to frequent or even regular punishment.

It is not surprising that the S.T.U. should show a higher proportion (26 per cent) than the normal (11 per cent) of those who did not like their teachers. There need be no general presumption of unsatisfactory relations between teacher and backward pupil— provided that the latter is with his equals, where his pace is that of the class as a whole. But, in a class of normal children, the backward boy and his teacher may well become mutual afflictions. The answers to the question, 'Did your teachers know their job?'

show how fair-minded the S.T.U. men, despite their unhappy recollections, were prepared to be; 81 per cent of them thought that their teachers were efficient (cf. only 54 per cent who liked them). Mac concedes, 'The teachers knew their jobs but I suppose we did not pay much attention,' and another writes: '— they must have had all the patience in the world to put up with all we did.' The following are some of the criticisms: 'Some were too strict', '—they were too easy', '— treated us too much like little kids', and '— too old-fashioned'. Another says, '— liked them a bit but got fed up with them because they never learned me anything about the outside life.'

Answers to the question 'Were you much afraid of being late, or of doing wrong?' show a significant difference of figures between the groups (32 per cent of offenders were afraid, cf. 19 per cent of controls). Many of the S.T.U. men who gave negative answers, reveal—sometimes in other answers—that fear did play a big part in their school life. The man, for example, who was interested in the brick kiln, states—in the passage already quoted—that he and his companions left it just in time to reach school without being late, because they '— knew there was the stick waiting . . .' And yet he, and many others who had described similar strong fear of breaking rules, stated that they were not afraid. The figures, therefore, probably tend to minimize the role of fear in school life. Many of those who had not been afraid, claimed to have defied the school: 'They used to threaten me with the police', 'They never used to hurt me. I was the big guy in the school', 'I never took notice of any teacher', and 'I liked getting into trouble'. The fear affirmed in the positive answers was mostly of the sort that could not be ensured against—as, for example, lateness, truancy or the deliberate infringement of any similar rule normally could be—by any action that the child was capable of taking. Backwardness appeared to be the major cause of the punishment that inspired active fear, since poor work and inattention are explained by the men as the common occasions of punishment. One man observes, 'I think it was a mistake as we were too scared to use our own ideas.' Even those who do not admit fear reveal, on the whole, a school life morbidly dominated by the fight against it. To capitulate was shameful: 'The class of chaps I was brought up with considered you a cissy if you were scared.' It is also true that fear holds a place in the normal child's sentiment towards his school, but, even so, the rules of reasonable punctuality and tolerable conduct acquire for him the smoothness of habit. The ordinary pupil does not goad himself to school each morning with reflections on what is waiting for him should he be 'a minute late'.

Over three-quarters of the S.T.U. men (the question was abandoned for the control groups because of ambiguities) agreed that their schools did not prepare them for any special civilian job. On the surface, this indicates a very reasonable state of affairs, since primary education is not designed to fit one for a specific vocation. But the numerous riders added to the answers make it clear that most of the men considered their answers as criticisms of their schooling. The majority seemed to discount the vocational value of ordinary primary school subjects. Some of the answers reflect the shock of the drastic change from school to work. One writes, 'They never learned me anything about the outside life which I think they ought to.' Dissatisfaction was expressed at the continuance of only primary subjects throughout school life; 'All we learned was to read and write' and '. . . too dry all I learned was how to write and do maths'. This suggests a gulf between school and adult life. The ability to read or write the occasional message or letter met with at work or in private life is, no doubt, taken for granted as a benefit of schooling, but, in many cases, there appears to be consciousness of a continuous development, in either work or leisure, from school life into the new life that begins when school days end. With release from school, the superfluous load of classroom knowledge is, in such cases, shed by disuse down to the minimum maintained by the scanning of ephemeral reading matter and the odd occasion to write a note. Such skill and knowledge as may have been painfully accumulated during school years thus becomes the inert and dwindling residue of the past, rather than the embryo of maturer growth.

In this investigation of the school lives of the men at the S.T.U., many points have arisen, some of general interest and some of relevance to the question of delinquency and crime. Many of these were indicated as they arose, without the intention of any further attempt at assessing their significance. But the biographical accounts of school days have served to clarify some matters that had proved of consequence in the men's army experience, and that would have been of corresponding significance in civil life. The two stages— school and army—are seen as complementary. The development of the educational backwardness observed in the army has been traced through the years of schooling. The finding of army tests that this backwardness was not explicable by intellectual disability was confirmed by the revelation of other adequate factors. Low morale and frequent absence in the army are seen to have had corresponding traits in school life.

The lag of educational attainment behind ability was too prominent a condition in the S.T.U. to be regarded lightly. The men's disclosures have shown how part of this can be brought about by adverse school conditions (though in Chapter XXI other more vital factors are revealed). Absence, large classes and classes of mixed ability appear as important conditions encouraging the drift into backwardness. The bright child with helpful home conditions may, by his own exertions and his parents' help, be able to make good a lapse due to sickness, but the child who is duller, or who lacks the opportunity of learning much at home, has little chance of making up any such leeway, and may, without individual attention, fall hopelessly behind. Such attainment as the backward child has on leaving school is held but slenderly and may soon trickle down to virtual illiteracy. Experiences of this type were by no means rare at the S.T.U. The disparity between ability and attainment in education is, by its nature, preventable. Although prevention in childhood is vastly preferable, it can still be tackled later. Lack of opportunity for instruction and reluctance to disclose what is regarded as a shameful thing no doubt prevent many adults from closing the gap between their potentialities and their attainments.

CHAPTER XXI

THE FAMILY

THE earliest and most impressionable period of a boy's life, when his habits are formed and his character is laid down, will long have passed by the time his delinquencies come to the notice of the investigator. One can then only look, as the Probation Officers or the research workers have to do, at the conditions of the later home—the type of house, the financial position, the completeness of the family, the parents' attitude towards each other so far as that can be deduced from one or two interviews, and their attitude to the young offender. But the vital evidence of the earlier years, when the seeds of action are implanted, can only be guessed at or gleaned from hearsay or from the young man's own reminiscences. Sometimes a chance remark, like 'I was dragged up', or 'a mother doesn't always want to look after her children', would uncover a glimpse. Occasionally a man's memory would reach back and gather a whole sequence of meaningful images, such as:

I can remember my first happy memory when I was about three years of age and my mother gave me a party and I wore a little sailor suit, and I was really happy. My second one was when I was 5 years when I was able to go to school and learn to spell and play with the other boys and change comics. Then I remember reaching the age of ten when I used to club with the other boys and buy five 'snouts' (cigarettes) and go round the back behind the shed and try to smoke them. My next one was when I used to go to the seaside for the weekend and when I went to a party. My next memory was leaving school and I brought my wage packet home with 18 bob in it, then my mother used to give me a certain amount of pocket money.

My first unpleasant memory was when I piddled on my Father's lap, he didn't like it. Next time was when I was in school and I got the stick for putting pins on teachers chair, she got caught up in them somehow. My next was when I came home with two black eyes and my best suit was torn, and my hat was in a tree. My next was when I pissed me trousers and me mother whacked me. My last what I remember of was when I broke in a shop and pinched some mouth organs. That was alright but I went outside the shop next day and me and my mates started playing them, then we had to run because the cops were after us.

The selection of incidents is significant: the moment of 'real' happiness when he wore a sailor suit at a party; the beginning of school life was to this boy a highlight, a happy occasion marking the entry into a world of books and learning, a world of adventure and day-dreams conjured up by the lurid pictures of 'comics'; then comes the companionship of other boys leading eventually into trouble. On the other side of the picture he puts his incontinence—itself a sign of emotional frustration—provoking anger and even a 'whacking' from his parents. The rest of the long story one can only guess at. And only an odd man here and there was able to recall so much. So that although the general pattern is much the same in nearly all these early recollections, the material is too vague, too subjective and haphazard to serve as evidence in any scheme of inquiry. What is needed is a thorough study of the home conditions of those families which may seem likely to produce delinquent members. Such a study would have to extend over many years and would require thorough and first-hand knowledge of the cases concerned. One can, therefore, only look at the offender's home and family as they were at the time of his offence, and see whether they differ in any very marked degree from those of normal young men, sketching in where one can, in the men's own words, details of the earlier years of childhood.

How the families were constituted

An unusual thing about the men's families was their size. They included, on an average, 6·3 children per family, compared with an average of 3·6 children amongst the control groups.[1] As many as 88 per cent came from homes of four or more children, and 56 per cent from homes with six or more children. There may have been

[1] See 'Report on the Present Problem of Juvenile Delinquency', Birmingham Education Committee, 1937, where the 229 offenders' families averaged 6·9 persons, while the average family in Birmingham consisted of 3·4 persons. Also Bagot, op. cit., who quotes the mean numbers of living children in delinquents' families as 5·18 in 1934 and 5·28 in 1936. The S.T.U. figure of 6·3 included deceased children of whom there were several in a number of families. The Home Office inquiry (op. cit.) shows the size of 'families at home' but only for those offenders from normally constituted families with normal home atmosphere (just over 40 per cent of all the offenders examined). No comparison can therefore be made, but for this restricted and obviously least abnormal group the figure is about 4·5 (see also Appendix A). The figure for H. Mannheim's Cambridge sample was 4·4 children.

a slight falsification of the figures through men from broken homes counting as part of the family the brothers and sisters who had gone away with the absconding parent and those with step-parents counting the influx of children of other unions. But the average size of family stands much too high to be affected very much by such distortions. Only about a quarter of the general population derives from families of six or more persons (including parents) among which nine-tenths of the offenders are found.

One's impression was that the homes with the larger families were also the poorer, apart from the obvious fact that there would be more mouths to feed, but it was not possible to establish this link. Certainly the few offenders from middle-class homes belonged to small families and several were only-children. It has sometimes been thought that only-children are more likely to prove wayward, but no such tendency was found in this group. There were rather more younger than older members of families in the S.T.U. group. Out of 171 young soldiers (excluding only-children and middle children, i.e. second of three, third of five, etc.) 95 were later (younger) and 76 earlier (or older) members. The following table sets out the proportions of first-born, second-born, third-born and last-born children. The fourth-born, *et seq.* are not included because there was nothing abnormal about their proportions. The first line shows the proportions that might be expected in a normal group, calculated from the sizes of the families concerned, and the second line shows the actual proportions amongst the offenders. The control groups were close to the normal throughout.

	1st-born	*2nd-born*	*3rd-born*	*last-born*
	%	%	%	%
Normal, expected	19·1	16·8	13·5	19·1
Obtained	18·6	11·4	13·4	25·4

Thus, there were slightly fewer second-born children and more last-born children than would have been expected from a normal group.[1]

[1] Dr. Charles Goring, in *The English Convict*, found that first and second-born children are more liable to become delinquent than younger members of families. W. L. Chinn, *A Brief Survey of Nearly One Thousand Juvenile Delinquents*, 1938, found that the greatest proportion (20·7 per cent) were second-born children. J. H. Bagot, *Juvenile Delinquency*, states that there was a tendency for delinquent boys in Liverpool to be older members of the family. See also Karl Pearson, *On the Handicapping of the First Born*, and M. Fortes, *Economica*, 1933.

Hereditary Traits

In trying to teach these men the rudiments of behaviour one often wondered, especially with the more obstinate, how far their weaknesses were inherited from earlier generations. Only on one small factor in their hereditary influence does this inquiry throw any light—the sizes of their parents' families. The replies to questions showed that the average size of the fathers' families was 8·7 persons, and their mothers' 8·8. And since many of the men said they did not know how many uncles or aunts they had because they were so numerous, the true figures may well have been higher.

A number of the men were aware of having inherited physical disabilities and a few were afraid of a recrudescence from the parents of venereal disease. The investigator encountered only one case of the fear of criminal inheritance (see Table 10, No. 12). The man's father, grandfather, two uncles and several cousins had been criminals. His father, for whom he had quite a strong regard, almost a morbid fascination in fact, had served several prison sentences and had taken the boy along on several of his escapades. In the course of three marriages, and between prison sentences and visits to the hospital for 'fits of blindness', he had begotten sixteen children. The boy was brought up by his grandparents from the age of seven, but he continued to see his father. He left school at thirteen, was married at sixteen and had two children by the time he was eighteen. Like his father, he was subject to moods of fury and he had twice broken up much of his home in wild fits. According to the Army tests he was dull and backward[1]. He had no interest in military training—he had been a deserter for eight months—but he finally found a vocation in sanitary work at the S.T.U., and for a year faithfully discharged the duties of '2 i/c Sanitary', and became quite a different being. But the old fears and habits still haunted him though one tried to show him by diagrams and analogies from dog breeding that the criminal traits in his heredity were probably no more potent than the non-criminal! His genealogy, as he reconstructed it, was as follows, the black symbols representing the criminal members (δ males, φ females) and the white the non-criminal, the man himself being marked (A).

---

[1] In one or two cases, and this was one, the tests of intelligence and aptitudes showed men as very dull when their general behaviour and spoken responses suggested that they were not at all backward or dull. An emotional situation may occasionally have inhibited their powers of expression, see articles by H. C. Günzburg and B. G. Schmidt; references in List of Books on page 218.

N

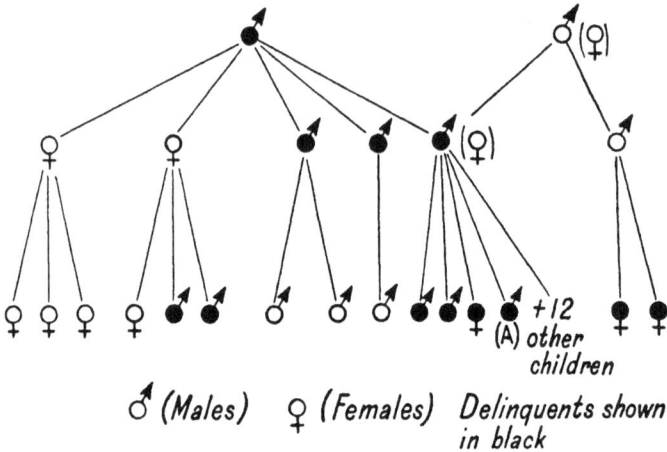

♂ (Males)   ♀ (Females)   Delinquents shown
                            in black

After a year at the S.T.U., unbroken by a single offence, he became restless and began to display his old fits of anger and to boast of his father's misdeeds. So, with much misgiving, he was posted away to a field battalion from which he was later discharged as a psychopathic personality.

Defective Homes

If we look at the structure of the offenders' homes we find an astonishingly large number (as many as 57 per cent) with broken or incomplete families, i.e. they had either no home, that is to say they were brought up in institutions (10 per cent), or by grand-parents (4 per cent), or else one or both of the parents had died (25 per cent),[1] or they had been reared by a step-parent, or their parents were separated, or the father had been away from the home for long periods (14 per cent)[2]—(for example, serving with the forces overseas, excluding wartime service). The contrast with the control groups is here most striking, for only 12 per cent of them came from similarly broken homes.[3]

[1] E. & S. Glueck found the same proportion in *One Thousand Juvenile Delinquents.*

[2] The percentages in brackets overlap slightly because some of the men's homes were incomplete in more ways than one.

[3] The corresponding figures cited by Rhodes in the Home Office inquiry (op. cit.) are 28 per cent for the delinquents and 16 per cent for the controls. They do not however include any cases where the father had been absent for long periods. Burt's classification does include prolonged absence, and also the only-child relationship, and he finds 57·9 per cent amongst delinquents and 25·7 per cent amongst non-delinquents. W. L. Chinn's Birmingham inquiry (op. cit.) found 31·5 per cent of the cases in broken homes. Bowlby records prolonged separation from the mother in 17 of his 44 cases.

Another source of weakness in the home environment was the prolonged illness of one of the parents. This was often a misfortune more damaging in its effect on the other parent and on the children than total loss or separation would have been. Several of the parents had been invalided in the first World War. Altogether an invalid parent (or parents) was noted in the records of 22 per cent of the men. To compare with this large figure one found only 7·5 per cent amongst the control groups. Of the 22 per cent, 8 per cent were already included amongst the 57 per cent with broken homes, but if the remaining 14 per cent are added to this figure we have a total of 71 per cent of all offenders with incomplete or defective homes (compared with 19 per cent in the control groups).

Another defect, perhaps quite as serious as any of those already mentioned, is the parents' serious neglect of a child's moral and physical welfare, expressed by indifference or hostility or even brutality to the child. This was one of the most difficult of all factors to trace, for the young man would try to hide it, or to avoid remembering it, or perhaps he even failed to recognize it himself. It was clearly established in 53 per cent of the offenders: 36 per cent were amongst those already quoted as having defective homes, and if the rest (53 − 36 = 17 per cent) are added to the cumulative figure of 71 per cent we have a total of 88 per cent affected. Still further defects could be added to the reckoning—cases of over-indulgence or serious friction between the parents—until very few men would remain without some abnormality in the home background. One or two among this small residue were not really delinquent at all—one had got into trouble because his hearing was impaired and two or three others were emotionally quite immature or much under Army age, and there were only incomplete records of nearly all the rest. It would therefore be true to say that some serious weakness in the home environment was present in practically every case, and that no other factor that one could observe was so common to all. At this point no direct comparison can be made with the control groups because it was clearly impossible to question them about any neglect or over-indulgence for which their parents could be held responsible. But from the figures already given it is plain that only a small proportion suffered the same disadvantages of home life as the offenders.

The mere counting of cases will not take us far towards understanding what the effect of such disadvantages of environment must have been on the behaviour of these young people. We were

viewing these events at a great distance in time, and could not say
with what force the original disturbances had affected their minds,
nor how far they had influenced, if at all, their later waywardness.
It may be profitable to set down some impressions of the way these
less fortunate men talked about their homes and of their reactions
to their misfortunes, beginning with the homeless.

The Homeless

The men who had known Homes but no home might be thought
most in need of sympathy. Yet the orphans that one saw did not
appear to be emotionally as unstable as some of the other men.
They were, however, often only too well aware of what they had
missed. If they were intelligent they were generally able to view
their situation sensibly, without self-pity, with some sense of proportion, and they responded warmly to any friendliness and advice.
Yet their confidence in themselves was weak and easily extinguished.
They had no comforting store of memories to sustain them in their
worst moments. Other men could escape into a phantasy world
embroidered out of the brighter threads of their past, or they could
literally run away from the harshness of the present to home and the
imagined comforts of childhood. For the orphan the past was
impersonal and friendless, and there was no home to which he could
escape, so that he was forced to stay in the present. So long as
things were running smoothly he acted quite normally, but if things
went wrong he tended to react more violently than most. He
would then direct his bitterness and pent-up feelings against even
those who had done most to help him, and would sometimes commit
acts of desperate folly.

The man without a home was often difficult enough in the Army,
though the comradeship of campaign life and the noisy chatter in
canteens offered him some sort of substitute for the loss of home,
and at least he knew that he was at no great disadvantage compared
with his fellow soldiers. It was when the time came for him to
return to civilian life that he suffered most.

It is perhaps not out of place to record the situation of one of
these S.T.U. men on his release from the Army in 1946. Within
a month of his release he had spent the whole of his gratuity in
indiscriminate hospitality and drinking. He frequented a London
Services canteen where he felt that his face was welcome and he
still enjoyed the privileges of soldiering without any of its responsibilities. He had banknotes in his pocket and he found that he

made friends easily. He took no trouble to get a job, and indeed he looked askance at any 'menial' jobs—his own word—that were offered him, though he was only qualified for labouring or domestic work. He had long cherished ambitions to become a music-hall artist or a film star. He had wit and was something of a clown, but he could not write his own lines and laughed excessively at his own clumsy jokes. His Army tests had shown him as below average in intelligence. He tried his charms on theatrical agents and on some of his newly-found friends who promised him lavish help, without success. At last reality began to close in on him. His money ran out; his release leave expired; and he had to put aside his uniform, and the services club could no longer admit him, for he was a civilian. To raise money he sold the coat he had been given on demobilization and all his clothing coupons. Winter came in suddenly with a cold spell and he had to buy a reconverted coat at an exorbitant price, through weekly payments. Soon his last shilling was exhausted and he was destitute. He failed to keep up payments on the coat and so had to give it up. An acquaintance asked him to sell somebody else's coat, without coupons, which he did, pocketing the proceeds. Finally, in desperation he walked into the cloak-room of an hotel and stole a coat, but was detected and arrested.

At the Court an Army friend intervened and spoke for him and he was discharged. His next misfortune was losing all his demobilization papers and his identity card—through putting on the wrong jacket by mistake (or so he said). He was exceedingly shortsighted but would not wear glasses because he felt they would mar his appearance. At this time he was washing up dishes for a large catering firm. He made the acquaintance of the irresponsible daughter of a professional man and was invited to her home. He told her family of his stage ambitions, of some imaginary successes and of his influential connexions. He spoke of a well-to-do uncle and a widowed mother, though he was the son of a prostitute who would not own him and had been brought up in a Home run by a large religious denomination. At last the young woman discovered his deceptions and gave him up. Then the Army friend found him a domestic job in a good household where he had a room of his own, good pay and regular hours of work. But he was dirty, he seldom washed his body or his clothes and was untidy and unpunctual. Within a few days of Christmas he was dismissed and was destitute again. He had nowhere to go for Christmas so he applied to his old orphanage for hospitality but they told him that he was too old to be admitted. He had no friends, for he had little to offer in friendship, besides being unkempt, unmannered and backward. He had no hobbies, he read little and craved human company. He smoked heavily whenever he could beg, borrow or buy a packet of cigarettes. He was continually drifting into the company of unsavoury characters, who seemed to smell out the putrefaction of his spirit. 'Everything is against me,' he would say, 'I must get a break sometime.' At last, having lost another good job through his own irresponsibility, he was caught up by a gang who were breaking into houses and employed him to get to know younger members of families who were to be the victims of their raids. Among these was the professional man whose daughter he had known, and whose kindness he now repaid by assisting in the burglary of his house. He was soon detected, as was inevitable because of his dullness and his weak sight, and was sentenced to a term of imprisonment.

So he passed, for a time, beyond the reach of those who wanted to help him. He could not see that his deprivations were the result of his own shortcomings, and that these in turn were the product of his upbringing and his own innate weaknesses. He could not see, though his few friends often tried to tell him, that only through the slow and laborious process of working at a job within his competence could he acquire self-respect, learn moderation in living and earn the right to friendship. He could not see all this because his outlook was hopelessly cramped by his upbringing and by the limits of his intelligence. So the chances of his redemption were slight. The weaknesses were apparent when he was at the Special Training Unit; the surprising thing is that he kept out of the Courts so long. But his story is not yet finished; good friends will go on helping him and trying to put their trust in him, but it is difficult to see what use hardship and confinement and the company of thieves will be to him in the meantime.

This man's story has been told at some length because it illustrates the inner helplessness of such offenders; perhaps it conveys, too, something of the size of the problem confronting the social worker in this field. How different was the sweet reasonableness of another orphan, a man of brighter intelligence, less warped mentally, who was well aware of the limitations of his upbringing but tried to turn them to account, and even imagined, though mistakenly, that he had done well out of it all. It is best told in his own words:

I can't remember my parents and my mum died when I was 7 years old, and of course Dad put us in a home. Well I did not see him till I was 13 and I have not seen him since. Well I was in the Liverpool branch of Dr. Barnardo's Homes. I don't remember much about it as I was too young. Then I went to Stepney, the headquarters of the Homes and from there to Kingston-on-Thames. I was there till I was 12 years and 6 months. We were like ordinary boys except we all went to school together, marched down to church with our own pipe band. I really think that this was a good foundation to set your life on as you have no one to spoil you. And it makes you appreciate a good home. When I was 14 years old I went to Gloucestershire on a farm. This I think is the bad part of them as you work for 5 shillings a week and your keep and buy your own clothes. Well I packed it in and went to Cheltenham and I got a lift with a cattle truck and I have always wanted to be a driver and the chap as owned it said he wanted a boy to work as driver's mate, so I took the job and I have been with him ever since. I started off without parents but I think Mr. and Mrs. S. (belated foster-parents to whom he was recommended by one of the staff at the Special Training Unit) are as good as any parents to me. That is my home now and they are my dad and mum.

Others were under no illusions as to what they had missed. 'Well, as long as I can remember', wrote one man, 'I have been in a Home or an Orphanage. I've been through all kinds of what they call mother's care but I never remember ever calling anybody Daddy.' The man who wrote that was a tough and experienced offender.

In some of the worst cases the youngster had felt incarcerated in the institution and the wrongdoing seems to have started soon after leaving it. 'My earliest happiest memory', wrote one, 'was being allowed to walk about freely after ten years in an orphanage.'

Perhaps the most interesting expression of an orphan's view came from a man who arrived at the Special Training Unit a sickly (see Table 10, No. 5), complaining youth, 'exhibiting neurotic traits, weak-kneed and liable to become easily depressed and despondent in face of difficulty" as the psychiatrist's report put it. A few months later he had changed out of all knowledge. He looked robust, spoke with a tone of quiet self-confidence, and was quick to learn. He was fortunate in having a bright intelligence, as his story shows:

I don't think I could say much about my home because at the age of 5 my mother died, that was in 1929. After this my father sent me to one of his brothers in Wales as he had to go to sea. At the age of six I ran away from him and went to live with my mother's only sister. By this time my father had gone to sea and had left my two brothers and sister with auntie. She did her best to be a mother to the four of us. But in 1931 she realised she could not do it as her sister, my mother, would have done, so she sent us to an orphanage and I think that was the most that could have been expected of her as she had four sons and a daughter of her own. In seven years at the orphanage I was reasonably happy as I had my two brothers with me but all that time I realised there was something and someone missing from my life. I could not think what it was at the time as I could not remember my mother, and I saw very little of my father. And when he did come, he was continually speaking of my mother. My brother, the eldest of the three of us, left in 1936 to join the Army, that left me to look after my youngest brother, to fight his battles and help him along generally. But I could see that he also was missing my mother, and I did my best to help him. It was not until 1937 that I saw my sister and by that time I had forgotten her and it was a shock when, one Sunday, my auntie brought with her a girl of about 17 and told me that she was my sister. After talking with her for about two hours I began to realize what it was that I had missed for so long.

After seeing the moral poverty of so many of these orphaned offenders one could not help reflecting on the total inadequacy of any system of charitable adoption, however well intentioned its sponsors might be, that nurtures the child's body until it is adult only to send it into the world without the warmth of affection, without a home to come back to and often without the moral strength or the emotional resources to cope with the problems of living. These orphaned offenders were possibly exceptional, and the more intelligent were generally able to recognize and so overcome their limitations, but one is forced to the conclusion that the less fortunate were starting life with reduced chances of a successful outcome.

Broken Homes

The step-mother of folk tales is harsh and cruel; perhaps she symbolized, for the child, the contrast between the mother's love and the harshness of the outside world. But the real step-mother could be harsh too. Several of the men, as children, had weighed up the substitute against the original and found her wanting: 'I think my father would have been better sticking to the first one', or 'I am afraid I never liked her from the beginning and we never got on well together. So after four years of it I went to live at my grandma's.' Even one of the most wayward men wrote: 'Since my mother died I have been brought up by my father's Lady Companion, sought-of a wife but not married, but she is not the same as my mother.' (Perhaps the man himself could not be held entirely responsible for his character which, according to the headmaster of his Approved School was 'one of the most plausible and self-confident youths in school. You are dealing with a personality who will use you to the limit of his requirements and then laugh when he has cheated his best friend'). If one change of partner was a tragedy a second might appear as a farce to the child: 'My first mother was very nice. Father has been married three times, a proper Henry VIII as you might say.'

Some men had clearly been much affected by the loss of a parent.[1] They still brooded over it and it seemed as though the death was too terrible to be accepted:

> When my father pass away all in our house was up set and I was very up set with being his only pal. Why I call him pal because I took him out every where I went. When my farther pass away I did not want to go because if I went to see him at the cemtry I would not get over it but I have got over a bit but I will never forget it and so my mum wore black and we are still sad.

and again:

> The most unpleasant memory of all was my father's death. Well, after that I never went anywhere because my mother was left at home and was worrying about my father.

and again:

> When my Farther died it was a big shock to my mother as she was with him on the Saturday an Sunday in North Wales. It was in the summer. When my Farther went home on Sunday night he hurt himself at work on Monday morning and he died Monday night. That was a very big shock to my mother has he was one of the best and we shall all still love him.

Prolonged Absence of the Father

One man in every seven had a father in regular service with the armed forces, or in the Merchant Navy. In nearly every case the father had been away from home for long periods, sometimes many years at a time, and the result must have been additional responsibilities for the mother, especially where the family was large, and, for the child, increased dependence on the mother and sometimes lack of discipline. 'Well, father was in the Army so it was no good to tell him anything,' said one man contemptuously. Another man's father, who had served as a regular soldier for many

---

[1] Bowlby records a 'recent traumatic event' in 11 of his 44 cases of young delinquents (see also footnote 3, page 197).

years before the war, came to visit the camp. He was stiff and regimental in manner and seemed more concerned to establish his own respectability by abusing the boy than to know how the lad was getting on. He left with the threat that he would turn his son out of home if he went absent again. For some weeks the young soldier had been much better behaved and reasonably contented, but the father's visit distressed him and two days later he went absent. So much for the authority of the martinet.

Fostering by Grandparents

If there is any disruption of the home a parent will often turn to the grandparents and sometimes send the child away to be brought up by them. In every case of this sort that came to our notice, the boy had become devoted to the grandmother and showed signs of childish dependence on her. It was as though he knew she could not live long and yet could not bear the thought of her loss. So the death of a fostering grandmother might seriously affect a man. It was the same with two or three men whose parents were very old—the fathers would have been over fifty years of age at the birth of the child. Here is an account of a man who, according to the psychiatrist, developed a mild neurotic state on hearing of his grandmother's death.

At the age of 7 years I went to live with my Granma. She was my best and only one I ever loved. I don't remember much about my ma and pa. I never seen much of them. At the age of 15 I went to live with my mother and father I found a hell of a lot of differans. At the age of 16½ I join the Army. I made pals with a feller not very good, he had no mother or father, it was pretty bad for him, he never had any mail, and so I let him write to my sister. One day I ran away from the army with him for about 10 days, this is what happen. We got home O.K. and the first thing my mother said was, your Granmother is dead, Jack. At the time I felt very bad being brought up with my granma. She was almost my mother.

Illness of Parents

If either parent in a working-class family became a chronic invalid it was likely to bear heavily on the other. Without adequate social insurance the partner would often have to endure hardship. The care of the children would fall to the oldest child. If it was the father who was ill the mother would have to go out to work and try to struggle with the arrears of housework in the evenings. She would then have little time and less patience to devote to the children. If the mother was an invalid the situation was as bad, for

the husband would try to take on the domestic duties, and his temper
and affections would certainly suffer in the process. It is surely a
matter of note that more than one in every five of the offenders
suffered such a calamity.

Friction between Parents

A question was put to the offenders and to the control groups
about friction between the parents. It ran 'Did your parents have
many cross words', and the word 'many' was given spoken emphasis.
Now the ambiguities in open questions of this sort are manifold,
for what one boy would call 'many' another would describe as the
usual number. Nor is one much better off if the decision is left to
a number of investigators (as was done for the Home Office inquiry,
Young Offenders). Admittedly one is a subjective and the other
an objective assessment, but how is one to define a 'normal attitude'
or a 'state of friction' (*Young Offenders*); how much friction can
be counted as normal and on what evidence does one decide the
matter? One point to be said in support of the present inquiry is
that the question was put to all the men concerned by the same
person and with the same emphasis and with the same interpreta-
tions of meaning. The results showed that 57 per cent of the
offenders answered 'yes' compared with 22 per cent of the controls.
All that one can conclude from these figures, however, is that there
was a sharp difference between the two groups.

Some of the offenders described their situations at home in
such detail as to leave no doubt of the seriousness of the disagree-
ments, and the very force of their descriptions indicated that the
friction had left a deep impression on them. One little fellow, who
still looked nagged and wretched, wrote: 'Father threw the dinners
across the table at mum. I can't forget it though they're better
now.' And another: 'Nearly every night a battle started between the
old man and the old girl. I have no interest in any of them. Was
always running away from home. I have never obeyed them and
I never will.' And another described an intractable dilemma,
though his reaction was milder: 'My Mum and Dad do not like
each other as he will not let her go out when she like. And my
dad don't like my mum has she stop him going out two.'

Sometimes the friction led to a split between the parents, and
the child naturally looked on the quarrelling as the cause of his loss
rather than as a symptom of an underlying cause. One man,
whose father had been a drunkard, wrote with obvious restraint:

'My home life was not so great as my parents were very sort of head-strong at one another so I did not enjoy myself at home but I really appreciate it now.'   The last words would be misleading if one did not know that his parents had finally separated seven years before and that he went 'home' to his mother.   The effect of all this, and of course there may have been other influences, was little short of disastrous for the boy.   He suffered from fits of crying, was a bed-wetter, was ridiculed by the other men, and his 'combatant tempera-ment' (or guts) was rated by a Personnel Selection Officer as 'one of the lowest ever encountered'.

The wartime evacuation of families and young children from big cities scarcely affected the S.T.U. men because most of them were at least fourteen years of age by the time of the first dispersions. There were one or two who mentioned it as a disturbing influence in their earlier lives, but it could not have been a root cause of emotional troubles.

Parents' attitude to the Child

The public conscience is easily aroused over cruelty to a child. For it is commonly and rightly held that undue harshness injures the personality, sometimes producing violent reactions at a later date. Yet it is often objected by those whose vision is fixed on the short-comings rather than the potentialities of criminals that a generation or two back harsh treatment of young children was deemed the proper and privileged duty of the parent, without having any very obvious harmful effect.   But one cannot read of the early lives of Samuel Butler, of Ruskin, Hazlitt and Wesley, to mention but a few, without feeling the hurt and resentment that was implanted in their young minds by callous upbringing, and as Mr. de la Mare has observed,[1] one does not know how many youthful spirits were degraded and extinguished by the cruelties of pre-Victorian up-bringing.

There were several offenders who spoke of cruelties they had endured.   'I had plenty of hits about the head and ears,' said one, and 'I got both ear drums burst from where my mother hit me.' And 'they always had a cane on the table every meal time, or else they'd bang me with spoons', wrote a wretched-looking fellow. It was impossible to know exactly how many men have suffered from harshness of this sort for many would conceal it, even from them-selves.   One question: 'did your parents have to correct you much

[1] Walter de la Mare, *Early One Morning* (Faber).

as a boy?' was answered affirmatively by 72 per cent of the offenders compared with 35 per cent amongst the controls. It is interesting to notice that nearly half of the 28 per cent who said they were not corrected much were the youngest members of the families. 'Correction' may however be taken to mean anything from a spoken reprimand to a thrashing, and the question tells us little except that the offenders apparently got more 'correction' than the others.

There was a good deal of evidence that a number of the men as children had been neglected by their parents.[1] The parents' treatment must indeed have been callous for a son to write: 'My father died when I was 13 years of age and I was not sorry to see the back of him. I was fetched up the hard way—I had to work, if not it was my lot.' Another wrote: 'My mother was strict and father had no time for me.' And another: 'Father was a very hard man'. One fellow, who wrote 'Mother and father didn't think much of me. I was always having rows with them, nearly every night', was in continual trouble, even after he had been at the Special Training Unit. One day, on being given a court-martial sentence, he swallowed a tube of anti-gas ointment in order to poison himself, but fortunately its effects were not fatal. Another uncovered his misery in a few words when he wrote: 'When my mother died of cancer nothing in the house seemed organized and my father stayed out to the early hours in the morning. You may think that has nothing to do with me. Well I did when I had a crippled brother to be looked after. I think it was his duty towards us and my mother to be with his son.'

Sometimes a man would repeat an expression like 'I was a bloody nuisance' time after time—that particular expression occurred four times in a single page of writing—as though it had been thrown at him day after day as long as he could remember. A normal, fairly contented domestic scene such as is conveyed by the following quotation, was comparatively rare in these descriptions:

'Well, I think I like mum best of all because she makes all the puddings in the house and washing up, etc. when the old man just comes home from work and smokes a pipe by the fire.'

A certain reaction away from the parents was occasionally seen, perhaps faintly in a statement like: 'Mother is of middle age, about 5 feet tall, dark hair, fair complexion, blue eyes, very good set of teeth, and she's got a very good figure. That's all I can tell you.'

[1] John Bowlby, in *Forty-four Juvenile Thieves*, recorded ambivalent or hostile attitudes in the mothers of 21 of the 44 cases in his study.

Or more pointedly in: 'I thought at the time my Mother was always telling tales. They tried to stop me but I think I nearly always got my own way.' Or the completely callous: 'It's only natural to think a little bit more of your mother because you can get things from your mother that you couldn't get from your father such has a couple of shillings when your broke.' And, 'I liked mum and dad when I was young because I could always get money to go to the pictures on a Saturday afternoon.'

Home Relationships of Emotional 'Types' and others

The attitudes of the offenders to their parents, and of the parents to the offenders have been recorded for all the 203 men in the S.T.U. sample. The assessments were made from protracted interviews of the welfare staff and the writer with the men, and from the men's own statements in the course of the present inquiry and on other occasions, including their answers to a questionnaire on family life.

Five conditions were noted, as follows:

(*a*) The offender's attitude to his home—
    (1) unduly strongly attached (bordering on the hysterical)
    (2) normally affectionate or indifferent.

(*b*) the parent(s)' attitude to the offender as a child—
    (1) neglectful, hostile or vacillating
    (2) normally affectionate but the home broken
    (3) normally affectionate in normal homes (i.e. both parents living together without undue friction).

In making this analysis it was found that the men who had been listed as emotional 'types' in Chapter X had a markedly different set of relationships from those of the rest of the sample. They are therefore shown separately as follows:

TABLE 17

Types	Parents affectionate in normal homes		Parents affectionate in broken homes		Parents neglectful		Totals
	Sons unduly attached	Sons not unduly attached	Sons unduly attached	Sons not unduly attached	Sons unduly att'd	Sons not unduly attached	
Aggressive	—	1	—	—	2	5	8
Introspective	—	—	—	1	7	7	15
Immature	4	—	4	—	25	7	40
Wanderers	3	—	1	—	11	1	16
Drifters	1	—	—	—	2	2	5
Totals	8	1	5	1	47	22	84

The interesting features here are that a large majority of these 'types' came from neglectful homes and that 33 out of the 40 immature men, and 15 out of the 16 wanderers, were unduly 'attached' to their parents, in most cases notwithstanding the neglect. The full significance of the relationships may best be seen by setting out the proportions for both the 'types' and the rest of the sample:

TABLE 18

Attitudes of men classified as emotional types and those not so 'classified' to their parents, and of the parents to their sons.

Object	Attitude of sons				Totals	
	— undue attachment		— normal or no attachment			
	(a) Types	(b) Others	(a) Types	(b) Others	(a)	(b)
	%	%	%	%	%	%
— Neglectful parents	56	23	26	38	82	61
— Affectionate parents						
(1) in broken homes	6	9	1	6	7	15
(2) in normal homes	10	7	1	17	11	24
Totals	72	39	28	61	100	100

The figures referring to the 'types' differ significantly (by chi-square tests) in two respects from those for the rest of the sample. The total of the first column shows that 72 per cent of them were abnormally attached to their homes (cf. 39 per cent of the un-classified men). Yet from the total of the first line it can be seen that 82 per cent of the 'types' grew up in neglectful homes (compared with 61 per cent of the others). Perhaps the most striking entries in the table are those against the third and fourth columns, third line. These show the percentages of cases who are *normal* in the sense that their homes were not broken and their parents were not neglectful, and who themselves were not abnormally attached to their homes. The percentages are only 1 among the 'types' and 17 among the others.

Two general conclusions may be drawn from this summarized material.

(1) Undue attachment to the home is observed not, as one might suppose, in the sons of normally affectionate parents but in the sons of neglectful parents, and

(2) An unsatisfactory home relationship is associated with almost all (99 per cent) of the emotionally abnormal 'types'.

The Child's attitude to the Parents

There is matter for speculation in the tendency for youths who had been treated harshly at home to show more 'affection' for their parents than those who had been indulged. It might be argued that the boy who has been deprived of affection is harking back to what he feels he has missed because he still has need of it, and that the other who is surfeited with affection and care is resentful because it has left him unprepared to deal single-handed with the realities of the world outside his home. Both situations can best be illustrated by the men's own words. Take the second case:

'Being the only boy I got everything I wanted. I only had to ask for a thing and in a few days if it is humanly possible it arrives. I hate to think what would have happened in my life if I had never had Father and Mother.' That man was one of the few from a middle-class home. Others were less fortunate:

'As a child I remember them as paying too much attention to me, their only child. I don't think its wise to pet children too much. Because I know, in my case, *I* soon realized *their* mistake, when, at the age of 16, my job found me in different parts of the country looking after myself. *I* wont make *their* mistake.' The distinction of 'I' and 'they' only serves to underline the separation. One man revealed a dual attitude, for on one occasion he spoke of his attachment to his mother and wrote 'Mother thinks there is nobody like me and I think a lot of her', but at another time he wrote 'when I went to work, then I was out of her way'. Perhaps, in one or two cases, this ambivalence sprang from a division in the mother herself. If a fond mother tries to run the home under the strain of poverty or illness she may become so distracted as to ill-treat the child one moment only to repent a little later and try to comfort it with an outburst of remorse. This vacillation appeared to harass some boys beyond endurance; thus one wrote:

'Sometimes I would get half-strangled and kicked round the room and at other times my mother would just spoil me.' This was the same youth (mentioned in Chapter X on pp. 81–2) whose father was bedridden, leaving the mother to bring up four children on a pension of 36/- a week.

The first situation mentioned above, that of the neglected youth harking back to home, has already been illustrated by earlier

quotations (pp. 71, 76, 83).   Another man, who had been badly neglected as a child wrote: 'I would willingly die to write any wrongs I
have done to my parents.'   And the soldier who is quoted on p. 183
as saying: 'have no interest in any of them', contradicted himself a
few days later: 'She thought the world of me.   I would give anything to be back with them.'

The explanation for these contradictory statements and for
this obsession with home lies partly in the man's own mental condition and partly in the enforced separation of Army life.   On first
considering the matter one might have expected the unfortunate
youngster who had been neglected or ill-treated at home to look
upon recruitment as an opportunity to shake the dust of home life
off his feet and to find his consolation in the comradeship of Army
life.   In fact quite the opposite happened.   He often refused to
join in with the life of his unit and he developed a consuming passion
to return to the source of his discontent which he now represented
to himself as all that was desirable:

'I don't want to soldier and I don't want to get married.   I
want to pay my people back for letting them down earlier.'   The
craving for home elevated the parents to fantastic heights—as one
put it when he scribbled meditatively:

'Not my opinions, but my thoughts—
Not my parents, but my idols.'

The yearning was generally centred on the mother:
'I'm married and I'm very young, 17½ to be right.   So my
Mum haven't got any benefit from me.   But now I'm married and
cant change the course now.   I'm wishing I have stayed single.
I'm quite happy with my wife but I think the only Sweetheart for
me was my Mum.   And if anything ever happened to her I know I
should loose my head.'

Another, who was married, said that whenever he went home
on leave he always called to see his mother and stayed there the
night before going on to see his wife and child.   Yet another wrote:
'My mum is the best person in the world.   Father is quite nice.'

He then goes on to say: 'Father is 10 year older than mother
but that is best as I want mother to live the longest as I dread
the day she will depart as she is all I have got in the world and the
best.'

And a dry little Scots lad wrote:
'I won't marry.   I'll stick to me old mum.'

o

Sometimes there was a suggestion of guilt, of wishing to atone for the pain they may have given their parents:

'There's one thing I would never do if they were living, it would not matter how old I was, I would not answer them back.' Perhaps the most unusual example was written out, as though in a dream, by one man:

> I love my mother and father,
> I adore my mother and father,
> I would die willingly for my mother and father,
> I would kill anyone who tried to harm my mother and father,
> I would not let anyone say anything about my mother and father,
> I insulted my mother once and I will regret it as long as I live.

An instructive commentary on this statement is the fact that the boy's parents took him before a Court when he was fourteen for stealing his father's ring.

The same pattern is repeated over and over again—the mother's early anxieties or serious neglect of the child, or poverty in the home: the son's waywardness, generally around the ages of 10 to 14; this adds to the mother's worries and distresses her, or if she is indifferent the son imagines it does, or it causes quarrels between mother and father; the son quarrels with the parents, perhaps joining the Army in a fit of pique; separation from home arouses the old feelings of deprivation and guilt; he needs to be comforted by the very love he had denied or that had been denied him.[1]

The focusing of his attention on the home tended to exclude all others from any claim on the young soldier's loyalty; thus he became impatient of Army discipline, out of step with his comrades and contemptuous of his superiors. Army regulations become mere shibboleths; his officers are unsympathetic and tyrannical, his comrades are shadows whose movements seem illogical and craven. 'No, I do everything for them (my parents) but no everyone else,' wrote one young Scotsman. Another man who had just written 'My parents are the best in the world and I love them both' and had been answering the questions sensibly, in a clear even hand, came to the question 'Would you make a son of your own do

---

[1] D. H. Stott (op. cit.) observes: "Every one of these (9) boys was dominated by an anxiety for his parents' affection. In some this took an obsessional, uncontrollable form and was accompanied by acute emotional distress. Such boys became persistent absconders. . . . All were in addition obsessionally homesick. . . . This acute conflict of attitude towards his parents made him a prey to impulsive irrational acts. At times when the lad felt the emotional situation quite intolerable he might make an attempt to join the Army or Navy."

exactly what he was told' and scribbled across the page 'Out of order', venting his feelings on the paper with scratched lines and 'no thanks to you' and 'but does not go for you'. The question had reminded him of contradictions in his home relationship. In defying this unjust world, or better still escaping from it, the offender thinks he is demonstrating his superiority over it. Even though it stretch out the hand of the law to seize him and lock him away in prisons, he will never bow to its authority for to do so would be to deny the all-importance of his sorrows and his home. Such, in his more revealing moments, is the mood of many an offender.

We have seen something of the condition of the offender's home life. Loss of home, home broken by separation of parents, the illness of parents, the prolonged absence of the father, bitter quarrels between parents, neglect, over-indulgence, the sudden death of a parent: these conditions were so common that only very few of the Army offenders were untouched by one or more of them. By comparison, the non-offenders in the control groups were much less affected; 71 per cent of the offenders were either homeless, or came from broken homes, or their parents were chronic invalids, or their parents had been away from home for long periods: only 19 per cent of the non-offenders were similarly affected. Even these figures do not bring out the real differences between the two groups for there was relatively much more friction between the offenders' parents and they were punished more by their parents. Little was known about the non-offenders apart from their own submissions and the true difference in security and affection between their home backgrounds and the offenders' may well have been greater than a mere counting of factors can show.

Links between the home background and various forms of misbehaviour

It has been shown in the preceding chapters that the Army offender does not suddenly become a miscreant when plunged into Army life. In most cases there are early weaknesses and lapses which show that the trouble is deep-seated, and within the man rather than an irritation from the conditions of Army life. The early pointers are truancy and youthful delinquencies. There are also other symptoms, harmless in themselves, but seeming to point to an inner conflict and an eventual clash with authority. Such are the absence of any hobby, excessive changing of jobs, a wanderlust, and very frequent visiting of the cinema. Since a defective home background has proved to be the most common abnormality amongst these Army offenders (compared with its normal incidence amongst the control groups) one wonders, for purposes of prediction, how far the several sorts of home trouble are linked with early symptoms and expressions of delinquency. One may roughly divide the home troubles into five kinds—lack of a home, broken home, invalid parent(s), friction between parents, and neglect (or indulgence). The degree of association has been calculated[1] between each in turn of these five conditions, on the one hand, and the various symptoms and expression of delinquency, including persistent absence from Army units and continual Army crime, on the other. Thus it might have been shown that an orphan was, say, less likely to be an absentee than a man with a home of his own to run to, and so on. Only two combinations showed any significant linkage and both included neglectful homes: thus, an offender from such a home was more likely to have been a school truant than an offender from a more satisfactory home; and was also more likely to have had a conviction for a civilian offence. But even here only a tendency is disclosed and it is merely one factor in a whole grouping of factors, which will now be considered.

[1] By chi-square test.

PART FIVE : CONCLUSIONS

CHAPTER XXII

TRACING THE CAUSES

IN the course of the earlier chapters we have noted any cases where a cause of waywardness could be traced. Thus, a few men were found to be physically so handicapped that this fact alone was thought to have accounted for their offending. Others were found to be suffering from psychoses so acute that they were discharged from the Army on medical grounds and one could obviously not attempt any analysis of further causes with them. One or two others showed no evidence of any real delinquency and were probably too young (under the minimum Army age) or physically too retarded to be able to keep up with the rigours of training. But the rest, the great majority, have remained outside any detection of single causes.

The method that has been employed in this inquiry—comparing the incidence of separate factors in the sample of offenders side by side with those of a normal control group—could only claim to have found a single conditioning cause when it had identified a factor as present in every one of the offenders and entirely absent from the controls. No such factor has come to light, nor is it likely to. There is strong evidence for asserting that delinquency is seldom if ever the result of any one of the conditions traced in this study. A number of conditions are evidently at work in shaping the delinquent's course of action; the statistical method can point to some of these by isolating factors which figure more prominently among the offenders than among the controls. As many as twenty-four conditions of this sort have been identified, but their combinations in the lives of the individual offenders are extremely varied. Thus some men show evidence of many of the twenty-four factors; others show only one, and the average is between three and four; and every one of the same factors is present in the control groups, though to a lesser extent. There are serious limitations to this method of considering each separate factor in isolation, even though an attempt has been made in preceding chapters to trace any links between one factor and another. If delinquency (Army or civilian) emerges from a complex of causes, then it is important that these should be considered together as far as possible, with their interactions: the innate tendencies considered in relation to the influence of the environment, the complex interplay of emotion between child and parents, the earlier acquired characteristics against the later ones. From the wealth of material which has been accumulated in the course of this work, it is possible to examine each case in turn and to look for elements common to all or to a number of them.

An attempt has, therefore, been made to weigh the relative strengths of early conditioning factors in each individual case. All the evidence relating to each of the 200 men has been considered together—his case-history papers, letters, questionnaires and drawings. A chart was constructed and against the name of each man was recorded any of the 24 causal factors and 25 background conditions that had been traced in his case. The estimated importance of each factor was indicated by symbols—a red cross for a probable major cause, a red circle for a possible major cause, a blue cross for a probable contributory cause, and a black cross for a contingent factor. Twenty-four cases were excluded from the sample because there were gaps in the evidence. The results for the 176 that remained may conveniently be summarized in Table 19.

All the figures in columns (a) and (b) refer to separate individuals, so that major factors are traced in 137 cases altogether (77·8 per cent). The figures in columns (c) and (d) overlap considerably, as between one factor and another, but not within any one factor. If additions are made across the page the totals (in column (e)) may be taken to represent separate individuals in whom those factors have been traced.

In about half the cases no more than three of these defective conditions were revealed. The average number was 3·6 per man and the greatest number was ten. The following table (20) shows in what proportions they were distributed throughout the whole group. No corresponding table can be prepared from the evidence of the control groups because only twelve of the twenty-four conditions could possibly be detected by the questionnaire method.

If we take the figures in the first two columns of Table 19, showing the probable and possible major factors among 77·8 per cent of the cases (excluding, however, the 9 psychopathic cases in the second

TABLE 19

Summary of causal conditions traced among
S.T.U. offenders (sample of 176)

Condition	(a) Probable major factor	(b) Possible major factor	(c) Probable contributory factor	(d) Possible contributory factor	(e) Totals	(f) Percentage of group
No home	6	6	7	1	20	11
Broken home	2	6	17	20	45	26
Parental neglect	28	33	15	2	78	45
Over-indulgence by parents	6	6	4	—	16	9
Lack of parental discipline (father's prolonged absence)	2	7	10	1	20	11
Invalid parent(s)	—	—	17	24	41	23
Abnormal friction between parents	—	—	11	57	68	39
Poverty at home	—	—	20	6	26	15
Shock of parental loss	1	—	6	—	7	4
Excessive punishment by parent(s)	—	—	11	73	84	48
Disturbance from evacuation	—	—	1	3	4	2
Psychotic	2	—	—	—	2	1
Psychopathic	10[1]	(9)	14	—	33	19
Hereditary defects	4	—	6	2	10	6
Physical deficiency	4	1	21	10	36	21
Malnutrition[2]	—	—	2	3	5	3
Bed wetting	—	—	—	5	5	3
Accidental injury	—	—	1	3	4	2
Mental dullness	—	—	7	2	9	5
Illiteracy	—	—	7	28	35	20
Loss of schooling	—	—	—	36	36	21
Excessive punishment (school)	—	—	1[3]	—	1	—
Persecution by schoolfellows	—	—	—	19	19	11
Army misfit	—	1	—	—	1	—
No essential delinquency	(3)	—	—	—	3	2
Totals	68	69	178	295	608	347
Totals (percentage)	38·6	39·2				

[1] After the table had been constructed from an examination of each of the two hundred case-histories, the military records were made available and it was then seen that 10 cases which had been discharged as psychopathic personalities had previously been listed under 'no cause traced'. They are therefore included now under 'Probable major factor' on the evidence of the Army psychiatrists. In 9 of the remaining 23 psychopathic cases only a 'possible major (environmental) factor', and no probable factor, had been listed. The same 9 are therefore shown in brackets under 'Possible major factor', and the remaining 14 are listed as 'Probable contributory factors'.

(Continued overleaf)

TABLE 20

Distribution of causal factors among 176 S.T.U. offenders

Number per person		Percentage of group affected %
1	..	12
2	..	16
3	..	23
4	..	22
5	..	10·6
6	..	9
7	..	4
8	..	2·2
9	..	0·6
10	..	0·6
		100·0

column), we find that 103 out of 128 (80 per cent) refer to home conditions, including 61 (48 per cent) to neglect at home, 12 (9 per cent) to having no home, and 12 (9 per cent) to over-indulgence by the parents. If to these 103 cases where home conditions have proved a possible major factor are added the cases where the same conditions are a probable *contributory* cause (affecting a further 28 men, the other factors overlapping on the same men), the total of 131 represents 74 per cent of the whole sample. Among the other probable contributory factors the more common were poverty in the home (20 cases), invalid parent(s) (17 cases), and physical deficiency (21 cases). Among the possible contributory factors, the most frequently recorded was excessive punishment by parents (though little importance is attached to this figure—see previous chapter); next were friction between parents (57 cases), loss of schooling (36 cases), illiteracy (28), invalid parents (24) and persecution at school (19). All these figures are exclusive of those recorded as probable contributory causes, and the total number of cases revealing each condition out of the 176 is shown in column (*e*).

We have broadly stated that a defective or broken relationship between the young offender and his parents was almost universal, in fact it probably accounts for 103 out of 128 cases where a major factor has been traced. But the actual situations which have been labelled 'neglect' or 'indulgence' or 'lack of discipline' are very

---

[2] This factor was probably much more widespread but only serious cases were likely to come to light in the present inquiry.

[3] It has been shown in Chapter XX that the S.T.U. men were punished a great deal at school, but it is impossible to determine the degree of influence of this factor, except in one case.

varied when one looks into them. Some are not so very difficult
to understand. Thus, where either parent has neglected the home
physically and morally and the children have grown up without any
sense of security or of the close comfort of a family circle, or without any moral training, it is only to be expected that the child will
bear the marks into its later life.[1] And where a parent has bru-
talized or continually hurt the child it will not only suffer but will
become corrupted by such treatment,[2] like the young Huckleberry
Finn under the influence of his father. Where a parent has indulged
and shielded the child against every puff of adversity he will grow
up weak and ill-equipped to face the elements of the outside world
single-handed. Where a child has suffered a severe shock like the
sudden loss of a parent, and has not the strength of a comfortable
home background to sustain him, he may recoil from the situation
and refuse to recognize it.[3] Such situations were commonly found
among these men, and they are not difficult to understand. But
there are others where the attitude of the child to the parents and
to the outside world is less straightforward, where early experiences
have left emotional disturbances that in the adult turn anti-social
and do not yield easily to treatment.

It may be wondered why more attention has not been paid to the
'psychopathic' traits in earlier chapters. Nineteen per cent of the
S.T.U. men were eventually discharged as 'psychopathic' personalities,[4] and these make up a large proportion of the total 'failures'.
This present inquiry has been mainly concerned with environmental
factors, and a 'psychopathic' condition is not one that the
author has attempted to recognize. It may be useful, however, to
isolate the psychopathic group and see whether they differ in any
significant way from the other offenders. Unfortunately the group

[1] Bowlby concludes from his study of young delinquents: 'Prolonged
separation of a child from his mother (or mother-substitute) during the first
5 years of life stands foremost among the causes of delinquent character
development and persistent misbehaviour.'

[2] During the recent trial of a man and wife who were accused of cruelty
towards a young girl of 16, the defence called a psychologist to witness that
during the course of an interview with the young girl he noticed that she
showed signs of untruthfulness and lightness of conduct. This evidence was
put forward to support the man's claim of innocence, but it could have been
claimed with equal justification by the prosecution, for cruelty often begets
immorality and untruthfulness.

[3] Freud, *Introductory Lectures on Psycho-analysis*, describes this state:
'It is as though these persons had not yet been able to deal adequately with the
situation, as if this task were still actually before them unaccomplished.'

[4] S. and E. T. Glueck classified 17·7 per cent of 384 young-adult criminals
as 'psychopathic personalities' (op. cit.).

numbers only 38 cases so that sub-division according to various factors is not likely to be very fruitful.   The following comparisons have been made:

Proportions of	Psychopaths %	Whole sample %
— broken homes	66	57
— neglectful parents	58	53
— excessive friction between parents	52	57
— emotional 'types'	61	42
— excessive attachment to home	53	53
— truancy	50	57
— excessive cinema attendance	35	30
— excessive job-changing	65	44
— civilian delinquency	38	36

One can only conclude from the general resemblance between the two sets of figures that so far as environmental and other factors are concerned the psychopaths do not represent a different population.

Hereditary or inborn traits were probably much more important in shaping the characters of the offenders than the figures in Table 19 suggest.   There was no opportunity to study the behaviour of the S.T.U. men's families and the only examples of inheritable factors that came to one's notice were provided by the evidence of the men themselves.

We have now arrived at the extreme edge of our knowledge of the beginnings of waywardness in this sample of Army offenders. There are hints of earlier disturbances and frustrations; but one cannot advance much further along the whole front of the inquiry by the simple method of question and answer, or by private interview, or even by using the men's own accounts of their earlier lives. The search into their background has established that the troubles were present in the early years of life, say from five onwards—at school, at work, and at home.   It is true that in many cases the shock of Army discipline jolted them back to an earlier state of mind, so that they became, as it were, children again, but the effect was only to aggravate an existing condition of retarded development.

At this stage, it may be useful to list some of the important factors that have emerged in the course of this inquiry as strongly associated with delinquency:

(1) There was a very high proportion of broken and unsatisfactory homes;

(2) there was a very large majority of cases where the relations between the parent(s) and the son were abnormal;

(3) the abnormal attachment to home, so commonly observed, increases as the parents' neglect of the child;

(4) a large proportion of the offenders' families were living near the poverty line;

(5) the great majority of offenders came from large families;

(6) the men from the larger families included more truants, job-changers and civilian delinquents;

(7) a very great majority were living in overcrowded homes (a consequence of large families);

(8) their intelligence was not markedly below normal;

(9) educationally a large majority were very backward indeed;

(10) physically they were slightly defective;

(11) even among the physically very defective men many other background conditions were observed;

(12) offenders generally suffered more early ill-health than the controls;

(13) they experienced more accidents;

(14) they were more anxious about their health;

(15) they suffered more persecution from other boys at school;

(16) they missed more schooling through ill-health;

(17) they included many more school truants;

(18) the truants tended to become job-changers;

(19) few of the offenders had a hobby, those with hobbies being less delinquent;

(20) they attended the cinema much more often than the controls;

(21) they were inclined to change their jobs frequently;

(22) there was a tendency to seek driving jobs or to go to sea;

(23) the lag of educational attainments behind innate ability tended to encourage truancy, job-changing and recidivism in crime;

(24) they were generally more restless than the controls;

(25) they mostly volunteered for the Army;

(26) their most common offence in the Army was unauthorized absence.

The way these and many other factors are scattered over the whole group suggests that it is not any single one or any particular combination of factors that is responsible for delinquency, but the general weakening effect of a number of these factors acting upon the

personality of the child.[1] And the evidence put forward in Appendix
A further suggests that such concatenations of influences are
common to a certain impoverished, overcrowded section of the
community among whom delinquency may be considered endemic.

There is thus a prima facie case for believing that environmental
factors, though not the sole determinants, are powerful forces in
shaping the development of the youthful delinquent. These environmental conditions press on the parents and the children, breeding
neglect, harshness, indifference, undernourishment and emotional
instability. From such inimical conditions the stronger and more
intelligent members may escape into more profitable employment as
soon as they are able. The weaker or more backward members are
trapped by them and by emotional disorders that set them against
society. In this situation the congenital and environmental factors
seem to be inextricably mingled. No doubt their relative strengths
at varying stages of the child's development could be measured but,
on common-sense grounds, the environmental influences, especially
poverty and overcrowding, appear so much the more important
and the more easily controlled.[2]

One must be watchful, however, lest in sifting the evidence of
the various environmental conditions one lets the essential truth

[1] C. Burt, *The Young Delinquent*, finds the average delinquent burdened
with 9 defective conditions, whereas the average non-delinquent control has
only 3. S. & E. T. Glueck (*After-Conduct, etc.*) write: 'Rarely, in the develop-
mental careers of delinquents and criminals, have only one or two of the
many influences referred to been operative. The usual situation is rather a
clustering of deleterious traits and circumstances in a demoralizing dynamic
interplay . . . it is the interplay of forces of the kind described, rather than,
or at least more than, the grossly oversimplified "freewill" and "criminal
intent" of tradition, that generates delinquency and crime.'

[2] Dr. K. Friedlander, op. cit., page 103, writes: 'adverse environmental
conditions will after the age of six lead to anti-social behaviour only if a
state of "latent" delinquency or anti-social character formation has previously existed.' It may still be true that environmental conditions contribute
to a state of 'latent' delinquency, just as in a majority of cases environmental
conditions can redeem the delinquent.

The Rev. W. S. Morrison (in 1895) gave some thought to this problem:
'It is not to be supposed that an improvement in economic surroundings alone
will ever banish criminal propensities from the human heart. Nevertheless it
is equally indisputable that if it were possible to effect some permanent
improvement in the economic circumstances of the most impoverished section
of the juvenile population offences against property would undoubtedly mani-
fest a distinct tendency to diminish. The only way in which it seems possible
to effect this improvement is by raising the standard of industrial efficiency
among the least favoured members of the juvenile population. How this
reform is to be accomplished is undoubtedly a most formidable problem. It
will never be accomplished if left to the parents of such children, in cases
where they have parents. It is a reform which must proceed from collective
action on the part of the community' (op. cit.).

slip through one's fingers. What, after all, does all this waywardness amount to? In every case, whether the offence be housebreaking, or neglect to polish one's boots, whether it be absence without leave or an attack upon the body of the Sergeant-Major, it is an assertion of impulses against the code of the society in which the offender finds himself. It is an inability to bow to social sanctions, to come back to camp when it is more 'comfortable' to stay away, to restrain one's anger when circumstances provoke, to polish one's boots because the Army has decreed that you must. Against all these imperatives the offender rebels, generally without counting the cost, often despite the consequences.

It seems that, on the one hand, there is an emotional state, not perhaps clearly realized, which produces wretchedness, restlessness and feelings of inadequacy in the man, driving him to anti-social acts[1]; on the other hand, there is a partly conscious reflection of the social code of behaviour (or conscience), which may be embryonic or highly developed to accord to social standards, but is continually being shot through by eruptions from the emotional situation. This upper crust of morality is continually in conflict with the emotional unrest beneath, and unless it is nourished and deepened by outside encouragement it will lose its sanction and may indeed become a secondary object of attack. Then, it may be subjugated and absorbed and become a mere self-justification for blind, instinctive, anti-social urges.

It is idle to say that the offender is merely more selfish, more wilful than other men. He suffers for his crimes and they can seldom be worth the punishments they invoke. No, the offender's fault is that he submits to an immediate impulse and is unable to restrain his feelings in the interests of his own comfort or anyone else's. Here, he acts like a child, in fact as he has continually acted since he was a child. And, to understand his actions one has to go back over the years of waywardness to those early years in which the pattern of his behaviour was first moulded. We have seen some of the particular influences in this man's early life that have made it so difficult for him to conform in the way that others do. To some extent they may be constitutional traits. Partly, we have seen, they are defects in the parental relations from which the child gains its first lessons in respect for authority. Partly, too, they lie in the

[1] D. H. Stott (op. cit.) writes: 'My thesis . . . was that this (delinquent) breakdown resulted from the boy's finding himself in what was for him, with all those factors predisposing him to anxieties and uncertainties in his basic affective needs, an intolerable emotional situation.'.

common crowded and squalid conditions where privacy is unknown, where there is no room for the finer things of life, and birth, copulation and death are familiar, and sometimes terrifying, realities. Some or most of these factors, as we have seen, press upon the delinquent in his earlier years.

We have, in this study, been mainly considering the influences that have shaped the offender in the past. Is he then left as a victim of his own impulses? How far, one may ask, has he any freedom of choice in what he does? The law assumes that he has freewill, for otherwise it would have to speak of prescriptions and treatments instead of sentences and punishments. It is undeniable that the individual is shaped by a combination of external and internal influences, though how far they are independent of his consciousness it is difficult to say; perhaps his will is free only to the extent that he has understood and learned to select or control such influences. The offender has hardly begun to do this and so presumably he has little real freedom of choice.

It is not that he cannot recognize the difference between right and wrong. He does nearly always recognize it and will fully acknowledge the validity of the moral code. 'What you say is quite right,' he will say, speaking of some moral point, 'but it's no good to me. I can't keep that up.' Sometimes, of course, he will choose to steal for his own gain, knowing that it is wrong, but he would not suggest that everybody should do the same. Then there are a few in whom a moral sense seems almost entirely lacking or paralysed, who are almost incapable of pity or fellow-feeling and whose object in life is to gratify their instinctive cravings with least harm to themselves. But such inhuman creatures are not often seen. In the main, as the evidence of the men themselves has shown in these pages, the offender does not act from any ulterior motive but rather, in desperation or defiance, from a sense of inadequacy or a need for evasion, or because he cannot meet the demands of the outside world.

But, even if he retains little freedom of will, the offender does, in most cases, still retain a striving for conformity, a yearning to be at one with the social world around him. It is this striving that produces his discontent and sets him against himself. Where there is no struggle, no anxieties, and the man is resigned to his fate or his phantasies, he is then a case for the mental physician alone. In practically every one there is some respect for the sanctions of society and some positive, redeeming quality—it may be a tenderness of moral fibre, a gentleness of manner or a sense of compassion, or at the least a feeling of discontentment with the wretchedness of his condition.

It is this divine discontent upon which the social worker must pin all his hopes and concentrate his treatment. It is the motive force by which he can bring the fears and evasions to the light of consciousness and introduce new, formative habits. And if, upon learning that the troubles go so far back into the past and arise from such appalling circumstances as the present study has suggested, he should be inclined to doubt whether much can be done for the offender, let him take fresh heart from those young soldiers who, encouraged by only a few months' shelter and re-education in the Special Training Units, went overseas to prove their worth as useful and sometimes heroic members of the community.

APPENDIX A

An Estimate of the Incidence Of Delinquency in England and Wales[1]

BY JOSEPH TRENAMAN AND B. P. EMMETT

THE conclusions drawn below show that one in every nine male persons becomes a delinquent, over a whole generation, and that amongst those sections of the population where delinquency is found to be concentrated the proportion rises as high as one in every three.

The incidence of delinquency is usually measured as the ratio borne by the number of persons found guilty of offences in the courts in any one year to the total number of persons in the population, or any part of the population (e.g. sex or age group), and is expressed as so many delinquents per 10,000 of the population. Two weaknesses of that method are that it masks the true extent of delinquency in the population and that it tends to suggest that crime occurs accidentally. If delinquency is a function of conditions lying deep within the personality of the individual or acquired after a considerable number of years—as recent research has suggested—then at whatever age the offender comes into contact with the law, the cause of his delinquency may, in many instances, be traced back to similar beginnings. The offender may, and in most cases does, begin his 'official' delinquency fairly early in life, before he is 15, or he may escape recognition until much later on, or perhaps he may not have occasion to transgress until later years although the delinquent condition may be latent within him.

Therefore, in order to estimate the incidence of delinquency, one needs to know more than just the annual ratio of offenders to population. One needs to consider the outcropping of crime throughout the lifetime of a whole generation. One needs to know the probability of any child born at any given time becoming a delinquent some time during his life. To estimate such a probability, we must consider the number of children born each year—numbers which may conveniently be referred to as 'generations'—and count year by year the individuals of each generation who are convicted in the courts for first offences. When all the members of a particular generation are dead, it will then be possible to express the probability as a ratio of the total number who were convicted at least once to the total number in the generation at birth. Clearly the probability will be different for each generation, owing to changes in the law (e.g. the 1933 Act), in mortality rates, in social conditions and so on, so that it would be hazardous to apply a

[1] Reproduced from *The Howard Journal* by kind permission.

probability figure for a past generation to one of which most members were still living. And even if a fairly typical past generation could be selected, it would nevertheless be impossible to make the necessary calculations, since prior to 1937 Criminal Statistics only classified offenders according to broad age groups.

A very rough estimate of the probability for generations born during the 1930s could, however, be made by estimating that delinquency and mortality rates for each age group will be constant at, say, the 1938 level for the succeeding sixty years. In fact, the 1938 figures stand a good deal higher than those for earlier years, but lower than those for the succeeding war years, as the following table shows:

Numbers of male persons convicted for indictable offences at all courts of England and Wales.

1930	..	49,678	1940	..	76,566
1932	..	57,196	1941	..	90,434
1934	..	57,701	1942	..	88,509
1936	..	63,852	1943	..	86,003
1938	..	68,679	1944	..	88,657
1939	..	68,100	1945	..	99,055
			1946	..	92,925

It is probable that given steady domestic and social conditions for some years to come, the figures will fall as they did after the 1914–18 war, and unless important changes are introduced in the law, may drop below the 1938 level. It is not unreasonable to take the 1938 mortality rates as a basis for this estimate. The fairly steady decrease in the death rate in the period between the two world wars may well continue, but probably it will be mainly confined to infant mortality. Already, by 1938 those males who had survived to the age of 8 years had an expectation of a further 54 years of life (for females the figure was even higher), so that no substantial changes can be expected from that age onwards. Using these mortality rates, we can estimate the percentage of a given generation surviving to various ages, i.e. the size of the generation at any given age. Applying the 1938 delinquency rates for each age group we can then estimate the numbers of offenders which the generation can be expected to furnish year by year and the problem reduces to computing how many of them are first offenders.

We may now proceed to make an estimate of the probability for males only. Females will not be considered within the scope of the present inquiry. We are, moreover, only concerned with delinquency which we may for convenience define as the condition in which a person comes to be convicted by the courts for an indictable offence. We are not concerned here with the hundreds of thousands of persons convicted in the courts every year for contravening regulations of revenue, traffic, trading, etc., nor has any account been taken of those non-indictable offences which are akin to indictable offences.

Consider one thousand boys aged eight years, the minimum age at which they can be brought before the courts. The number of offenders which this generation will produce in each succeeding year is easily calculated by the method outlined above. The age group figures in Criminal Statistics, however, do not distinguish between first and recurrent offenders, so that it is necessary to turn to other sources for our estimates of the numbers of first offenders. Neither the Prison Commissioners nor the Home Office have been able to provide this information, which was eventually obtained from two sources, the first being a table prepared by Dr. E. C. Rhodes (*Young Offenders*, page 100) giving the age and number of previous offences of 1,951 delinquents between eight and sixteen years old, convicted in juvenile courts in London and six provincial towns in 1938, and the second an analysis of the subsequent criminal history of persons first found guilty of finger printable offences in 1937. This latter deals with males aged 17 and over (finger prints are not recorded at an earlier age) and was prepared by the statistical department of the Metropolitan Police. The table in *Young Offenders* yields estimates of the percentage of offenders at each age from eight to sixteen years who were first offenders. Unfortunately, we wish to know not the percentage who were being convicted for the first time, but the percentage who were first offenders at the same age. Thus from Rhodes' figures it appears that about $\frac{1}{10}$ of the eight-year-old delinquents had at least one previous conviction. Yet they must, all of them, necessarily have been first offenders at that age. If, therefore, we increase the proportion of first offenders derived from Rhodes' figures by a fixed amount, we in effect allow for the number of delinquents who committed more than one offence at the same age. By this means, and smoothing out irregularities introduced by the smallness of some of Rhodes' samples, we arrive at the estimates for the percentage of delinquents at each age from eight to sixteen years who were first offenders at that age.

TABLE I

Age	Number of First Offenders per 100 delinquents
8	100
9	96
10	92
11	88
12	84
13	80
14	76
15	73
16	70
17–20	58
20–24	48
25–29	38
30–39	33
40–49	30
50–59	28
60–69	26
70–79	25

This 'First Offender ratio' curve can be tentatively extended to cover the entire life span of the generation in a number of ways. The validity of such 'extensions' can, however, be measured against information contained in the second of the above-mentioned sources. This gave proportions of males first finger-printed in 1937 classified in broad age-groups from 17 onwards. The particular 'extension' given in Table I, though of necessity approximate, was found to lead to proportions agreeing closely with the Metropolitan Police figures.

The table below shows the complete calculations for determining the number of new delinquents which the generation consisting of 1,000 eight-year-old boys could be expected to furnish each year. The numbers of survivors are calculated from the 1938 mortality rates for males (see *The Annual Abstract of Stat.stics*). The 'offences committed' are taken from *Criminal Statistics* for 1938, and the numbers of first offenders from the estimates given in the Table above.

TABLE II

Age	Number of Survivors	Offences Committed	First Offenders	Cumulative Total First Offenders
8	1,000	2·2	2·2	2·2
9	998	4·6	4·2	6·4
10	997	7·0	6·0	12·4
11	996	9·5	7·9	20·3
12	995	11·5	9·1	29·4
13	994	13·2	10·0	39.4
14	993	11·2	8·0	47·4
15	991	11·2	7·1	54·5
16	989	10·5	6·6	61·1
17–20	980	29·4	16·5	77·6
21–24	968	23·0	11·0	88·6
25–29	953	20·0	7·6	96·2
30–39	910	28·0	9·2	105·4
40–49	856	15·0	4·5	109·9
50–59	649	7·5	2·1	112·0
60–69	466 }	1·5	0·4	112·4
70–79	46 }			

185·4 TOTAL 112·4

We see, therefore, that among eight-year-old boys about one in every nine can be expected to become an offender at least once during his lifetime. This probability relates to no specific generation but is unlikely to be far wrong for any of the 1930–39 generations. Sixty years or more may seem to be a long period to budget for but the 1930 generation, for example, has already passed through its period of maximum criminal activity with the peak in 1943. Since the incidence of delinquency was so high in this period, our estimate will, to that extent, be conservative for at least the 1930 or 1931 generations.

Such a proportion is alarming enough, considering the limitations that have been placed on the definition of delinquency, but it is already

P*

established that delinquents are not drawn in equal proportions from all classes of the community, and in order to arrive at a more valid assessment one needs to weigh the probability, not against the whole generation, but against that part of it from which delinquents are mainly drawn. As suggestions for further lines of inquiry one might consider place of residence and size of family as two possible criteria.

The *New Survey of London Life and Labour*, for example, shows the number of arrests (not convictions) for indictable offences in 1929 in terms of the population dwelling in streets of five broad social classes. Thus arrests per 10,000 of the population vary from 41 in the streets of the lowest class to 6 in the middle class districts, with 13 as the average for all London streets. Assuming that the proportions of convictions to arrests are equal for all social groups (if anything, they are likely to be greater among the lower classes), the ratio of offenders per generation may be expressed in terms of each class, as follows:

Social class	Number of Arrests (1929)	Population in London streets	Arrests per 10,000	Probability of male delinquency
Lowest (degraded)	392	95,400	41	1 : 2·7
Living below poverty line	1,100	369,100	30	1 : 3·8
Mass of unskilled labourers	1,832	1,341,900	14	1 : 8·8
Skilled workers	2,881	2,641,500	11	1 : 10·3
Middle class	552	918,100	6	1 : 18·7

The population group could be narrowed down in another way by considering the sizes of families from which offenders are drawn. Most recent inquiries have suggested that delinquents come from large families and a fair estimate would be that 70 per cent derive from families of four or more children.[1] On this assumption one could break down the probability of 1 : 9 for the whole male population into one for delinquents born in families of four or more children and another for those born in smaller families. 'The Home Market' (London Press Exchange 1937) estimated that 26·4 per cent of the population were drawn from families of six or more persons. At a rough estimate we may take such families as including four or more children and only two adults. The probability is that 26·4 per cent is an over-estimate of the proportion of persons living in families of four or more *children*. The ratio of offenders per generation may, therefore, be expressed as:

[1] J. H. Bagot (Liverpool) finds 79 per cent of delinquents' families have four or more children; W. L. Chinn (Birmingham) says most offenders in his sample come from homes with five or more children; the Birmingham Education Committee's report, in 1937, shows that the offenders' families average 6·9 persons; Breckinridge and Abbott (New York, 1912) state that in Chicago 74 per cent of offenders come from homes with four or more children; S. and E. T. Glueck (Boston) find 57·9 per cent of delinquent children in homes of five or more children; C. C. Van Vechten, Jr. (Chicago), records 55 per cent of delinquents from homes with four or more children. This present study shows 88 per cent from families of four or more children with an average of 6·3 children per family. Leo Page, *The Young Lag* (Faber, 1950) mentions that 14 out of 19 young offenders come from families of four or more children; the average number being 4·9.

*Ratio of offenders
to population
(male)*

Among families of 4 or more children   1: 3·3
     „   „   of less than 4 children   1: 24·4

This factor of family size cannot be applied to the table of ratios for various classes of London streets because it is not known how family size varied from one class of street to another though even in the lowest class of street the average size of family can hardly be greater than among offenders.

However, if the two sets of figures were combined—i.e. for family size and geographical area—it is clear from the existing tables that the ratio would vary from more than 1: 3 to something like 1: 100, in itself a most significant fact.

Enough has been said, however, to demonstrate that amongst that section of the population where size of family is an index of poverty, court convictions for indictable offences touch practically every other person, more than one in every household on average.[1] If the definition of delinquency were widened to include all those who commit such offences but escape the vigilance of the police (and they have been put at two or three times the number brought into the courts) we are confronted, not with an individual problem, but what can only be described as a mass phenomenon.

[1] S. and E. T. Glueck, *One Thousand Juvenile Delinquents*, state that over four-fifths of their offenders' homes were in regions which were centres of vice and crime, with street gangs and 'few opportunities for wholesome recreation'. They also report elsewhere (*After-conduct of Discharged Offenders*) that among 500 young-adult criminals 85 per cent come from families 'found to have been immoral, delinquent or criminal'.

See also D. H. Stott, *Delinquency and Human Nature* (Carnegie U. K. Trust, 1950): 'The second social aspect of treatment is impressed upon us by the much greater frequency of delinquency among the siblings of these 102 boys than among adolescents as a whole. Of their 126 brothers over ten years no less than 34 had appeared in court up to the time of writing. This is a proportion of under 1 in 4. During the year 1947 (that during which most of the 102 were sent to us) the proportion of boys aged 10 to 20 inclusive among the population as a whole who committed indictable offences was 1 in 77. The corresponding proportions for girls were 1 in 18 for the sisters of my boys as compared with 1 in 620 within the whole female population of 10- to 20-year-olds.'

APPENDIX B

(In the column headed 'Significance' the differences between the two sets of answers have been tested by chi-square. ** indicate a probability of 1 per cent or less that the differences have arisen by purely chance errors, and * indicates a 5 per cent probability. Such measures assume that the two samples are drawn at random from their respective populations. Since neither sample was taken at random it will be safer to assume that only those differences marked with ** are probably real.)

1. *Family Background.*	Answer	Offenders %	Controls %	Significance
Size of family (number of children)		(6·3)	(3·6)	**
Abnormally constituted home (only one parent or no parent in the home)		57	12	**
Invalid parent(s)		22	7·5	**
Both parents 'now enjoying good health'		41	79	**
'When you were young did you like your mother more than your dad?'	Yes	47(a)	32	**
'Did your parents have *many* cross words?'	Yes	57(b)	22	**
'Did your parents have to correct you much?'	Yes	72(c)	35	**
'Do you feel that you were ever a nuisance to your family as a child, through your own fault?'	Yes	67	35	**
'Do you think your mother had difficulties in bringing you up, through no fault of hers or your own?'	Yes	44(d)	33	*
'When you left school, did your parents let you have all your own way?'	Yes	29(e)	27	
'Do you think you should still obey your parents?'	Yes	64	67	

(a) 21 per cent did not reply. (b) 23 per cent did not reply. (c) 47 per cent of 'noes' were youngest children. (d) 41 per cent did not reply. (e) 29 per cent did not reply.

	Answer	Offenders %	Controls %	Significance
2. Health.				
'Have you ever been in hospital and for what illnesses?'	At least once	64	59	
'Have you had any speech troubles, (stuttering, lisping)?'	Yes	15	10	*
'Did you ever go rather short of food through your mother finding it difficult to make both ends meet?'	Yes	14	10	
'Do you think early ill-health has left any harmful effects?'	Yes	25	14	**
'Do you worry or get anxious about whether you are well or not?'	Yes	39	25	**
'Has any sickness or defect in your family been passed on to you (like weak eyes, flat feet, baldness)?'	Yes	15	9	*
'Have you ever had any serious accidents like broken bones or injury to the head?'	Yes	42	27	**
3. Civilian Employment.				
'Did you feel you had settled down to a job for life before you joined up?' (Or 'Do you now?')	Yes	59	82	**
'Have you served any trade apprenticeship or completed any skilled training for your job?'	Yes	36	57	**
'Is your trade different from your father's?'	Yes	59	88	**
'Has your mother gone out to work?'	Yes	32	33	
'Do you think women should be allowed to go out to work?'	Yes	47	54	*
'How do you think your employer treats you?'	Very well	64	65	
	All right	32	29	

	Answer	Offenders %	Controls %	Significance
'How many different jobs have you had?'	(Average number)	(4·5)	(2·3)	**

4. Leisure Activities

	Answer	Offenders	Controls	Significance
'Did you spend most evenings outdoors, in the street (as a boy)?'	Outdoors	79	59	**
	Indoors	13	41	**
	At the cinema	8	—	
'What were your spare-time hobbies?'	(Mentioning a hobby)	32	80	**
'How often did you go to the pictures?'	(Av. no. of times per week)	(2·7)	(1·1)	**
'How often to the theatre, circus or pantomime?'	At least once	70	70	
'What club did you belong to?'	(Belonging to a youth organization)	49	44(a)	
'Any betting?'	Some	43	31	**
'How late did you stay out? Was it all right at home?'	Up to 9 p.m.	16	32	
	Up to 10 p.m.	13	38	**
	Up to 11 p.m.	60	25	
	Later	11	5	
'Did you go dancing?'	Yes	44	51	*
'Spend much of your spare time with girls, or with boys?'	Girls	30	10(b)	**
	Boys	24	56	
	Both	41	32	
	Neither	5	2	
'Did you get pocket money at school? Was it more than 1/6 a week?'	>1/6 a week	42	36	
	<1/6 a week	45	44	
	None	13	20	
'After you went to work did you keep enough of your earnings to pay for your amusements?'	Yes	96	90	*

(a) An estimate of club membership for the whole country.

(b) Many of these belonged to boys' clubs and so for this question they are not an adequate control.

5. Schooling

	Answer	Offenders	Controls	Significance
'Did you like school?'	No	29	18	**
'Did you like the lessons?'	No	27	8	**
	Only some	23	38	
'Did you like the teachers?'	No	26	11	**
	Only some	20	21	
'Did you like your school fellows?'	No	5	2·5	
	Only some	14	12	
'Was the work too hard, or did you find it easy?'	Hard	43	13	
	About right	32	60	**
	Easy	25	27	

	Answer	Offenders %	Controls %	Significance
'Was the school too strict?'	Yes	45	15	**
'Did you find Arithmetic difficult to pick up?'	Yes	48	27	**
'Did you find you were in difficulties with the writing?'	Yes	34	13	**
'Did you enjoy and take part in the games?'	Yes	91	87	
'Were you picked on by the others, and why?'	Yes	21	11	**
'Were you much afraid of being late, or of doing wrong?'	Yes	32	19	**
'Were you ever caned or punished much?' .	Yes	94	81	**
'How many classes from the top were you on school?'	Top	45	74	**
	One down	24	12	
	Two down	11	9	
	Three + down	20	5	
'Was your school building pleasant inside?'	Yes	80	83	
'Did you attend evening school after leaving school? How long?'	More than one month	14	40	**
'Were you away from school much because of sickness?'	6 months +	46	13	**
'Were you absent much because you didn't want to go?'	Yes	57	15	**
'Was yours a church school?'	Yes	48	15	**

6. *Punishment.*

	Answer	Offenders %	Controls %	Significance
'Have you ever been punished for anything you didn't do, at school, at home, in a civvy job, or in the Army?'	Yes	61	17	**
'Have you felt that you usually deserved all the punishment you got?'	Yes	51	82	**
'Have you ever really been victimized, either in civilian life or in the Army? Could you explain how it happened?'	Yes	43	11	**

APPENDIX C

ANTHROPOMETRIC TABLES FOR OFFENDERS AND NON-OFFENDERS

Height

Height distributions of sample of 200 soldiers at the Special Training Unit, of 1,000 convicts measured by Dr. Charles Goring (1913), and of normal Army intake (December, 1942).

Height in Inches	S.T.U. sample %	1,000 convicts %	Army intake %
60 and under	0·6	4·3	0·5
61	2·5	5·0	0·8
62	3·8	7·9	1·9
63	8·3	12·8	3·7
64	12·6	13·1	7·0
65	12·8	14·7	10·9
66	22·3	14·7	13·4
67	15·3	9·9	15·5
68	8·9	8·9	14·9
69	5·2	4·6	12·0
70	6·5	2·4	8·4
71	0·6	0·7	5·5
72	0·6	0·4	3·0
73 and over	—	0·6	2·5
	100·0	100·0	100·0

Height distributions of the S.T.U. sample compared with the distributions for normal Army intake (aged 18 years) and for 1,000 convicts (1913).

Height in Inches	S.T.U. sample %	1,000 convicts %	Army intake %
60 and under	0·6	4·3	0·5
61–3	14·6	25·7	6·2
64–6	47·7	42·5	30·3
67–9	29·4	23·4	44·3
70–2	7·7	3·5	16·6
73 and over	—	0·6	2·1
	100·0	100·0	100·0
Mean height	65·86″	65·47″	67·30″

Weight

Weight distribution of sample of 200 soldiers at the Special Training Unit, and for normal Army intake (all ages) in December, 1942.

Pounds	S.T.U. sample %	Normal Army intake (all ages) %
100 and under	2.6	4.9
101–10	8.3	13.6
111–20	25.6	22.5
121–30	28.2	23.6
131–40	23.8	18.2
141–50	10.3	9.4
151–60	1.2	4.5
Over 160	—	3.3

Weight distribution of sample of soldiers at the Special Training Unit compared with distribution for normal Army intakes aged 18 years.

Pounds	S.T.U. sample %	Normal Army (aged 18) %
99 and under	1·3	0·6
100–14	17·3	13·2
115–29	45·4	39·6
130–49	34·0	37·9
150–69	2·0	7·8
170 and over	—	0·9
Mean weights	125·35	129·4 lbs.

Comparison of Lesser and Greater Samples of Offenders

Statistics from the sample of 200 delinquent soldiers studied in this inquiry and for a larger sample of 700 delinquents drawn from the same Unit.

Army records		Larger Sample %	Smaller Sample %
Medical categories:	A1	86·9	87·3
	A2	3·6	2·9
	A3 and A4	2·4	1·5
	B1	3·3	4·9
	B2	1·8	1·5
	B5–7	1·1	1·5
	C	0·9	0·4
Religion: Church of England		70·7	65·4
Church of Scotland & Presbyterian		5·3	6·0
Methodist		2·0	1·9
Baptist, Congregationalist, etc.		1·0	0·5
Jew		1·0	1·0
Roman Catholic		20·0	25·2

			Larger Sample %	Smaller Sample %
Army records				
Intelligence (Matrix Test) Group I	(high)		7	6
„ II	(above average)		19	15
„ III	(average)		47	52
„ IV	(below average)		21	23
„ V	(low)		6	4
Follow-up reports after posting:				
Disciplinary record, average or above			81·7	83·2
Conduct in unit, average or above			81·9	86·7
Willingness to do uncongenial work, average or above.			81·1	90·1

Background data		
Broken or defective homes	51·4	71·0
Civilian delinquents	21·3	36·0
Borstal sentences (pre-Army)	4·3	3·3
Approved School sentences	10·5	12·0
Borstal or Approved School or both	12·4	14·3
Father's prolonged absence from home	8·0	14·0
Request for sea service or driving job	33·5	44·4

The two sets of figures for medical categories show no significant differences (by chi-square test) beyond normal sampling errors. The differences between the proportions of Roman Catholics are explained by an influx shortly before the smaller sample was selected. The figure of 20 per cent is, therefore, probably nearer the true figure for the total S.T.U. intakes. The differences between the Intelligence test results, too, lie within the range of sampling errors. With all three factors it is clearly preferable to take the distributions from the larger sample as the basis for discussion in these chapters.

The differences between the follow-up results for the two groups may indicate that the Special Training Unit was achieving better results in 1944 when the sample was taken than in 1942, when the Unit was formed. The type of man being posted into the Unit in 1944 was no less difficult, in fact the Commanding Officer has suggested that the best men came at the beginning. The improvement in the proportions of men willing to do uncongenial work (from 81·1 to 90·1 per cent) is strongly suggestive of more successful methods being employed in the later period of the S.T.U. when the smaller sample was taken.

The contrast between the variations in the figures taken, on the one hand, from Army documents where data are available for every man, and on the other, from observations made by the investigator, are striking indeed. Thus the figures for the abnormalities listed under 'Background data' are in every case except one (Borstal sentences, where the incidence is so small that sampling errors easily produce a freak difference) higher in the smaller group, sometimes by more than fifty per cent. Both sets of figures are based on personal interviews with the men, but in the case of the smaller group the interviews were more searching, were made with the active co-operation of the men, covered a wide range of subjects and included the written testimony and answers to questionnaires by the men themselves. The findings of the smaller group are taken as nearer the true figures here because they are so consistently higher and also because, in several of the cases which were included in both groups, some factors (e.g. defective homes, civilian delinquencies), were revealed under examination in the smaller group but had not come to light in the larger group. Delinquents naturally tend to conceal the defections of their past, and only by winning their confidence and by regular contact with them and, where possible, with their homes, will the full knowledge of such conditions be gained. In all of these background factors, therefore, the figures from the inner sample have been quoted in the chapters above.

BOOKS QUOTED IN THE TEXT

ABRAMS, MARK: *The Home Market*, (London Press Exchange, 1937).

BAGOT, J. H.: *Juvenile Delinquency in Liverpool*, (Cape, 1941).

BIRMINGHAM EDUCATION COMMITTEE: *Report on the Present Problem of Juvenile Delinquency*, 1937.

BOWLBY, JOHN: *Forty-four Juvenile Thieves*, (Bailliere Tindall & Cox, 1948).

BRECKINRIDGE & ABBOTT: *The Delinquent Child and the Home*, (New York, 1912).

BRITISH ASSOCIATION FOR THE ADVANCEMENT OF SCIENCE: *Report of Anthropometric Committee under Sir Francis Galton*, 1883.

BRITISH BROADCASTING CORPORATION: *A Youth Inquiry*, (Further Education Experiment, BBC, 1951).

BURT, SIR CYRIL: *Mental and Scholastic Tests*, (P. S. King, 1922).

BURT, SIR CYRIL: *The Young Delinquent*, (Un. of London Press, 1945).

BURT, SIR CYRIL: *Education of Illiterate Adults*, (B. J. Ed. Psy., Feb. 1945).

BURT, SIR CYRIL: *Intelligence and Fertility*, (Hamish Hamilton, 1946).

CARR-SAUNDERS, SIR A. M., MANNHEIM, H., and RHODES, E. C.: *Young Offenders*, the Home Office Inquiry, (Cambridge, 1942).

CHINN, W. L.: *A Brief Survey of Nearly One Thousand Juvenile Delinquents*, (B. J. Ed. Psy., Vol. VIII, Feb. 1938).

Criminal Statistics, 1938 (H.M.S.O., 1939).

DE LA MARE, W.: *Early One Morning*, (Faber, 1935).

FORTES, M.: *The Influence of Position in Sibship on Juvenile Delinquency*, (Economica, Aug. 1933).

FRANKEL, H.: *The Industrial Distribution of the Population of Great Britain in July*, 1939, (J. R. Stats. Soc. CVIII, Pts. III–IV, 1945).

FREUD, S.: *Introductory Lectures on Psycho-Analysis*, (Allen & Unwin, 1922).

FRIEDLANDER, K.: *The Psycho-Analytical Approach to Juvenile Delinquency*, (Kegan Paul, 1947).

GALTON, SIR F.: *Inquiries Into Human Faculty*, (Dent, Everyman).

GLUECK, E. & S.: *One Thousand Juvenile Delinquents*, (Cambridge, Harvard Univ. Press, U.S.A., 1934).

GLUECK, E. & S.: *After-Conduct of Discharged Offenders*, (Macmillan, 1945).

GORING, C.: *The English Convict*, (H.M.S.O., 1913).

GUNZBÜRG, G. C.: *Can Intelligence be Raised?* (Modern Education, Sep. 1948).

GUNZBÜRG, G. C.: *The Unsuccessful Reader*, (Mental Health, VIII, 2, 1948).

HEALY & BRONNER: *Delinquents and Criminals*, (New York, Macmillan, 1926).

HEALY & BRONNER: *New Light on Delinquency and its Treatment*, (Yale Univ. Press, 1936).

HOME OFFICE: *Report on Juvenile Delinquency*, (H.M.S.O., 1920).

HOME OFFICE INQUIRY: see Carr-Saunders, Mannheim and Rhodes.

JACKSON, LYDIA: *Emotional Attitudes of Delinquent Children*, (B. J. Psy., Vol. XLII, 3 and 4, Dec. 1950).

LINDNER, R. M.: *Rebel Without a Cause*, (Introduction by E. & S. Glueck) (Research Books, Ltd., London, 1945).

LOMBROSO, C.: *Homme Criminel*, (Paris, 1895).

LOMBROSO, C.: *Speech at Sixth Congress of Criminal Anthropology*, (Turin, 1906).

LOMBROSO, C.: *Crime, Its Causes and Remedies*, (Heinemann, 1911).

L.C.C. EDUCATION COMMITTEE: *Juvenile Delinquency in London*, (P. S. King, 2441, 1926).

L.C.C.: *Report of the L.C.C.'s School Medical Officer*, (P. S. King, 1930, Vol. II, 2).

L.C.C.: *Report of the School Medical Officer of the L.C.C.*, (L.C.C., 1951).

LUMMIS, C.: *School Attendance, Employment and Army Records*, (B. J. Ed. Psy., Feb., 1946).

MAKARENKO, A.: *Road to Life*, (Nott, 1936).

MANNHEIM, H.: *Juvenile Delinquency in an English Middletown*, (Kegan Paul, 1948).

METROPOLITAN POLICE, DISTRICT RETURN: *Arrests for Indictable Offences*, 1938, (S. 2 Branch, 1939).

MIDLOTHIAN EDUCATION COMMITTEE: *Survey of the Sixteens*, (1942).

MORRISON, REV. W. D.: *Juvenile Offenders*, (London, 1896).

New Survey of London Life and Labour, Vols. III and IX, (P. S. King, 1931).

PAGE, LEO: *The Young Lag*, (Faber & Faber, 1950).

PEARSE, I. and CROCKER, L.: *The Peckham Experiment*, (Allen & Unwin, 1943).

PEARSON, KARL: *On the Handicapping of the FirstBorn*, (Dulan, 1914).

PENTON, J. C.: *A Study In the Psychology of Desertion and Absenteeism in Wartime and its relation to the Problem of Morale*, (unpublished).

PINTNER, R.: *Foundations of Experimental Psychology*, ed. Murchison, (Clark University Press, 1929).

PRISON COMMISSIONERS: *Report of the Commissioners of Prisons*, (H.M.S.O., 1942–4).

Psychologists and Psychiatrists in the Services, Report of an Expert Committee on, (H.M.S.O., 1947).

REES, J. R.: *The Shaping of Psychiatry by War*, (Duckworth, 1947).

REEVES, J. W., and SLATER, P.: *The Leisure Interests of 500 A.T.S.*, (Occupational Psy., Jul., 1947).

RHODES, E. C.: *Juvenile Delinquency*, (J. R. Stats. Soc., Part III, 1939).

RODGER, A.: *A Borstal Experiment in Vocational Guidance*, M.R.C., 78, (H.M.S.O., 1937)

ROYDS, A.: *Report on an Enquiry into the Relationship of Juvenile Delinquency and Environment in an Industrial Town*, (Oldham, 1936).

SCHMIDT, B. G.: *Changes in Personal, Social and Intellectual Behaviour of Children Originally Classified as Feeble Minded*, (Psy. Mon. Vol. 60, No. 5, Am. Psy. Ass. Inc.).

STOTT, D. H.: *Delinquency and Human Nature*, (Carnegie U.K. Trust, 1950).

TRADE, BOARD OF: *Journal*, (25 Nov., 1950).

VAN VECHTEN, C. C. JR.: *The Study of Success and Failure of One Thousand Delinquents Committed to a Boys' Republic*, (Chicago, 1935).

VERNON, P. E.: *Research on Personnel Selection in the R. Navy and the British Army*, (The American Psychologist, Feb. 1947).

VERNON, P. E.: *Psychological Tests in the R. Navy, Army and R.A.F.*, (Occupational Psychology, April, 1947).

VERNON, P. E.: *Reading Ability*, Min. of Education C'ttee. (H.M.S.O., 1950).

WOMEN'S GROUP ON PUBLIC WELFARE: *Our Towns—a Close-up*, (Oxford Un. Press, 1943).

INDEX

(y.s. = young soldiers)

For Product Safety Concerns and Information please contact our EU
representative GPSR@taylorandfrancis.com
Taylor & Francis Verlag GmbH, Kaufingerstraße 24, 80331 München, Germany